SEPARATE BUT EQUAL?

The debate about post-16 provision has been and remains highly contentious. Very damaging effects are attributed to the deep divide between academic and vocational post-compulsory education which has marked the English education system. It has been blamed for keeping one side too narrowly academic and the other too narrowly practical. More worryingly, a persistent belief that 'real' education post-16 is properly reserved for an academically minded minority has kept participation rates well below those of most comparable countries, thereby producing an under-educated workforce.

This book looks in detail at the strong contrasts in the provision traditionally made for 'vocationally' and 'academically' minded students, and looks at differences and similarities in practice. The chapters report on how those students prefer to learn, how their teachers define the kinds of learning appropriate for particular qualifications, and how the organisation of learning for 'different but equal' qualifications was observed in forty different schools and colleges.

The book's main focus is on the objectives and processes of learning at a stage that is certainly being transformed, but that is still powerfully shaped by myths about the sixth form and the education of 'leaders'.

Tony Edwards, **Frank Hardman**, **Roy Haywood** and **Nick Meagher** are all in the Department of Education at the University of Newcastle upon Tyne, and **Carol Taylor Fitz-Gibbon** is Professor of Education and Director of the Curriculum, Evaluation and Management Centre at the University of Durham.

SEPARATE BUT EQUAL?

A Levels and GNVQs

Tony Edwards,
Carol Taylor Fitz-Gibbon,
Frank Hardman, Roy Haywood and
Nick Meagher

London and New York

First published 1997
by Routledge
11 New Fetter Lane, London EC4P 4EE

Simultaneously published in the USA and Canada
by Routledge
29 West 35th Street, New York, NY 10001

© 1997 Tony Edwards, Carol Taylor Fitz-Gibbon, Frank Hardman, Roy Haywood
and Nick Meagher

Typeset in Garamond by Keystroke, Jacaranda Lodge, Wolverhampton
Printed and bound in Great Britain by Creative Print and Design (Wales), Ebbw Vale

British Library Cataloguing in Publication Data
A catalogue record for this book is available from the British Library

Library of Congress Cataloging in Publication Data
Separate but equal? : A-levels and GNVQs / Tony Edwards . . . [*et al.*].
    p.   cm. — (Further education)
  Includes bibliographical references (p.).
    1. Post-compulsory education—Great Britain. 2. Vocational education—Great
  Britain. 3. Post-compulsory education—Great Britain—Curricula.
    4. Vocational education—Great Britain—Curricula. I. Edwards, A. D. (Anthony
  Davies) II. Series: Further education (London, England)
LC1039.8.G7S46 1997
373.238′0941—dc21   97–12119
                                                                            CIP

ISBN 0–415–15297–6
ISBN 0–415–15298–4 (pbk)

CONTENTS

List of figures   vii
List of tables   ix
Acknowledgements   xi

1 CONTRASTS IN LEARNING?
Tony Edwards   1

2 EDUCATING LEADERS AND TRAINING FOLLOWERS
Tony Edwards   8

3 LISTENING TO STUDENTS AND THE 50 PER CENT FRAMEWORK
Carol Taylor Fitz-Gibbon   29

4 CLASSROOM OBSERVATION IN ACADEMIC AND VOCATIONAL COURSES POST-16
Nick Meagher   62

5 A LEVEL ENGLISH LANGUAGE AND ENGLISH LITERATURE: CONTRASTS IN TEACHING AND LEARNING
Frank Hardman   96

6 LINKS BETWEEN LEARNING STYLES, TEACHING METHODS AND COURSE REQUIREMENTS IN GNVQ AND A LEVEL
Roy Haywood   126

7 CONCENTRATED AND DISTRIBUTED RESEARCH: REFLECTIVE OBSERVATIONS ON METHODOLOGY
Carol Taylor Fitz-Gibbon   163

8 CONCLUSION: DIFFERENT AND UNEQUAL?   169

References   177

Index   187

FIGURES

3.1   Per cent of the sample of Advanced GNVQ students who were
      enrolled on four courses, by gender   33
3.2   Per cent enrolled in each of the four Advanced GNVQ courses,
      1995   33
3.3   Intake for Advanced GNVQs and three A levels, described by
      GCSE average scores   34
3.4   Advanced GNVQ intake in 1994 and 1995, described by GCSE
      average scores   35
3.5   Age distribution of Advanced GNVQ students   38
3.6   Reported teaching and learning activities in Advanced GNVQs and
      three related A levels   42
3.7   Perceived learning activities, 1996   45
3.8   The awards made to Advanced GNVQ students   49
3.9   The GCSE average score of students with various awards   50
3.10 Chances graphs for A level Business Studies and Human Biology
      for students who had approximately a D average grade at GCSE   53
3.11a Regression line for A level Business Studies, 1994   54
3.11b Regression line for A level Human Biology, 1994   55
3.12 Regression lines for Advanced GNVQ courses   55
3.13 Equating Advanced GNVQs with A levels using the 50 per cent
      framework   57
3.14 BTEC National Diploma awards compared with Advanced
      GNVQs   58
4.1   An Observer record of ten minutes from an A level Economics
      class   75
4.2   Percentage of time spent on various classroom activities for
      students on four A level courses   77
4.3   Percentage of time spent on various classroom activities for
      students on four Advanced GNVQ courses   81
4.4   Comparison of classroom activities for A level and Advanced
      GNVQ classes   86

4.5   Balance of classroom activities as perceived by A level students in
      one school   89
4.6   Balance of classroom activities as perceived by Advanced GNVQ
      Health & Social Care students   90
4.7   Comparison of the balance of classroom activities as perceived by
      A level and Advanced GNVQ students   91
5.1   Students' perceptions of learning activities in A level Mathematics
      and English Literature lessons   99
5.2   Students' perceptions of learning activities in A level English
      Literature and English Language   101
5.3   Patterning of teaching exchanges for ten teachers of A level
      English Literature and English Language   109
5.4   Patterning of teaching exchanges for Teacher A   115
5.5   Patterning of teaching exchanges for Teacher J   117
6.1   Model of three epistemological orientations   133
6.2   The shifting teaching and learning process   135
6.3   Kolb summarised   139
6.4   Observed percentage differences between A level and Advanced
      GNVQ activities   142
6.5   Observer record of frequency of classroom activities for A level and
      Advanced GNVQ subjects   143
6.6   Kolb LSI records for A level and Advanced GNVQ students   145
6.7   Kolb LSI records for an A level Physics and an Advanced GNVQ
      Business Studies class   146
6.8   Bar charts showing how A level and Advanced GNVQ students
      prefer to gain and handle information   146
6.9   Bar charts showing different preferred learning styles of A level
      and Advanced GNVQ students   146
6.10 Student preferences compared between A level and Advanced
      GNVQ Business Studies   148
6.11 Differences between A level Science and Humanities classroom
      activities as reported by students   149
6.12 Comparison of classroom activities for Advanced GNVQ Business,
      A level Business and A level Economics   150
6.13 Advanced GNVQ Science FE cohort of staff and students' learning
      style practices   152
6.14 Learning preferences of Advanced GNVQ Business
      students   158
6.15 Teachers' answers to Kolb LSI questionnaires   160
6.16 Preferred learning styles of GNVQ Hospitality and Catering staff
      and students   161
6.17 Preferred learning styles of A level Physics and Chemistry staff
      and students   162
7.1   Kolb's learning cycle   164

TABLES

2.1   A level entries, 1996   17
3.1   Distribution of students between Advanced GNVQ courses   31
3.2   Reasons for taking Advanced GNVQ courses   32
3.3   Distribution of students by Advanced GNVQ course   33
3.4   Prior qualifications of students on Advanced GNVQ courses
       finishing in 1994   36
3.5   Significant differences between Advanced GNVQ and A level
       students in the same school or college   36
3.6   Percentages of students who had previously taken vocational
       qualifications   37
3.7   Percentages of students who were provided with work experience   40
3.8   Investigations of the per cent of variance in students' grades
       associated with the institution attended by the students   51
4.1   Numbers of lessons observed in different subjects   65
4.2   The links between sampling and recording classroom observations   69
4.3   ALIS descriptors showing significant differences between 'academic'
       and 'vocational' courses   70
4.4   'Continuum questionnaire' for the balance of classroom
       activities   72–73
4.5   Observer record of an A level Economics lesson summarised   76
4.6   Observer record of a BTEC National Diploma lesson summarised   76
4.7   Discourse and questioning activities in four A level subjects
       compared   78
4.8   Frequency and range of classroom activities in four A level subjects
       compared   79
4.9   Five most frequent classroom activities in four Advanced GNVQ
       courses compared   81
4.10   Frequency and range of classroom activities in four Advanced
       GNVQ courses compared   83
4.11   Observer record of an Advanced GNVQ Science lesson summarised   83
4.12   Frequency and range of classroom activities in A levels and Advanced
       GNVQ courses compared   84

4.13 Frequency and range of classroom activities in A level Business,
     A level Economics and Advanced GNVQ Business compared   85
4.14 Frequency and range of classroom activities in Advanced GNVQ
     Business in schools and colleges compared   87
5.1 Profile of teachers   103

ACKNOWLEDGEMENTS

The project cited in Chapter 1 (p. 5) was funded by the Economic and Social Research Council 1992–1995 (grant number R610/00453). Tony Edwards, Carol Taylor Fitz-Gibbon and Roy Haywood gratefully acknowledge the Council's support.

Two separate but related research projects on 'Effective learning for Advanced GNVQs' were funded by the National Council for Vocational Qualifications 1995–1996 (grant number GO1/GEN/XCVN01). The first project involved an observational study of GNVQ learning, and the second a value-added analysis of statistical data on GNVQ students' attitudes and performance. NCVQ support is again gratefully acknowledged.

Nick Meagher is to be thanked for providing and sharing observations, analysis and the graphical representation of the data presented in Chapter 6.

1

CONTRASTS IN LEARNING?

Tony Edwards

Very damaging effects are attributed to that deep 'divide' between 'academic' and 'vocational' post-compulsory education which has marked the English education system. It has been blamed for keeping one side too narrowly academic and the other too narrowly practical. Even worse, a persistent belief that 'real' education post-16 is properly reserved for an academically minded minority has kept participation rates well below those of most comparable countries, thereby producing an under-educated and under-skilled workforce. Variations on those bleak conclusions have been repeated many times.

Recent ministerial descriptions of the divide as false, artificial and unnecessary make the damage attributed to it seem readily repairable by sensible curriculum reform, and no educational 'engineer' could be more sensible than Sir Ron Dearing. Yet although his review of post-16 qualifications (1996: 1.13) recognises the 'cultural obstacles' to reform created by 'pervasive attitudes inherited from the past about the relative worth of achievement in the academic and vocational pathways', in particular their association with separated provision for 'the able and the less able', it makes only passing reference to the size of those obstacles and almost none to the long record of failure to surmount them. The persistent devaluing of vocational education, although increasingly challenged in policy rhetoric, reflects entrenched assumptions about the kinds of learning appropriate for future leaders and for even their most skilled followers. Different qualifications, or the lack of any qualifications at all, have served to allocate young people to different levels in the labour market. It has been assumed that an able minority are best prepared for high-status occupations by studying a few academic subjects in depth, the capacity of that specialised curriculum to survive fierce and persistent criticism being incomprehensible without an understanding of its association with preparing an elite. In contrast, vocational education has been provided largely for those regarded as being less able, as needing to be motivated by seeing direct connections between what they are learning now and their future employment, and as likely to enter technician-level occupations for which higher-order cognitive skills were taken to be largely irrelevant. It was the route for those judged to be unsuitable or who deemed themselves unsuited for advanced academic study, and it was almost entirely separated from extended general education (Green 1995).

1

Reviewing educational provision for the 15–18 age-group at a time when a trend to longer school life was just becoming apparent, the Crowther Committee (1959) identified 'the education of the ablest' as being 'what the English system does best'. It also saw the high cost of that preoccupation as a neglect of the rest which was especially conspicuous at the post-compulsory stage. Yet even though most 16–19 year olds are now in education and training rather than in employment, which is the transformation Crowther hoped for, remarkably similar conclusions continue to be drawn. The system is still seen as 'mainly geared to developing academic talents in a minority', whose success then 'casts a long shadow' because it so accentuates one kind of educational achievement that alternatives are stigmatised as suitable only for those who have failed at something else (Smithers and Robinson 1991). Two 'quite different traditions' are described as co-existing almost without touching, one based on 'an agreed content of [subject] knowledge and the abstract principles behind it' and the other on 'specific skills and competencies which are necessary to perform a job' (National Union of Teachers 1996: 3). To the extent that those traditions continue to be divided not only by curriculum and modes of learning but also by the prospects open to students working within them, then the 'cultural obstacles' to accepting them as different but not unequal appear formidable indeed. Large changes in the scale and scope of post-compulsory education may be blurring but are not yet covering the sides of the divide.

When the Crowther Committee deplored the waste of ability created by a highly selective education system, only 10 per cent of 17 year olds were in full-time education, compared with 60 per cent in 1996, and only 4 per cent were going on to higher education, compared with almost a third of the age-group who do so now. That growth, especially rapid during the years 1987–1993, has made staying on in many places the normal thing to do and turned not doing so into 'a new counter-cultural form of dropping out' (Green and Ainley 1995: 15). While enough of the stayers have left full-time education at 17 to maintain unfavourable comparisons with (for example) Japan, Germany and France, claims to a 'revolution in participation rates' are largely justified from a more insular perspective (*Department for Education* press release, 27 July 1994). It is a revolution partly brought about by young people who remain in school or enter college because they have nowhere else to go. The steep decline in job opportunities for young people lacking the educational qualifications used by employers to screen applicants has brought a rising demand for at least an educational waiting room. But it also reflects rising levels of achievement at 16, and consequent aspirations for further credentials to confer relative advantage in the search for jobs (Ashford *et al.* 1993). Emphasis on GCSE A–C grades in school performance tables and elsewhere sustains a widespread perception of lower-grade passes as 'failures' and so depresses the ambitions of many in the middle range (Cockett and Callaghan 1996). Yet in 1996, 44 per cent of the mass entry for GCSE achieved five or more of those 'good passes' and so met the traditional requirement for progressing to A level that was being attained in the early

1960s by only 15 per cent of the age-group. Attributing that three-fold 'rise in productivity' to less rigorous examining or the popularity of easier subjects, which are the explanations favoured by believers in a 'natural' rationing of 'real' educational achievement, has to take account of the fact that A level results have risen in parallel despite that examination's continuing (if sometimes questioned) reputation as a remaining bastion of academic standards. Higher education has itself become 'a popular undertaking' that draws in a third of the age-group at 18 compared with only 15 per cent even as recently as 1987, allowing the government to claim in its (1995) White Paper on *Competitiveness* that the United Kingdom has become 'a European leader in graduate output' . Hopes of further expansion are therefore focused on the preceding stage, and that remains no more than a 'medium participation system'. Indeed, relative success in graduate output highlights the relative failure to keep pace with the National Education and Training Target which prescribes that 60 per cent of the population should achieve by the age of 21 the level of educational performance (two A level passes or their equivalent) traditionally associated with academically and socially selected sixth forms.

The phrase 'or equivalent' indicates a main consequence of expansion, both the expansion already achieved and that intended. A level entries have risen three-fold in thirty years. In two authoritative but inconsistent judgements, either they 'may now be approaching the ceiling of academically-minded young people for whom A levels were designed' or they have already expanded well beyond 'the purposes for which they were created' (Dearing 1995: 5; 1996: 3.5). Those seem notable understatements of how an exclusive model has been adapted to a mass market. The initial design was intended for the more academically inclined pupils among the 'top 20 per cent' of the ability range that the grammar schools recruited. Even that selected minority were never as 'reasonably homogeneous in their academic abilities, inclinations and aspirations' as universities found it convenient to assume when they were resisting any significant broadening of the sixth form curriculum (Schools Council 1980: 29), and their diversity raised persistent objections that using the same examination as both an entry qualification for universities and a higher school leaving certificate forced large numbers of students into an inappropriately specialised and academic mould (Edwards 1983a). In the 1960s, rising numbers of so-called 'new' sixth formers, lacking the traditional prior achievement and academic aspirations, reinforced those objections and brought renewed demands for a less specialised (though not necessarily more vocational) alternative to A level. Thirty years later it had become generally agreed that the magnetic attraction of A level draws in far too many students who are not suited to the 'A level approach' and for whom the risk of 'disappointment' is high (Dearing 1996: 3.5). A necessary condition for reaching national targets that constitute a huge break with the traditional exclusiveness of English post-16 education is therefore seen as the successful introduction of qualifications offering different kinds of learning to new kinds of 'advanced' student, who would not previously have continued in full-time education. In an especially sharp break with the past, these 'vocational' or 'applied' alternatives to A level have to be both distinctively different in form and content and yet 'equal' (or 'equivalent' or 'comparable', these terms being used almost interchangeably) in the opportunities that they make available.

This is the challenge that the Dearing Report diminishes by giving it little attention. The traditional channelling of academically and socially selected cohorts along educationally stratified routes towards different levels of the labour market is exemplified in the Certificate of Pre-Vocational Education, which was explicitly offered to students described (by the government) as being 'of broadly average ability with modest examination achievements at 16' who would normally enter employment a year later. That its credential value was set even below that of O level explains why its more ambitious takers saw these pre-vocational courses as a way back to the 'academic' track rather than as an alternative way forward (Atkins 1984). In contrast, the BTEC National qualification was designed as a real alternative for students, many of whom were expected to be as able and ambitious as their A level contemporaries but who were also assumed to want their studies to be more practical and to have a direct bearing on their future employment. The promise of comparable prospects was then enhanced in publicity for Advanced GNVQs, hence the label of 'new vocational A levels' highlighted in the Department for Education's 'brief guide' to the new qualification (August 1993) and the accompanying assurance that its holders could move either into employment or into higher education. In Dearing's definition of its fitness for purpose, it is well suited to students 'whose approach to learning is by doing and finding out' and to employers with a high regard for core skills and 'more interactive learning styles' (Dearing 1995: 14). The promise is clear: a form of vocationally oriented but still general education is now available without the career disadvantages traditionally associated with it. It is to provide a bridge between two previously divided traditions.

Between promise and reality, however, lies the shadow thrown by A level's 'long life and innate quality' (Dearing 1996: 3.5). Its pedigree stretches back to 1951, and beyond that to a Higher School Certificate which also embodied the virtues attributed to specialised academic study. But while Dearing recognised the advantage bestowed on A level by appearing as the 'gold standard' qualification, he understated it in emphasising GNVQs' especial relevance to employers. The competition between ancient and modern would be much less unequal if it were indeed true that – 'Employers generally had limited interest in A levels and even less in AS . . . [which] were therefore seen as primarily relevant to higher education' (Dearing 1996, Appendices: 12, para. 21). That conclusion distorts A level's power as a multi-purpose credential. It may well be that most young people employed at 18 'were entering jobs for which the specific knowledge gained from A levels was not relevant', but that qualification has been heavily used as a proxy measure of 'promising' applicants' ambition, self-reliance, capacity for hard work, and capacity to learn. It has therefore been and remains by far the most marketable credential. It is noted in the Dearing Report that although A level students felt less well prepared than their GNVQ contemporaries for entering employment, they had no doubts at all about the market value of good A level passes. Advanced GNVQs therefore have to win parity of esteem with a long-established market leader that attracts almost all the students judged academically capable of following that traditional academic route. They have to provide the same 'level' of qualification for students who are generally weaker academically. They have to resemble the established academic model in the opportunities to which they give access, but they also have to be sufficiently unlike A levels in how knowledge is organised, transmitted and assessed to appeal to the much wider constituency of students on which the attainment of ambitious national education targets depends.

That formulation of fitness for purpose serves to introduce the research on which this book is largely based. It is research that reflects the writers' varied but complementary interests in approaches to learning that have traditionally marked off the 'academic' from the 'vocational' in English post-compulsory education. Carol Taylor Fitz-Gibbon had long been investigating students' performance at A level, her research indicating differences in the 'difficulty' of subjects as well as in how they were taught. The extension of an already very large database to include the teaching of BTEC National was partly to see whether the different purposes and structure of that qualification were evident in the organisation of students' learning, and also to see whether there were significant differences from A level in methods associated with successful performance. That evidence came largely from students' reports of the frequency of various classroom activities. In their earlier work on the uniqueness of the English pattern of 'study in depth' and its capacity to resist change, both Tony Edwards and Roy Haywood had noticed how little was known directly about pedagogic practice on either side of the curriculum 'divide', despite the confidence with which generalisations were exchanged. In an application to the Economic and Social Research Council for funding to investigate 'methods and effectiveness in post-16 teaching and learning', Carol Taylor Fitz-Gibbon and they emphasised this lack of observational evidence and the potential benefits of combining it with statistical data derived from the A level Information System. Nick Meagher was the Resarch Associate for that project. Previously director of studies in an inner-city comprehensive school, he had a particular interest in the effects of broadening access to post-16 education by diversifying the kinds of learning experience it offered. Building on the ESRC-funded project, he subsequently carried out for the NCVQ (in collaboration with Roy Haywood) an intensive programme of classroom observation of Advanced GNVQ in twenty-four schools and colleges in England, Wales and Northern Ireland. Carol Taylor Fitz-Gibbon's parallel contract with the NCVQ involved reanalysis of extensive statistical data on GNVQ practice. Work from both these later projects has also been drawn on in the book. Simultaneously with the ESRC research, Frank Hardman was comparing pedagogic practice in A level English Language and English Literature. As two of the 'easier' A levels identified by Dearing, they might not be expected to show large differences. Yet English Language was introduced as a separate A level in the mid-1980s as a deliberate move away from the academic study of literary texts and towards more 'applied' and even partly 'vocational' studies in which independent and collaborative learning would be strongly encouraged. Comparing how the two subjects were taught raised more general questions about how the nature of academic knowledge shapes its transmission. Before joining the staff of Newcastle University, Hardman had both co-ordinated the TVEI (Technical and Vocational Education Initiative) programme in a comprehensive school and headed its English department. Like many teachers, therefore, he had straddled the 'divide' between the academic and the vocational.

Although their perspectives and approaches differ considerably, all five contributors to the book are intrigued by the dilemma that pervades post-16 curricular reform. The versions of advanced general education embodied in GNVQs, more vocationally oriented and more applied than the established academic model, have to resemble this model sufficiently in market value that prospective students will not be diverted onto a less suitable pathway by the greater rewards to which it may lead. But GNVQs also have to be sufficiently unlike the established model to appeal to the much wider constituency of students on which raising the educational level of the workforce depends. It may well seem that distinctiveness of 'approach' is much easier to achieve than parity of esteem, given the different kinds of provision traditionally made for 'academically' and 'vocationally' minded students and the different curriculum traditions in which A levels are embedded and from which Advanced GNVQ has emerged. Certainly the key terms in discourse about them are drawn from such different vocabularies that they are very unlikely to be different ways of defining rather similar learning experiences. And in the hectic debate about their respective merits, contrasts are often drawn very sharply indeed. This is understandable. While Advanced GNVQs have to establish their distinctiveness as well as their credibility, A levels attract support from educational conservatives for whom a preoccupation with practicality and relevance represents a betrayal of real education. Their advocates are therefore inclined to polarise the supposed characteristics of each, ignoring such inconvenient complications as the popularity of some 'applied' A levels, the attention now being paid to those transferable skills that academic study has been assumed to develop, and the weight now placed on underpinning knowledge and conceptual understanding in GNVQ. It is certainly commonplace to criticise A levels for neglecting skills and GNVQs for neglecting knowledge, views caricatured by a GNVQ student's complaint against a lecturer, presumably not yet socialised into GNVQ-approved ways of working, who continued to be 'more of an A level teacher expecting you to learn masses of stuff from books instead of letting you find out for yourself' (Chorlton 1994: 97–98). A rather similar, generalised contrast appears in the Dearing Report. The Advanced GNVQ students surveyed as part of that review tended to see their learning as having been organised around

6

independent study and 'research', while their A level contemporaries reported a predominance of 'lectures' (Dearing 1996, Appendices: 39–40).

A liking for sharp contrasts is also apparent among educational researchers. Fitz-Gibbon (1996) has criticised the tendency to pose research questions more realistically formulated as 'how much of A and how much of B?' in the stark form of 'is it A or is it B?'. But the debate about post-16 provision has been and remains highly contentious. Drawing the sides in black and white is much more likely to attract attention than doing so in shades of grey, as Alan Smithers (1993) demonstrated in his highly publicised attack on NVQ and GNVQ models of learning.

Although written with Fitz-Gibbon's warning in mind, Chapter 2 returns in more detail to the strong contrasts in the provision traditionally made for 'academically' and 'vocationally' minded students. From these are drawn expectations about practice, although reasons are also suggested as to why even these are less than clear cut. The chapters that follow are about differences and similarities in practice. They report evidence of how students on both sides of the curriculum 'divide', and from hundreds of schools and colleges, think they have been taught. They also report on how those students prefer to learn, how their teachers define the kinds of learning appropriate for particular qualifications, and how the organisation of learning for 'different but equal' qualifications was observed in forty schools and colleges. Although that evidence is placed in the context of current and recent changes in the scale and scope of post-compulsory provision, the book is not another account of already well-documented reforms and proposals for reform. Its focus is on the objectives and processes of learning at a stage which is certainly being transformed, but which is still powerfully shaped by myths about the sixth form and the education of 'leaders'. It is with these large historical residues that the next chapter begins.

2

EDUCATING LEADERS AND TRAINING FOLLOWERS

Tony Edwards

Contemplating the future of the English 'sixth form' when rising numbers were already challenging its elite image, Alec Peterson suggested abandoning the term altogether as an obstacle to rational discussion. For many of his pre-war generation who 'owe everything to the sixth form and will not forget it', it was too 'emotionally overloaded' with memories of a time when, 'with a handful of others,' they first tasted intellectual excitement and saw the possibility of a university place 'with all the accompanying visions of expanded ambitions and upward social mobility' (Peterson 1973: 2). That theme of irrational attachment to a partly mythical past appears in many accounts of resistance to change. For example, puzzled observers of the sixth form curriculum were advised to abandon any notion 'that a curriculum is a set of arrangements which rationality has called into being and which rationality can alter'; that peculiar pattern of studying a very few subjects in depth was so bound into the grammar school tradition of preparing an academic elite for high status occupations that it had remained immovable against all criticism of excessive specialisation (Taylor *et al.* 1974: 5). Deploring its immovability twenty years later, the first head of the National Curriculum Council recalled that debates about reforming A level had been 'second in irrationality' only to arguments about overcrowding the preceding stage. Thus reasonable proposals for curriculum space in which to develop core skills had been 'met with unsubstantiated assertion and, sadly, an implication that treason was afoot' (Graham 1993: 126).

In trying to explain that extreme response, Duncan Graham referred to the power of the private school lobby to hold ministers to the cause of A level conservation. Certainly that sector has a vested interest in retaining a qualification in which high success rates contribute substantially to schools' market appeal. Whether those rates are any higher than should be expected from such academically and socially selected intakes is questionable (Tymms 1992; West and West 1996), but the fact that a sector that contains only 8 per cent of 14 year olds produces about a third of school leavers with three A level passes is regularly highlighted in its publicity. The sector's leading schools certainly have no obvious interest in vocational alternatives to A level which they do not offer themselves, and which they are very unlikely to offer as long as these are seen as incompatible with marketing traditional academic excellence (Higham *et al.* 1996; Edwards and Whitty 1997). Yet in 1994, both the Headmasters' Conference and the Girls' Schools Association signed a joint declaration with other professional bodies in support of a national system of post-16 qualifications within which academic and vocational modules could be combined.

It is the relative status of those alternatives, however, that remains the critical issue. Duncan Graham's larger explanation for repeated failures to broaden A level was the continuing hold of that tradition of educating an elite 'through the acquisition of knowledge for its own sake' which it is seen to embody (Graham 1993: 126). That tradition has survived the facts that A levels are now taken by a third of the age-group rather than a select company of scholars of the kind recalled by Peterson, and that the proportion achieving at least two 'good passes' at A level is now several times larger than the entire sixth form cohort of forty years ago. Growth on that scale has aroused fierce objections from those who believe that true academic achievement is rationed by the 'natural' distribution of abilities, so that one response to it has been a strong inclination to preserve the academic route from deterioration by 'relegating' supposedly inappropriate students to 'membership in a low prestige or stigmatised curriculum' or, in a less caustic formulation of the same diversionary tactic, to construct 'a separate vocational ladder for less academic students to climb' (Reid and Holt 1986: 90; Raffe and Surridge 1995: 4). It was not surprising therefore that the Dearing review of post-16 qualifications was shackled from the start by a requirement 'first and foremost to ensure that the rigour of A-levels is maintained' (Dearing 1995: 16). Nor was it surprising that yet another reference to A levels as 'the gold standard' appeared in the Secretary of State's press release welcoming the final report (27 March 1996). That phrase has long been a cliché in curriculum debate, its users seeming not to notice that the country abandoned the real gold standard in 1931 and did so without any of the disasters predicted to follow that reluctant decision. Yet unless the traditionalism that it captures is understood, the long record of failed reforms will seem 'irrational' to the point of perversity.

It is in the context of A level's continuing dominance of the educational currency market that I first consider the traditional hierarchy of post-compulsory pathways in English education. A level has long been associated with selective preparation for 'middle-class' (professional and managerial) employment. That remains the case. What has changed dramatically has been the belief that only a small part of the workforce needs the qualities associated with such employment. Education and Training Targets are now set for a majority of the population at levels intended to accredit outcomes traditionally associated with high status occupations – notably those of initiative, self-reliance and a well-developed capacity to solve problems and take decisions. That majority educational experience is therefore intended to be very different indeed from the processes of induction into established working practices and habits that overtly characterised vocational education in the past (Chitty 1991; Hodkinson 1991). In an apparent convergence of learning objectives with those of the academic route, it is now expected to incorporate 'the value of conceptual study' and to promote 'general intellectual capacity' by developing the 'higher-order skills' of analysis and evaluation (SEAC 1992: 7). Yet such apparently similar outcomes are expected from very different forms of curriculum, pedagogy and assessment. As indicated in the opening chapter, this book is concerned with new vocationally oriented forms of advanced general education and not with the 'training' alternatives gathered within the NVQ framework. After outlining the difficulty in securing anything like parity of esteem for these alternatives, I consider what predominant forms of learning might be expected in the contrasting curriculum traditions in which A level is located and from which Advanced GNVQ has emerged. Although brief references are made to our own research, my purpose is to provide a context for the empirical chapters that follow.

PREPARATION FOR LEADERSHIP AND PARITY OF ESTEEM

Charles Handy (1984) has described the British education system as having outgrown the society that produced it, a society in which an 'educated' minority managed a barely literate majority. That model of a steep-sided pyramid became politically unacceptable in a democratic society. It has also come to seem economically disastrous, so that a remarkable level of agreement has been reached about the kind of workforce needed for a modern economy to prosper. Briefly, industries that needed only a small proportion of skilled workers have disappeared or declined, as have processes of mass production in which routine activities are managed from above. Professional, managerial and service employment is growing, especially in those 'knowledge jobs' that depend on manipulating and communicating information. At almost all levels of employment, the pace of technological change requires workers to be adept at acquiring new knowledge and new skills rather than at reliably repeating past methods. Adaptability and flexibility therefore appear as cardinal virtues in the new labour market.

I am not assuming the correctness of this analysis. Indeed, there are strong grounds for questioning whether the 'upskilling' of employment and the consequent decline of 'unskilled' labour are as pervasive as they are often taken to be; whether the supposedly 'tightening bonds' between qualifications and educational attainment are as visible beyond professional, managerial and technical occupations as is often assumed; and whether the attention given to investing in occupational know-how has served to divert attention from other economic and political failings (Ashton *et al.* 1990; Merson 1995; Brown and Lauder 1996; Hodkinson *et al.* 1996). What I am assuming is the influence of that analysis on post-compulsory education policy and the debates surrounding it. Most obvious has been the ending, for reasons that also include the social dangers of high youth unemployment, of that long neglect of 'half our future' for whom no serious educational provision had been made beyond the compulsory stage, as though whatever else they needed to know to be effective workers could be picked up as they went along (Holland 1979; Edwards 1983b). By 1989, the Confederation of British Industry could already expect agreement in principle, though certainly not in practice, that the employment of 16–18 year olds 'without training leading to nationally recognised qualifications' should be quickly abandoned. Its analysis of a 'skills revolution' demanding prompt educational response gave impetus to national targets that, however necessary by international standards, represented a very sharp break with the traditional exclusiveness of English post-compulsory education. Two A level passes or their equivalent was now expected from 60 per cent of the population, even though it represented a level of attainment reached by only 15 per cent as recently as 1985, because nothing less was deemed appropriate for entry to an ever-rising level of employment involving complex, non-routine activities, 'considerable individual responsibility' and some supervision of others. Writing to head-teachers of all maintained secondary schools about their obligation to help reach that target (25 May 1995), the Schools Minister Eric Forth referred to an increasingly sophisticated economy in which many employers, 'particularly those operating in international markets and those using modern technology, now see this as the basic level required by their employees'. So when an educational conservative expressed doubts about whether average standards needed to rise, provided that the top 20 per cent continued to be highly educated, his seemed a voice from a past age still committed to a steep pyramid of leaders and followers (O'Hear 1991).

Acceptance of the economic case for a better educated workforce has made rapid growth in post-compulsory provision an international phenomenon, causing disturbance to various national arrangements of educationally and socially segregated 'pathways for learning'. These pathways are typically arranged in a hierarchy that descends from the 'general' (or 'pre-academic' in the sense of being a preparation for higher education), through the 'technical' (for technician-level employment) to 'vocational' training for those entering manual or routine white-collar employment (OECD 1989). The ordering is hierarchical because these three routes give the readiest access to different levels in the labour market, and students are selected and self-selected accordingly. National education systems differ considerably in the relative size and status of the pathways, in ease of movement between them, and in the extent to which 'academic' qualifications are used for screening of potential employees as well as potential advanced students, though considerable relative advantages are normally conferred by success on the academic track (Wolf and Rapiau 1993). What has distinguished the English system has been the selectiveness of that track, and the lack of high status alternatives able to attract some of the ablest students (Sanderson 1994; McCulloch 1989).

The academic track leads furthest and fastest where successful outcomes are taken as evidence of high intellectual capacity, and so are given preference over credentials which may be more directly relevant to that area of employment but that are also taken as indicating a lower level of trainability (OECD 1989: 72–73). In the English system, the relative advantage bestowed by A level on those not entering higher education remained sufficiently uncertain as long as the youth labour market stayed buoyant. This uncertainty reinforced demands for less specialised, shorter or vocationally oriented alternatives for 'new' (or 'non-traditional') sixth formers and their college equivalents (Dean *et al.* 1979: 255–262). But although used most obviously by universities as evidence of fitness to proceed to a degree course, A level's increasing use for direct entry to professional, managerial and some 'technical' employment as evidence of intelligence, ambition and other 'useful' attributes meant that successive proposals for broader, less 'demanding' alternatives raised immediate objections that they would offer inferior opportunities (Drake and Edwards 1979; Maguire and Ashton 1981; Burchell 1992). This is why so many comprehensive schools have struggled to maintain a range of A level subjects not viable from a cool calculation of resource management. But the unique value of A level as a multi-purpose credential has also brought formidable dilemmas for schools and colleges in their counselling of students. Despite the bleak statistic that a third of those attempting it 'waste' two years by not completing their course at all or not achieving the level of qualification they sought (with Advanced GNVQs soon showing similar failure rates), it has been difficult to advise academically marginal students against taking that risk when the potential rewards are so high (Audit Commission 1993). This has worked against a national interest in encouraging 'some of the most able to follow a vocational pathway', and a national interest in discouraging those tempted to follow a route for which they are not suited (Dearing 1995: 7–10).

Clearly, the select company of subject-minded scholars portrayed in nostalgic evocations of the old sixth form has long become a large and diverse crowd. Even at a time when most sixth formers were still in grammar schools, a quarter of them and over 40 per cent of those in comprehensive schools were not intending to enter higher education, making it evident that 'the sixth form can no longer be thought of as the training ground for a narrow and clearly defined band of professions' (Schools Council 1972: 54). When not afflicted by doubts about lax assessment exaggerating the rise in attainment, government ministers have taken pride in the 'revolution' in participation rates since that time and sought further expansion. But they have also wished to hold the line around A level as the embodiment of traditional academic standards and values. To a critic, that conservationist approach has been 'an altar on which the enthusiasms, achievements and attitudes of the majority have been sacrificed' (Holland 1994: 6). But, as was argued earlier, the defence of A level has very deep cultural roots. They include 'old humanist' resistance both to vulgarising culture to make it more accessible, and to giving technical and vocational education anything like equality with a 'liberal' training of the mind. In that particular liberal tradition, technical knowledge is what the educated minority hire and direct but do not themselves possess (Mathieson and Bernbaum 1988; McCulloch 1991;

Sanderson 1994). Reactions to the expansion in full-time post-compulsory education have therefore ranged from regret at its continuing insufficiency in comparison with 'competitor' countries to disbelief that it can have occurred without a serious decline in 'real' educational standards.

Disbelief that so many are really entitled to take an academic route long kept exclusive has prompted support for vocational alternatives to A level from those wishing to divert unsuitable students on to supposedly less demanding routes. The more generous response has been to recognise that 'more means different' (Ball 1990). But does different mean equivalent? The difficulty of achieving anything like parity of esteem for arriviste qualifications contending with A level's aristocratic pedigree has seemed to some observers to be so insurmountable that they recommend a single 18-plus qualification into which A level would be submerged (Finegold *et al.* 1990; National Commission on Education 1995; Crombie-White *et al.* 1995). The Conservative Government, however, remained committed to 'three types of qualification which it is right should remain distinct' (Secretary of State Gillian Shephard, 9 November 1994), but which it has also wished to see accepted as different but equal. On the eve of the transition from BTEC National to Advanced GNVQs, a main theme throughout a conference organised by the Schools Examination and Assessment Council was the high risk that the distinctive purposes of alternative qualifications would become confused or obscured if 'spurious connections' are claimed which then appear merely as an expedient bid for status. 'Equivalence', it was concluded, is 'highly elusive' (SEAC 1992: 9).

Carol Taylor Fitz-Gibbon argues elsewhere in this book that the esteem in which a qualification is held depends on what its holders are believed from that evidence to know, understand and be able to do. But it also depends largely on the kinds of student it is believed to attract – their social origins, ability and likely occupational destinations. An Advanced GNVQ is intended to be worth the same as two A level passes as a qualification for entry to higher education or specialised vocational training or employment, with a Merit or Distinction equivalent to higher grades of A level pass. It should therefore 'tell' employers or admission tutors that its holders have reached the same 'level' of educational performance, even though they have done so through a very different kind of 'learning experience'. In the English system, in which a 'practical' curriculum has long been regarded as provision for the second-best, those two messages are not easily reconciled. It is therefore not surprising that most of those 'qualified' to take the academic route choose to do so, or that many less 'suitable' students also do so, or that Advanced GNVQ has recruited largely from 'the middle range of GCSE achievement' (FEU *et al.* 1994: 33). There is some overlap in prior achievements because some students who would have been accepted for A level choose the vocational route instead. There is no evidence, however, of the 'drift' of academically able students from A level that universities were warned about as GNVQ got underway (McNeill 1994). In so far as the two qualifications compete for the same students, they do so on very unequal terms which include persistent doubts about whether GNVQs compare with A levels in 'difficulty'. That particular lack of a recognised equivalence is explored by Carol Taylor Fitz-Gibbon, with due regard for her own evidence of differences in the 'difficulty' of A level subjects which complicate generalisations.

It is certainly easier to see the two qualifications as being complementary, with Advanced GNVQs attracting large numbers who would not previously have considered staying on at all. Yet there is no clear division of labour between them because overlapping functions are intended. As noted earlier, many 'successful' A level students enter employment at 18 confident in the market value of that credential, even though they may feel less well equipped than their GNVQ contemporaries with IT, presentational and some other skills relevant to beginning a job (Dearing 1996: 7). Many GNVQ students are attracted by an apparent and direct relevance to an area of employment (Green and Ainley 1995). But although that qualification was intended to lead naturally to employment or occupationally specific training, the fact that such a majority of its students hope to go on to college or university seems to indicate that it is 'evolving very much as an educational award'. To the extent that this is so, its rapid growth may be attributable more to 'a major change in young people's educational aspirations' than to pent-up demand for advanced vocational education or to other supposedly distinctive characteristics. The more it develops in that direction, the more its success will be judged 'largely by the numbers getting into higher education', despite the objections of those who see it primarily as bridging the gap between full-time academic education and work-based training (FEU *et al.* 1994: 6 and 35).

Urging industry to recognise and use the new qualification, the Higher Education Minister Tim Boswell accepted that 'parity cannot be conferred, it must be earned' (*The Times Educational Supplement* 28 February 1994). It can be argued that its sudden designation by ministers as 'Vocational A-levels' was a mistaken bid for prestige by association at the cost of diminishing the educational distinctiveness that its promoters were also keen to emphasise. Rejecting that particular designation because it brought confusion with NVQs gained mainly in the workplace, Dearing sought an alternative means of 'conferment' in renaming Advanced GNVQs as 'Applied A-levels'. He hoped that label would 'help give parents a better understanding of the value society placed on the GNVQ', while at the same time identifying 'a distinctive approach to learning based on the application of knowledge' (Dearing 1996: 9.14). That proposal has apparently been not only rejected by the government but withdrawn by Dearing himself, despite its warm welcome from (for example) the Labour Party and several teacher associations. One headline has referred to 'Applied A-levels' as 'set for the sidings'; another referred to a 'failure to redeem an ailing qualification' which the ensuing analysis attributed, predictably, to ministerial unwillingness 'to tarnish the "gold standard" of the A-level by broadening its scope' (*The Times Higher Education Supplement* 18 October 1996, *The Times Educational Supplement* 8 November 1996). Dearing's initial purpose, however, extended beyond the bolstering of GNVQs' market appeal. In so far as parity with A level is indeed 'earned' rather than arbitarily 'conferred', then different modes of teaching and learning would no longer be expected as a consequence of the lower ability or disinclination for academic study attributed to vocational students, nor explained by their probably lower-status destinations in the labour market. Instead, students would be advised on which route to take according to their educationally preferred mode of travel. That advice would not be based on matching a student's general ability against the level of intellectual demand associated with A level, but would be given after a much subtler diagnosis of suitability for particular kinds of learning and assessment. It is with these educational differences that the rest of the chapter is concerned.

DIFFERENCES IN CURRICULUM, ASSESSMENT AND PEDAGOGY

As forms of curriculum, A level and Advanced GNVQ represent sharply contrasting ways of selecting and organising knowledge. A level is made up from a collection of separate academic subjects, each chosen by the student within the constraints of what the school or college can offer and what future employers or admissions tutors may expect or prefer. Breadth or balance in that choice may be desirable, but neither is required. Nor are tangible benefits in the assessment of students' performance attached to their capacity to make cross-curricular links. Within each subject, knowledge and ways of knowing are selected from the concerns and working practices of what are mostly well-established academic disciplines within the liberal tradition of valuing 'knowledge for its own sake'. They therefore have their own internal criteria of relevance and worth which are deliberately detached from those of 'everyday' life, as they are from those of other disciplines. By comparison, GNVQs represent knowledge and skills 'regionalised' into 'areas of application' (Bernstein 1990: 63) – that is, selected primarily because of their presumed relevance as preparation for employment within a particular vocational field. Their usefulness is intended to be obvious to students who want to see fairly direct and fairly immediate application of what they are learning to the 'real world', in particular the 'world of work'. Advanced GNVQs are therefore vigorously promoted as appealing to students who 'prefer qualifications which are closely oriented to the requirements of employment' (NCVQ 1994: 8).

They are also typically described as suiting those who prefer more practical and collaborative and less desk-bound modes of learning (Chorlton 1994: 89). Both the assumed preferences of students and the extent to which these are met in practice are explored in Roy Haywood's chapter on different learning styles, and how far these seem to match in practice the apparent objectives and requirements of A levels and Advanced GNVQs. Part of the hard work needed to establish the credibility of the latter has been to give unusually explicit attention to the kinds of 'learning experience' their students can expect. These are therefore more easily visible for investigation than are the entrenched but diffuse beliefs surrounding A level about (for example) the qualities of leadership and independence that advanced academic study is presumed to develop. And although the bid for parity with A level has worked against some innovations, notably the initial attempt to do without any formal tests of 'under-pinning' knowledge and the continuing but increasingly questioned resistance to sub-stantial externally assessed written work, the Dearing Review retains notions of novelty and 'distinctiveness'. In exploring differences that have been intended if not necessarily achieved, I have kept in mind the warning cited earlier against translating 'more-or-less' questions into the more dramatic but less realistic form of 'either–or'. Indeed, explanations of why even expectations of difference are less than clear-cut anticipates the frequent blurring in practice apparent from classroom observation.

Knowledge 'pure' and knowledge 'applied'

Along with recommendations that transfer of students between routes and some mixing of academic and vocational studies should become easier, Dearing also insisted on the distinctiveness of the 'approach to learning' embodied in GNVQ and defined by the application of knowledge to real-life problems and tasks. As a way of marking the distance from A levels, that may seem an obvious strategy.

Despite its transformation from narrow track to broad highway, A level as a form of curriculum has shown remarkable resistance to being reconstructed. More subjects have become available, syllabuses have been reduced and subject cores established, coursework has been given a limited place in formal assess-ment, modular syllabuses have created possibilities for flexible programmes of study, and belated attention is being paid to developing and to assessing explicitly those generic skills that advanced academic study has been assumed to impart. Yet throughout these changes, recently described as 'creeping modernisation' (Higham *et al.* 1996: 53), A level remains essentially what it was when it replaced the similarly structured Higher School Certificate in 1951. A very few subjects are studied separately, then examined separately at the end of two years. A persis-tent academic bias keeps those subjects largely detached from considerations of usefulness, so that although (for example) Mathematics and the physical sciences are entry requirements for many vocational degrees, their content is very largely shaped by the pursuit of knowledge 'for its own sake' (Jones 1992). It is true that the 'modernising' process has recently brought sharply increased entries (though from a very low base) in such relatively applied subjects as Sociology and Psychology, and a proliferation of 'studies' (notably Business) that are not homogeneous disciplines but resemble the 'regionalised' knowledge mentioned earlier. As Frank Hardman shows in Chapter 5, the new A level subject of English Language was intended to be less arcane than English Literature in its frame of reference, to have some visible vocational relevance, and to encourage the development of some of those generic skills that Dearing located predominantly in GNVQs. Similarly, when HMI distinguish between Economics and Business Studies, in terms of the emphasis of the first on understanding 'concepts relating to the creation and use of resources and the exchange and distribution of wealth' and of the second on 'explaining how specific sectors of the economy operate', they are distinguishing between old and new choices within the A level range (Ofsted 1996a). Yet despite such 'modernising' changes, if General Studies is excluded as being a complement rather than an addition to students' specialised choices, then nearly two-thirds of the 1996 A level entries were in the same ten subjects that predominated forty years ago in the sixth forms of grammar schools. By comparison with their established presence, Table 2.1 shows most 'new' subjects still struggling to secure their niche.

It is true that attributing to A level students an eager 'subject-mindedness', a term that implies interest in knowledge for its own sake, has to take into account the capacity of traditional A levels to keep open a range of options for those who have not yet decided what to do next. For many such students, their A level programme is 'deferred vocationalism': they may not rate highly the usefulness or even the inherent interest of the knowledge being accredited, but they do not doubt its exchange value once they have decided what to exchange it for (Fuller *et al.* 1991). My concern here, however, is not with students' motivation but with how their studies are structured, and how traditional A levels are largely freed from an obligation to be useful by the priority given to acquiring knowledge and understanding according to the rules of that particular subject

Table 2.1 A level entries, 1996

Pure		Applied		General	
English	12.0	Art & Design	4.6	General Studies	8.6
Mathematics	9.1	Sociology	4.0		
Biology	7.0	Business Studies	3.9		
History	5.9	Psychology	3.2		
Geography	5.8	Law	1.6		
Chemistry	5.5	Technical Subjects	1.5		
Physics	4.4	Computing	1.4		
French	3.7	Expressive Arts	1.3		
Economics	3.3	Sport/PE	1.3		
		Media/Film	1.2		
Sub-total:	56.7	Communication Studies	0.7		
German	1.5	Home Economics	0.4		
Other foreign languages	1.4				
Religious Studies	1.2				
Classical Subjects	1.0				
Music	0.9				
Science	0.7				
TOTALS:	63.4		25.1		8.6

Note: Figures are percentages of all entries

(Lewis 1994; Pring 1993; Hirst 1993). This is why they have such strong appeal for 'cultural restorationists', who see them as bodies of literally 'disciplined' knowledge which should be authoritatively transmitted and traditionally examined. Rejecting integrated and other purportedly 'practical' studies even in mainstream secondary schooling as a mistaken bid for relevance, they find them especially deplorable at the post-compulsory stage when an able elite should be developing those qualities of mind appropriate to their future responsibilities. From that perspective, the preservation of A level in its traditional form is a necessary obstacle to the intrusion of 'progressive' tendencies to impoverish true education by confining it largely to what may appeal to students here and now (Pilkington 1991; O'Hear 1987, 1993). So when (for example) the Further Education Unit (1992) rejected the conventional boundaries between 'arts' and 'science' or the 'theoretical' and the 'practical' as damagingly restrictive, and proposed instead 'new study combinations . . . more relevant to an innovation culture', both diagnosis and remedy would be anathema to defenders of 'proper' academic knowledge 'properly' taught.

In sharp contrast, Advanced GNVQs have been openly promoted as useful knowledge. They too have been criticised as over-specialised, each 'vocational field' taking up so much of students' time that general education is reduced to the compulsory units of core skills supposedly integrated within the programme (Sparkes 1994). But, unlike A levels, their intended outcomes are derived from what is considered an appropriate general preparation for that field of employ-ment and are presented as attracting a different kind of student for that reason. Most GNVQs carry their claim to occupational relevance in their names (Health and Social Care, Manufacturing, Engineering, Retail and Distributive Services, and so on). Even in GNVQ Science, which has less of the appearance of applied knowledge, there is an overt emphasis on understanding 'the work of scientists and developing the skills which scientists use', and the mandatory units are defined largely by what students learn to do – to analyse, investigate, obtain, control, monitor, communicate. That emphasis is justified not only by its supposed appeal to students, but in relation to what employers expect of recruits with qualifications in science (Coles *et al.* 1995).

It also reflects a continuing belief in the motivating effects of more 'practical' studies on less 'academic' students, a belief that was conspicuous in the Norwood Report's notorious matching of three types of secondary schooling to three types of pupil. Destined for 'the learned professions . . . and higher administrative and business posts', the grammar school type was able to 'grasp an argument or follow a piece of reasoning', was interested in causes as well as actions and in 'how things came to be as well as how they are', and was 'sensi-tive to language as expression of thought'. This was the type that presumably came into its own in the sixth form. Below the gold of the grammar schools in Norwood's hierarchy, but above the practically minded majority to be catered for in the secondary modern schools, came the silver products of the secondary technical schools, whose 'interests and abilities lie markedly in the field of applied science and applied art' and for whom 'knowledge must be capable of immediate application' (Board of Education 1943: 2). That 'technical type' seems not unlike the kind of student whom Advanced GNVQ is intended to attract: more practically minded than those taking the A level route but also more theoretically inclined than those taking NVQs.

Forty years after Norwood, the prime mover in the Technical and Vocational Education Initiative defended his 'dawn raid on education' on similar grounds. To David Young, then heading the Manpower Services Commission, the existing secondary school curriculum was 'too academic and tends towards the universities'; it needed 'another line of development that is equally respectable and desirable, which leads to vocational qualifications' (*Education* 19 November 1982: 386). Although HMI later regretted the under-representation of the ablest pupils among those involved in TVEI, Young had not intended it for them but for those below them in the conventional hierarchy who would benefit from a technically oriented alternative to the usual watered-down version of the academic curriculum (Young 1990: 89–91). When city technology colleges (a 'logical extension' of TVEI to some of their advocates) later included in their mission the task of raising the staying-on rate in inner-city areas to levels usually associated with grammar schools or suburban comprehensives, the achievement of that objective was seen as dependent on breaking the academic and elitist mould of post-16 education by creating a new qualification for students 'who want to do things as well as know about them' and who ask 'always' to see relevance in what they learn (CTC Trust 1991; Jones 1992).

It is this kind of motivational effect that is claimed when GNVQ is described as providing for students 'whose abilities would not otherwise be properly developed or recognised' (NCVQ 1994: 8). As the Secretary of State explained to a conference of headteachers of traditionally academic private schools clearly assumed not to need such inducements, the government's policy for other kinds of children was 'to raise levels of achievement by motivating those pupils who do not respond best to a purely academic curriculum' (Gillian Shephard, speaking to the Girls' Schools Association, 9 November 1994). Although Dearing was required by the same Secretary of State to retain the 'purely academic' pathway represented by A level, his own justification for rejecting a single post-16 qualification was that it would be heavily skewed towards 'the proven A level approach . . . to the detriment of students who have not yet responded well to academic learning and who are stimulated by a different approach' involving 'the application of knowledge and skills in a broadly vocational context' and a systematic training in how to learn (Dearing 1995: 12–13). In his Final Report, he therefore proposed that the distinctiveness of the two qualifications should be clear and 'consistent'. While recognising a trend in some A levels towards 'relevance and application' which might cause them to be more appropriately allocated to the 'applied' pathway, he defined as the primary orientation of the academic route the development of knowledge, skills and understanding 'associated with a subject or discipline'. He then positioned Advanced GNVQs at the interface between them and that 'mastery of a trade or profession at the relevant level' which is the main purpose of NVQs. As an alternative form of general education rather than vocational training, GNVQs had nevertheless to be more practical than A levels in content and also in modes of learning, which 'combine classroom and workshop experience' and provide frequent opportunities for 'working with others and planning one's own study' (Dearing 1996: 3.21–3.25).

In practice, as argued earlier, the initial intention to keep GNVQs much closer to the vocational than to the academic side of the post-16 continuum came into conflict with the accompanying intention to achieve parity of esteem. The second objective has taken precedence, with uneasiness about departing too far from familiar forms of curriculum and assessment being reinforced by economic arguments about the high level of conceptual understanding required of 'thoughtful workers' in a modern labour force. Reforms since its introduction have therefore produced a broader view of the knowledge that should 'underpin' students' demonstrable process skills. They have also brought threshold testing of that knowledge, the grading of the final GNVQ award, the replacement of 'competences' by 'attainment' in the formulation of learning objectives, and current proposals (following the Capey review of weaknesses contributing to a continuing lack of credibility) for much more substantial external assessment. Even initially, the 'disregard for knowledge' that Smithers (1993) attributed to the NVQ model exaggerated the disregard displayed by the GNVQs adapted from that model for full-time students in schools and colleges. But that these could still be described by a 1995 NUS/UWT policy statement as having 'no syllabuses as such' illustrates how far they depart from A level notions of content prescribed and organised according to the nature of an academic discipline. When GNVQs first emerged, they reflected their NVQ origins by specifying learning outcomes relevant to a field of employment but not specifying how those outcomes were to be achieved. Knowledge relevant to achieving them might or might not have a disciplinary base; that was a matter for the teacher to determine, although it was very unlikely indeed to be found in a single discipline. The basic approach was fervently defended as a radical new model of learning appropriate to the modern world, 'a conceptual framework within which to rethink both content and delivery' (Wolf 1995: xii). Enthusiasts proclaimed it a model 'appropriate for education and training of all kinds' because it discarded old notions of prescribed content, prescribed periods of study, and forms of assessment which over-valued a facility in writing essays and formulating examination answers that had little relevance to the demands of non-academic contexts (Ball 1995; Jessup 1991, 1995). Critics dismissed it as so narrowly utilitarian in what was included as relevant skills, knowledge and understanding that it carried the dangers both of impoverished training and a widening of the academic–vocational divide (Smithers 1993; Hyland 1994; Eraut 1994; Bates 1995; Wolf 1995).

Among the damaging consequences that Smithers attributed to the new model's 'disdain for knowledge' was the discouragement of 'teaching in a conventional sense'. Lacking a syllabus, teachers of NVQ and GNVQ were described as consuming so much time in designing units of study and preparing materials to fit them that they had little time left for considering how to teach. Worse still, they were portrayed as being deliberately discouraged from using the 'only two methods known to be effective' – namely, whole-class teaching and direct instruction (Smithers 1993: 31). In its response to that attack, the NCVQ (1994) agreed that it intended to discourage 'conventional' teaching as Smithers defined it but rejected 'the notion that if knowledge is not imparted through instruction based on fully prescribed content it cannot properly be gained'. Both then and in subsequent publications, the Council's theme has been that 'unconventional' teaching is appropriate for the kinds of student taking GNVQs and is effective preparation for their entry to a modern, adaptable, workforce. In giving such prominence to student autonomy, self-reliance and capacity to acquire new knowledge and skills, the recommended 'approach' seems to converge on principal components in the rhetoric traditionally surrounding A level. It is with this apparent convergence and its implications for pedagogic practice that the rest of the chapter is concerned.

From teaching to learning?

In reporting statistical data indicating that Advanced GNVQ courses 'differ consistently' from A levels in their delivery, Carol Taylor Fitz-Gibbon asks what had given teachers the signal to teach in a different way when there is so much evidence of professional resistance to pedagogic change. The intention that Advanced GNVQs should offer a different kind of learning experience has been explicit from the start. How the promised differences are to be secured is not easily identified, because their origins lie in a model of learning premised on specifying required outcomes but not specifying either the content or the processes through which these outcomes are to be achieved. To its critics, this apparent flexibility is a serious weakness because it ignores what can be gained from building in the kinds of learning expected of students, rather than seeking merely to 'test them in' (Sparkes 1994: 7). It is nevertheless possible to generalise about modes of learning appropriate to Advanced GNVQs to an extent to which A levels are not amenable, despite Dearing's repeated references to two distinctive 'approaches'. For example, when the NCVQ's (1995) student guide to GNVQ Science describes the variety of individual and team projects built into it, it highlights both the 'out-of school contexts for gathering data' and (more generally) the frequent opportunities 'for you to decide what you do and how you go about doing it'. Similar prospects are offered in publicity for other GNVQs. I referred earlier to how greater student autonomy is portrayed as being especially attractive and motivating to students who have not succeeded by 'conventional' methods and 'whose abilities would not otherwise be developed or recognised' (NCVQ 1994: 8). To take another example, potential Advanced GNVQ students are invited to ask themselves whether (for example) they have coped well with GCSE coursework, whether they 'like the idea of working independently' and of sometimes carrying projects outside the classroom, and whether they both 'like the idea of working independently' and 'work well in teams'; positive answers to those questions indicate their suitability for programmes of study confidently expected to display those characteristics (Chorlton 1994: 88). The questions themselves may seem like an invitation to participate in the kinds of 'progressive', 'learner-centred' pedagogy that some of the government's education advisers have systematically denigrated. But the apparent contradiction can be reconciled by interpreting the 'vocational progressivism' embodied in Advanced GNVQ as a translation into economically desirable forms of attributes like self-direction which then appear as occupationally beneficial accomplishments (Chitty 1991; Hodkinson 1991). Thus GNVQs are described as 'encouraging students to work independently, use their initiative and make intelligent judgements about their work' because these are 'exactly the skills demanded by employers and universities alike' (*City and Guilds* Broadsheet no.131, 1994). The question remains, how are teachers 'signalled' to provide the kind of learning environment in which those 'skills' are likely to be developed? It is the 'testing in' referred to earlier that provides a large part of the answer.

How Advanced GNVQs are assessed has been highly controversial throughout the qualification's short life, receiving far more and far more critical attention than did its BTEC predecessor. An oppressively bureaucratic process is attributed to a mistaken attempt to 'cover' all 'relevant' aspects of student performance. The initial omission of any testing of under-pinning knowledge prompted such damaging comparisons with A level that it was reluctantly introduced, although in multiple-choice forms that seemed to lack the rigour ascribed to conventional examinations. But recent government announcements indicating a large move back to more selective examining of more substantial items of students' work seem to assume that A levels provide a 'gold standard' model of assessment, which a long history of criticism would not support. What certainly distinguishes the present GNVQ 'approach' are the prominence given to 'core and other cognitive skills'; the extent to which these are supposedly built in to the final assessment, in official definitions of learning outcomes; and especially the overt dependence of merit and distinction awards on students having demonstrated a sufficient independence in gathering and presenting portfolios of evidence of their academic performance. So when a teacher of GNVQ Business Studies in one of the visited comprehensive schools made herself available for advice on students' projects but did no class teaching, drew individual students' attention to their 'need to find out' but did no more than suggest where that information might be found (notably in businesses outside the school), she would seem to have been following the non-didactic approach so prominent in GNVQ publicity. She then explained her usual approach as a deliberate holding back from being directive, even though most of her students had mediocre GCSE results and (in her words) 'lacked confidence', because the mode of assessment required that they had frequent opportunities to demonstrate their independence. Other effects of 'testing in' a pedagogical 'approach' are described in the chapters that follow. Some of them may be glimpsed in the Dearing Report. A common university view is reported that Advanced GNVQ students should be better prepared than they are, which presumably means prepared more like those who have taken A levels, for the note taking and extended essay writing demanded in most degree programmes. Students themselves, however, perceived those taking GNVQs to have been better prepared in some aspects of what has been called 'workplace literacy' – in particular, experience of working in groups and in IT and other information gathering and presentational skills (Dearing 1996: 2.17, 2.35).

Viewed in this context, GNVQs appear to belong with other 'modernising' initiatives intended to shift the emphasis of schooling 'from teaching to learning', whether in response to perceived economic imperatives or from a general belief that it is pedagogically more effective (Hustler and Hodkinson 1996). That phrase was used by Geoffrey Holland (1994) in a tribute to what TVEI had achieved for the system at large. HMI's evaluation of that Initiative also refers approvingly to a 'shift in teaching styles away from abstract and theoretical approaches towards more practical work and other forms of practical participation' (HMI 1991: ix). The government's initial promotion of city technology colleges as 'a new choice of school' highlighted their suitability for children who like 'doing as well as knowing', and so carried an implication that conventional secondary schooling was overweighted with information and academic modes of transmitting it. Those schools' own subsequent publicity then emphasised how a lavish use of new technology would give more responsibility to students for managing their own learning, and greater priority to developing their skills of finding and using information (Whitty *et al.* 1993: 117–121). In the same vein, the Education 2000 Project originated in 1983 from a conviction that schools' traditional reliance on teacher-centred instruction failed to recognise how much 'the future belongs to those who know how to learn' and who are practised in finding for themselves what they need to know. Its principal instigator has also set the solitary study and emphasis on analytical writing he associates with academic study against the emphasis on working with others, mixing categories of knowledge, verbal skills and problem solving which he defines as the approach to learning suited to modern employment (Abbott 1994).

That GNVQs appear to fit into this modernising context is unlikely to per-suade conservative critics that their pursuit of relevance and consequent disregard for academic disciplines is anything other than a fatal undermining of a properly authoritative relationship between teacher and taught, in which the autonomy of the learner is quite properly limited by the distance between the teacher's knowledge and the student's ignorance. They are likely to regard those limits as best defined in the transmission of an established subject. But they may be no less prescriptive when drawn from some theme or topic around which knowledge is integrated, or from what are taken to be the requirements of an occupation or occupational area. But as Bernstein has argued, it is mistaken to assume a causal relationship between strongly defined (classified) academic knowledge and hierarchical (strongly framed) relationships between teacher and taught. 'Framing' refers to how students are positioned in relation to the knowledge being transmitted. It is strong wherever the teacher largely controls the content, sequence and pace of what is being learned, then evaluates students' performance against authoritative criteria of relevance and correctness. Some of the evidence reported in later chapters suggests that while GNVQ students tend to have more control over the pacing and even the sequence of their work than do their A level contemporaries, it is difficult to see much greater discretion in relation to *what* they are learning or to the teacher's overall management of the process.

This opens up the possibility that more important differences may lie in the nature of student autonomy than in a measure of its extent. Comparisons of A level Economics with BTEC Business and Finanance, made partly because of the obvious overlap in content, indicated a greater variety of learning activities in BTEC, much more use of IT, and more time spent on researching a topic. But there were no significant differences in dictated notes or teacher presentations of a topic, and less difference than might have been expected in preparing assignments and group discussion (Fitz-Gibbon and Lacy 1993). Similar results came from subsequent comparisons of A level and GNVQ. Dearing's own generalisations drew on A level information system (ALIS) data about both the wider range of activities and the more 'active' learning associated with GNVQ. But while it was the GNVQ students in a separate survey who described their learning as having been organised mainly around 'independent study' and 'research', it was the more 'lecture-dominated' A level students who also reported the more frequent opportunities to 'question what they read and were taught' (Dearing 1996, Appendices: 39–40). In Chapter 4, Nick Meagher reports his observations of considerable differences between the sides of the 'divide' in the range and especially the pace of learning activities. A level lessons were generally faster and busier, with students spending far more time engaged in the kinds of extended discourse ('discussion') that Frank Hardman (Chapter 5) has analysed. But Meagher still concludes that 'the pedagogic thrust . . . remains with the teachers who interpret meaning'. Generalisations about learner autonomy are therefore difficult to establish. A great deal of A level learning appears to be more heavily and pervasively teacher directed than much familiar rhetoric about independent learning would suggest. On the vocational side of the divide, critics of the outcomes model of learning have argued that concepts of 'learner autonomy' have been appropriated from the 'progressive' tradition only by expedient and substantial redefinition, so that once students have chosen their units, their learning is 'subordinated to the gathering of evidence to satisfy predetermined competence criteria' (Hyland 1994: 47). Yet the much more extensive use of IT in GNVQ courses would be expected from the modernising perspectives outlined earlier, to enable greater learner independence and to move the teaching role away from the direction of learning towards its support (Abbott 1994).

I return finally to the apparent gap between rhetoric and practice at A level. From the pedagogically conservative position I have outlined, the teacher's rightful authority comes from his or her expertise in an established body of academic knowledge. That authority is undermined when subjects are integrated, or when they are lost to sight within some vocational 'field', or wherever an excessive concern for relevance to students' current interests or to narrowly defined demands of employment creates undue scope for exchanges of opinion uninformed by disciplined knowledge (Edwards 1995). But in relation to study in depth by supposedly subject-minded students, that view of authoritative teaching is surely problematic. In Crowther's portrayal of the traditional sixth form, this was the stage at which 'pupils became students' and began to take that 'responsibility for their own learning', and at which 'an intellectual life shared between pupil and teacher' became possible (Ministry of Education 1959: 224). Thirty years later, HMI descriptions convey similar images of good practice. By comparison with the preceding stage, HMI expected A level teachers to lecture less, prescribe classroom tasks less closely, allow more scope for students' initiative, and create frequent opportunities for their students to 'explore and formulate ideas instead of merely listening to those of the teacher' (DES 1987b: 24–27). At least by implication, progressively greater autonomy is taken to be a natural consequence of 'growing into' the subject. Pedagogic conservatives see induction into part of the academic heritage as a long process in which the right to question what is being learned should be delayed until enough is known. They would therefore accept Macfarlane's description of the teacher–student relationship at A level as that of expert and initiate without any of his accompanying regrets; the expert instructs, the initiate receives instruction, and 'as the learner acquires knowledge and skill, so the pace and difficulty of the work increases thereby maintaining or appearing to maintain the need for a didactic approach' (Macfarlane 1993: 61). Yet even that image has connotations of a cultural and cognitive apprenticeship which should include increasingly frequent opportunities for students to display a developing mastery as they are inducted into the ways of the subject. HMI described good A level practice where teacher and students 'engage in extended conversation and discussion' and an 'interchange of ideas' (DES 1988a: 29). The more knowledgeable the student, the more that 'conversation' might be expected to include some questioning of the knowledge being acquired. While the boundaries around academic subjects limit students' opportunities to draw on their 'everyday' knowledge from which those subjects are systematically distanced, those students should also become progressively more competent at recognising the specialised rules governing (for example) how evidence is to be displayed and interpreted, an argument constructed, or a conclusion supported, and so at realising ever closer approximations to expert academic performances (Sheeran and Barnes 1991).

If that is a reasonable account of how things should be, HMI descriptions of how things often are would seem to support Macfarlane's generalisation (1993: 59) that 'the A-level learning experience remains largely didactic'. That is not necessarily a criticism. Indeed, recent Ofsted monitoring claims a higher proportion of A level lessons identified as 'satisfactory or better' than at any other stage of schooling. But they have also reported a great deal of 'presentation of information through a lecture supported by a teacher-directed question-and-answer session' – in short, of the teacher-controlled 'recitation' of prescribed knowledge that has been the predominant pedagogy in mainstream schooling (Edwards and Westgate 1994). What HMI clearly disliked when they saw it, at a time when any 'progressive' inclinations were not yet being curbed, was 'a narrow interpretation of the syllabus leading to over-directive teaching' and too much passive receiving of facts' (DES 1987b: 22).

A high frequency of such inappropriate practice is most often attributed to heavy pressures on teachers to play safe, and to end-of-course examinations that give too much credit to the recall of knowledge. The first explanation relates to the high market value of successful A level performance, and the consequent temptations for teachers not to 'waste' time that should be given to covering the syllabus. The second explanation is less obviously persuasive. A level is commended in the Dearing Review because it 'undoubtedly develops skills valued by employers, for example skills in analysis and the critical evaluation of information' (Dearing 1996: 7.48). Yet as preparation for high status employment, it has been consistently criticised for neither developing nor assessing such generic skills explicitly but simply assuming that 'all A levels already embodied all the necessary skills' and would merely be 'diluted by meddling' (Graham 1993: 126). Despite being vigorously supported by the National Curriculum Council as a potential bridge between the two sides of the divide, core (or key) skills have been locked into vocational qualifications, in their role as a substitute for general education, but locked out of A level as not sufficiently important to justify the diversion of effort (Green 1995). Worse still, critics have argued that the actual demands of A level work so much against the grain of what is intended that if desirable skills and personal qualities are indeed apparent in successful students, then they are more attributable to students' general ability than to value added by that particular form of intellectual training. A familiar charge, exemplified in the Higginson Report (DES 1988a, para. 2.4), is that A level examining gives students too much credit for their ability 'to memorise and recall facts and arguments', and too little for their capacity to 'exercise judgement, to reason, to stand on their own feet . . . and think for themselves'. Even when teachers appreciate the benefits of sometimes tempering didactic methods, they are prevented from acting accordingly by over-crowded syllabuses and 'a day-to-day pragmatism which works in the opposite direction' and which causes them to severely limit opportunities for 'open' discussion that may turn into unproductive diversions from a tight, instructional agenda (Macfarlane 1993: 60–61).

What complicates the diagnosis is the possibility that high grades may be achieved more effectively where students experience an 'interchange of ideas' and opportunities occasionally to challenge the knowledge being transmitted. Entwistle (1994) concludes that most learners adopt a 'strategic' approach to their learning and seek to invest their effort where it will be most productive. 'Surface' approaches to learning, focused on reproducing what has been taught and read, are likely where the recall of information is perceived as being sufficiently rewarded. The hard work needed to go more 'deeply' is likely where 'the assessment procedure requires the demonstration of conceptual understanding' by those seeking high grades (Entwistle 1994: 12). That distinction seemed to be clearly understood by some of the teachers we observed. For example, a teacher of A level Economics at a comprehensive school advised his class that they 'have to get into the techniques of writing essays', but also reminded them that it was not enough to 'put in a lot of content, you've got to go beyond that and analyse things'. In successive lessons on the conditions in which small businesses might prosper, bursts of exposition by that teacher were interspersed with demands that they 'did some thinking again' and with invitations to 'disagree with me if you think I'm wrong'. In an independent grammar school, conceptually demanding exposition by the teacher – for example, 'I'm going to continue this damning indictment of monopoly, then I'm going to turn around and argue that it's not as bad as all that' – was saved from being too much a teacher performance by the high level of interaction and his eagerness to be challenged. This was a potentially high performing class in a high performing school, frequently reminded that while the recall of information might be sufficient for a pass, much more was required to achieve high grades. Facility in the use of technical language might help a little, but it was 'understanding that the examiners are looking for to give top marks. . . . This is where you go beyond the simple definition. . . . So what is the effect of monopoly on economic efficiency? This is what I'm going to spend time on, because this is where the marks go.'

These brief glimpses of teaching serve to lead into the empirical accounts that follow by illustrating the difficulties of generalisation. Teachers and students vary in their aspirations and expectations of examination performance. Subjects themselves vary (as do syllabuses in the same subject) in their factual loading and the extent to which they seem visibly to reward displays of analytical and interpretative skill. With the exception of General Studies, 'hybrid' subjects appear to be easier. They therefore appeal to students who do not see themselves as 'academic' (Fitz-Gibbon and Vincent 1994; McCulloch et al. 1993). This may make it seem easier to take some pedagogic risks. Investigating subjects high in the hierarchy of difficulty, Hodgson (1994) found closely directed student exercises to be more common in the 'hard' (physical) sciences, and 'research' and 'class discussion' to be more common in the 'soft' sciences. But since the latter were also characterised by relatively more use of duplicated or closely prescribed notes, his evidence seemed to indicate various forms of teacher-centredness rather than a simple continuum from the more to the less didactic. Within the same subject, the teachers of English observed by Harrison and Mountford (1992) differed sharply in their approach to developing their students' skills of literary criticism. Some encouraged their active participation in forming judgements. Others preferred to demonstrate 'from the front of the class' techniques of textual analysis that there was no time to develop jointly, and which they seemed in practice to assume could be learned by imitation. Both 'versions of professionalism' were directed towards the achieving of high grades. That 'boxed-in curriculum' that the researchers describe as 'well-drilled, efficient and predictable' reflected the teachers' belief that even sophisticated inter-pretations could be given. The more time-consuming 'Socratic' search for understanding reflected a different view of what worked in achieving similar outcomes. These are similarities and contrasts within the same side of the divide. The rest of the book is largely about what happens to such generalisations when comparisons are extended to those different 'approaches' that supposedly characterise 'academic' and 'vocational' education post-16.

3

LISTENING TO STUDENTS AND THE 50 PER CENT FRAMEWORK

Carol Taylor Fitz-Gibbon

INTRODUCTION

Separate but equal was deemed to be impossible in the famous legal judgement on segregated schooling in the US. Can we in the UK have separate Advanced GNVQs that are nevertheless equal to A levels? How could we know? They are not delivered in separate institutions but are they delivered in separate ways? And how could equality of esteem be estimated and then monitored over time as the qualification 'proves' or does not prove itself? In terms of enrolments, Advanced GNVQs have been a great success and to that extent they have shown a fitness for purpose, even if that purpose might have been created by the lack of jobs and a flight from A levels to one of the few remaining alternatives.

In this chapter the two major themes addressed are: how Advanced GNVQs are operating, as seen from reports from students, and the extent to which Advanced GNVQs can be judged to earn parity of esteem. We draw on data, provided by Martin Wright, from the A level Information System, now called ALIS+ (meaning plus GNVQs) to signal that we are monitoring vocational qualifications in addition to A levels. To address the issue of how Advanced GNVQs are operating, we use some of the responses provided by students completing the extensive ALIS+ questionnaires. To address the issue of esteem, we use examination data, GCSEs, A levels and Advanced GNVQs in what we call the 50 per cent framework. This refers to the fact that 50 per cent of the variation in achievement can be predicted from a knowledge of prior levels of achievement of the students concerned.

This chapter deals with data arising from the first four Advanced GNVQs to recruit substantial numbers:

- Art & Design
- Business
- Health & Social Care
- Leisure & Tourism

Reference is made to two major reports by the Further Education Funding Council (FEFC) that provided information on the functioning of the GNVQ

29

system (FEFC 1994, 1995). These reports were based on inspections in forty-two FEFC-sector colleges. (Colleges accounted for two-thirds of all new registrations for GNVQs.) During these visits, discussions were held with college managers, teachers, support staff and students, and there were meetings with awarding bodies (BTEC, City Guilds and the Royal Society of Arts Examination Boards). Officers of NCVQ, Department for Education and Employment and Further Education Development Agency were also consulted.

In preparing this chapter it was also possible to draw on comparisons with a study of BTEC National Diploma in Business and Finance that had been undertaken in 1992–1993 and resulted in a series of reports by Lacy and Fitz-Gibbon which are referenced in the text.

Background – ALIS

The A-Level Information System (ALIS) was started in the academic year 1982–1983. The basic procedure is that datasets from questionnaires administered to students are analysed and combined with data on students' examination results for GCSEs and A levels. Starting from only twelve schools, the ALIS project has expanded to the point where it now analyses about a third of A level entries, i.e. results from about 70,000 A level candidates. However, some 30,000 students are in a small 'basic' version of ALIS which deals only with Value Added results. (The progress students make relative to that made by other students starting from the same baseline of prior achievement is called 'Value Added', although the ALIS project originally used the more neutral statistical term: 'residuals'.)

The full-scale version of ALIS considers students' levels of satisfaction on a variety of matters and also obtains reports of teaching and learning activities. It is this full-scale version of ALIS+ which was used in the current study.

The samples for this chapter

According to the FEFC survey, the number of colleges offering Advanced GNVQs, as of November 1994 , was about 300, and the students were distributed between each of the four Advanced GNVQ courses as shown in Table 3.1. Since the ALIS database includes schools as well as colleges, some discrepancies were to be expected and suggest that more schools are offering Business and fewer are offering Health & Social Care than is the case in the college sector. It would seem likely that the more strongly an Advanced GNVQ related to specific vocational areas, the more likely it was to be in colleges, particularly FE colleges that would have the necessary resources and experience. Unfortunately, FE colleges are under-represented in ALIS, partly due to the difficulties experienced in collecting the questionnaire data and partly due to the extensive work already undertaken by what was the Further Education Unit (FEU) in the use of student questionnaires. However, as more sixth form colleges undertake Advanced GNVQ work, the ALIS database will expand. For the present analyses Table 3.1

Table 3.1 Distribution of students between Advanced GNVQ courses as indicated by the numbers of graded results in the ALIS database compared with FEFC data for colleges

Adv. GNVQ	ALIS 1995	Participation as reported by FEFC 1995	ALIS 1995	Participation as reported by FEFC 1995
	Numbers of students		%	
Art & Design	89	1,975	8	11
Business	616	9,344	57	53
Health & Social care	143	3,068	13	17
Leisure & Tourism	231	3,395	21	19
TOTALS	1,079	17,782	100	100

Note: FEFC figures from FEFC 1995: 6

shows that the distribution of results that were available in 1995 was reasonably similar to the distribution reported by the FEFC.

The 1,079 students for whom results were available represented a considerable attrition from the sample of more than 3,000 students who had indicated on the first ALIS+ questionnaire, usually given at the beginning of the sixth form, that they were going to study for Advanced GNVQs. There are several reasons for believing that the loss was not all student drop-out: the questionnaire might frequently have been completed before course enrolments were finalised (November); a proportion of students might still have been working on their advanced GNVQs or the results might not have been returned to ALIS by the school or college.

a significant number of students who appeared to be non-completers intended to re-sit external tests and/or complete their portfolios of evidence. . . .

Inspectors found that up to 20% of students coming to the end of their courses in 1994–95 still had some work to do to complete their portfolios or had not yet passed one or more of the external tests. Many of these students finished their work during the summer months and most of them were expected to achieve the full award before the end of the autumn term.

(FEFC 1995: 32)

INTAKE

This section deals with reasons why students enrolled on Advanced GNVQ courses, the students' prior qualifications, both GCSE and vocational, and how they differed from A level students. The distribution of students between four Advanced GNVQ courses is also considered.

31

The normal entry requirements are four or five GCSEs at Grades A to C or an intermediate GNVQ.

Reasons for enrolling on the advanced GNVQ course

How did students come to choose to take an Advanced GNVQ? Students were asked to select responses to the question: 'I chose this course, rather than A levels because. . . . ' The percentages who answered 'fairly true' or 'very true' to the various options presented are shown in Table 3.2 for both 1994 and 1995.

The largest proportion, four out of five students, reported *the course sounded more interesting* as a positive factor. The two responses that are starred in Table 3.2 suggested academic insecurities as a reason for choosing GNVQ courses. There appeared to be slightly more than half the students for whom the preference for coursework, as opposed to examinations, was a factor in their choice. Although only about one in five reported lack of GCSEs as a factor, being advised to take the course was reported as a reason by more than a third of the students, and this advice may well have been based on GCSE performance. Only about one student in ten considered that their choice was influenced by friends taking the course.

Table 3.2 Reasons for taking Advanced GNVQ courses

I chose this course, rather than A levels because. . . .	% responding 'fairly true' or 'very true' 1994	% responding 'fairly true' or 'very true' 1995
The course sounded more interesting	84	85
I'm no good at exams, so coursework assessment suits me better*	54	52
I was advised	39	44
I couldn't do the subject(s) at A level	26	24
I didn't have enough GCSEs to do A level*	19	21
My friends did the course	13	12

* Academic concerns

Enrolment in four Advanced GNVQs

In the 1994 ALIS sample there were 1,797 students who appeared to be taking Advanced GNVQs, according to the first ALIS questionnaire. These were divided among four Advanced GNVQ courses as shown in Table 3.3. (A further 59 were taking Manufacturing, but these were dropped as the sample was so small.)

In 1995, the distribution of apparently enrolled students was similar but with Business dominating even more (57 per cent of our sample) and Art having a smaller share. Since both Business and Art have almost exact parallels in A levels,

Table 3.3 Distribution of students by Advanced GNVQ course

Subject	1994 % of 1,797	1995 % of 1,079
Art & Design	16	8
Business	45	57
Health & Social Care	18	13
Leisure & Tourism	21	22
Total	100	100

Source: ALIS 1994 and 1995 databases

it will be interesting to see if any clues are available as to the gains or losses suggested by these two years of data – gains for Business and losses for Art.

How relatively well subscribed were the four Advanced GNVQs? Figure 3.1 indicates the percentages taking each course. Business was the most heavily subscribed course, accounting for 45 per cent of the Advanced GNVQ enrolment, and Art & Design the least heavily subscribed. Two courses had enrolled considerably more females than males: Health & Social Care and Art & Design. The patterns were almost exactly the same in 1995 (Figure 3.2).

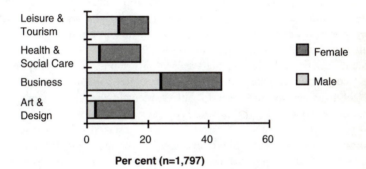

Figure 3.1 Per cent of the sample of Advanced GNVQ students who were enrolled on four courses, by gender

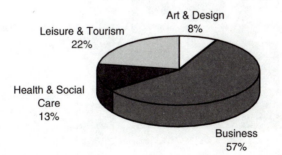

Figure 3.2 Per cent enrolled in each of the four Advanced GNVQ courses, 1995

33

Prior GCSE qualifications of Advanced GNVQ students

Three indicators were derived from the grades on GCSE examinations: the *average points score*, the *total points score* and the *number of subjects* taken at GCSE. The scores used the usual assignment of

A = 7 points
B = 6 points
C = 5 points
D = 4 points, etc.

The distribution of GCSE average scores among students taking Advanced GNVQs was heavily skewed, both in 1994 and in 1995, towards the lower end of the achievement range (the lowest quarter). Figure 3.3 shows the intake to all four Advanced GNVQ courses (Business, Health & Social Care, Leisure & Tourism and Art & Design) with three A levels for comparison: Art (one of the 'easiest' A levels) Business Studies (relevant to the largest proportion of Advanced GNVQ students who were Business students) and Chemistry (one of the 'hardest' or most severely graded A levels). In the Advanced GNVQ courses in 1994 there was a predominance of students with low GCSE grades (the lowest quarter) and only about 5 per cent above average, with barely 1 per cent in the top quarter. This highly skewed distribution was not seen in the A level groups which all had at least 15 per cent in the top quarter.

Figures 3.3 and 3.4 show that, for both 1994 and 1995, the courses drew predominantly from the lowest quarter of GCSE results. However, approaching 10 per cent each year were above average for A level students.

In 1994, the average Advanced GNVQ student in the ALIS+ database had a GCSE *average score* of 4.5 (D/C) while A level students typically had an average of 5.6 (C/B). The mean GCSE *total score* for Advanced GNVQ students was 34 points, whilst A level students averaged 47 points. The difference in the numbers of GCSEs taken was less than one, so the large differences in total

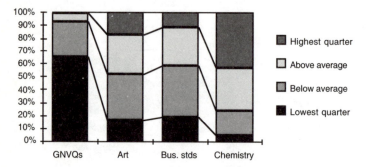

Figure 3.3 Intake for Advanced GNVQs and three A levels, described by GCSE average scores

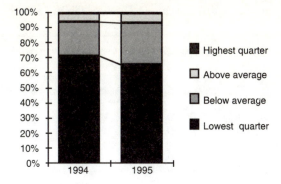

Figure 3.4 Advanced GNVQ intake in 1994 and 1995, described by GCSE average scores

scores seemed to be attributable to low grades rather than lack of entries. In 1995, the situation was very similar (see Figure 3.4) but with a slight increase in the numbers in the third quarter ('below average' but not in the lowest quarter).

Differences between the various Advanced GNVQs were small in terms of GCSE average points scores. The lowest average intake was in Health & Social Care in which students had a GCSE average score between D and C (4.4). The highest intake was in Art & Design, with a mean GCSE average score of 4.6, also between a D and a C. The difference was trivial in size.

The GCSE total scores and the numbers of GCSEs taken cast a slightly different light on the question of prior qualifications. Art & Design students were lowest on these measures due, apparently, to their tending to having taken seven rather than eight subjects. However, differences were again small in magnitude although statistically significant, with the GCSE total score ranging from generally 33 (Art & Design) to 36 (Business), overall differences of less than three points.

The extensive degree of overlap between the intakes to the four Advanced GNVQ courses is illustrated in Table 3.4.

The uptake of GNVQs must have varied partly because of availability. Of those students taking A levels in a sample matched on the basis of GCSE average scores, i.e. from a starting level equivalent to those taking Advanced GNVQs, 37 per cent were in institutions that did not appear to offer Advanced GNVQs. Some of these students must have taken A levels for want of any alternative. In order to study students who did have the choice of taking either Advanced GNVQs or A levels, a second matched sample was created from institutions that offered both A levels and Advanced GNVQs. A discriminant analysis showed the variables that best differentiated Advanced GNVQ students from A level students in those institutions in which there *was* a choice (Table 3.5).

Table 3.4 Prior qualifications of students on Advanced GNVQ courses finishing in 1994

				GCSE average score (F = 2.97 , p = 0.02)
Course	*N*	*Mean*	*SD*	*Means and confidence intervals*
Art & Design	282	4.57	0.75	(———-*——)
Business	812	4.49	0.80	(—-*—)
Health & Social Care	330	4.38	0.95	(———-*——-)
Leisure & Tourism	373	4.44	0.75	(———-*——)
				——+———————+———————+————————+—
				3.4 4.50 4.65 4.80

				GCSE total score (F = 3.79 , p = 0.01)
Course	*N*	*Mean*	*SD*	*Means and confidence intervals*
Art & Design	282	33.36	9.85	(———*——)
Business	812	35.89	9.95	(—-*——)
Health & Social Care	330	34.44	10.75	(———-*———)
Leisure & Tourism	373	35.04	9.07	(———-*——)
				———+——————+———————+———————

Table 3.5 Significant differences between Advanced GNVQ students and A level students in the same school or college

Variable	*Mean for Advanced GNVQ group*	*Mean for A level group*	*F ratio*	*Effect size*
GCSE average score in the sciences	4.21	4.48	43.51	0.24
Parental occupation	3.81	3.99	13.70	0.14
GCSE average score in humanities	4.71	4.86	23.58	0.18

Note: the analysis was run separately for each Advanced GNVQ but results were so similar that this single table is sufficient to represent the situation. All F ratios were highly statistically significant (p<.001)

Those who had chosen GNVQs were most different from those who had chosen A levels in the same institutions in

• having lower GCSE grades, particularly in the sciences
• having parents with lower status occupations

The average score on a measure of parental occupation was higher for A level students but the Effect Size was only 0.14. (Effect Size = standardised mean difference. In this case the distribution of parental occupations was 0.14 of a standard deviation higher for A level students than for Advanced GNVQ students. This means that the average A level student had parents in higher status jobs than 55 per cent of Advanced GNVQ students. Had the two groups been equivalent the figure would have been 50 per cent.) The most discriminating variable was the average GCSE score in the sciences.

Prior vocational qualifications

It might well be expected that those choosing Advanced GNVQs would be more likely to have already undertaken a vocational course. The percentages who had previously taken vocational qualifications are shown in Table 3.6.

To a greater extent than A level students, Advanced GNVQ students had shown an earlier interest in vocational qualifications. These findings fit well with the common perception that, for many students, attitudes affecting post-16 choices are determined earlier in the school than the GCSE year.

Table 3.6 Percentages of students who had previously taken vocational qualifications

Previously taken vocational qualifications	Schools and colleges with Advanced GNVQ courses		Schools and colleges without Advanced GNVQ courses
	Advanced GNVQ students	A level students	A level students
City and Guilds	9.3	3.3	2.8
BTEC first	8.9	0.4	0.4
CPVE	5.8	0.9	0.9
RSA	15.7	11.8	10.8

Source: ALIS 1994 database

Age distribution

About 36 per cent of Advanced GNVQ students were over the age of 20, indicating that they were probably returning to education after a year or two spent on other activities, or had taken considerably longer than usual to reach the level of an Advanced GNVQ. There were no students older than 24 in the ALIS sample.

PROCESSES ON ADVANCED GNVQ COURSES

In the second ALIS questionnaire, which is answered in the second term of the second year, students were asked numerous questions about their courses. While

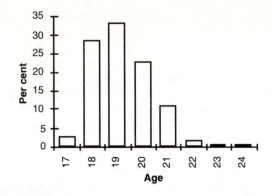

Figure 3.5 Age distribution of Advanced GNVQ students

their answers are interesting in absolute terms, they are more interesting when interpreted alongside answers provided to similar questions by A level students.

Responses from each Advanced GNVQ course completed in 1995 were compared with those from a relevant A level course.

- Art & Design was compared with A level Art
- Business was compared A level Business Studies
- Leisure & Tourism was compared with A level Business Studies
- Health & Social Care was compared with A level Social Biology

The general pattern of the responses will vary from college to college and school to school. Schools and colleges participating in ALIS+ receive detailed reports with their own institution's data from items including those shown below in italics. The following summaries were based on examining all the data for each pair of subjects, looking at a number of concerns about how courses are delivered.

Induction

General levels of satisfaction with support received in all four Advanced GNVQs were low, as they were on the corresponding A levels also. The per cent responding 'fairly satisfied' or 'very satisfied' was quite low, around 30 per cent level with respect to *assessment processes, understanding demands of the course,* and an *explanation of the course*. Only in Health & Social Care did the percentage of students 'fairly' or 'very satisfied' approach near to 50 per cent. This seems to imply some need to improve the induction procedures, explaining the course and its demands, for both Advanced GNVQs and A levels.

Leisure & Tourism was considerably less favourably viewed on these issues than was A level Business Studies.

Support received during the course

Levels of satisfaction as indicated by responses to '*I got the help I needed on the course*' and '*I knew the work I had to do for the course*' were considerably more positive than those relating to induction, with between 60 and 75 per cent choosing the top two categories in response levels, almost exactly the same as for the relevant A levels.

Careers

Since GNVQs are considered to be vocational courses, one might expect particular success in advising students on careers. This seemed to be the case with Advanced GNVQ Art & Design, with about half the students reporting that they were 'fairly satisfied' or 'very satisfied' with *advice in career choice*, as opposed to only 35 per cent on A level Art. The same discrepancy applied to the items '*I learned more about industry*' and '*I learned more about business*'. With regard to *learning about the community* and '*I got a better idea of the job I would like*', the percentages were very much in line with those found in A level Art.

Advanced GNVQ Business showed levels of satisfaction that were particularly high in *learning about industry and business* and that were similar throughout to responses in A level Business Studies.

Health & Social Care Advanced GNVQ appeared to be particularly strong in teaching students about *the community* and weak in *industry and business*, which seems entirely reasonable. On the *advice in career* choice and the item '*I got a better idea of the job I would like*', satisfaction was 50 per cent or over, very similar to the levels in A level Social Biology.

Leisure & Tourism was not perceived as producing as much knowledge of *industry and business* as A level Business Studies apparently, but levels of satisfaction on the item '*I got a better idea of the job I would like*' stood at 58 per cent who were 'fairly satisfied' or 'very satisfied', exactly equal to the responses in A level Business Studies.

With regard to the general levels of satisfaction with a variety of other kinds of *help*, provided more specifically by the college than by the course itself, the responses were fairly similar to those of A level students. Again Leisure & Tourism students appeared a little less satisfied than those on A level Business Studies.

Active learning and core skills

The general satisfaction of our sample of Art & Design students was again demonstrated in that they attributed their learning to the *coursework assignments, school and college staff, responsibility for self study* and *workshop support for coursework*.

Advanced GNVQ Business students also showed very high levels of satisfaction with the *responsibility for self study* and *working as a team*, as did Health &

Social Care and Leisure & Tourism with respect to *working as a team*. There does seem to be evidence that Advanced GNVQs are providing students with well-appreciated chances to work in teams, an experience/skill to which employers from business and industry have been drawing attention (CBI, 1995).

Work experience

According to the FEFC report for colleges, work experience featured in 75 per cent of GNVQ courses, with the amount varying from subject to subject:

> Almost all Business GNVQs included relevant work experience which reflects the tradition inherited from previous vocational courses in the subject and the widespread availability of potential placements.
> ... Teachers on a number of GNVQ courses in Business, Health & Social Care, Science and Leisure & Tourism have identified units that could be achieved by students in the workplace. Regular visits from teachers were used to confirm assessments made by workplace supervisors and the whole experience was an integral part of the student's course. The students on these courses were frequently enthusiastic about their placements, often able to relate their experience to the content of their courses.

(FEFC, 1995: 20, 21)

Work experience would seem to be particularly relevant to Advanced GNVQs. Table 3.7 shows that greater proportions of Advanced GNVQ students were provided with work experience than was true of A level students even in reasonably 'vocational' A levels. Business via the GNVQ route had 61 per cent reporting work experience whereas A level Business Studies reported only 22 per cent. On average, students on an Advanced GNVQ course seemed to have a 35 per cent greater chance of obtaining a work experience placement than A level students on similar courses.

Table 3.7 Percentages of students who were provided with work experience

Subject	% with work experience	% difference in favour of Advanced GNVQ course
Art Advanced GNVQ	34	13
Art A level	21	
Business Advanced GNVQ	61	39
Business Studies A level	22	
Health & Social Care Advanced GNVQ	71	59
Social Biology A level	12	
Leisure & Tourism Advanced GNVQ	47	35
Business Studies A level	22	

A striking feature of students' responses to questions about work experience was how much more likely Advanced GNVQ students were to have been *assessed by an employer* and to have had *staff from the school or college visit them* during their work experience. For example, in the largest sample, Advanced GNVQ Business, 77 per cent reported that staff visited them as opposed to only 30 per cent in A level Business Studies.

Resources

Students were asked about resource problems, such as equipment being broken or not available. In general fewer than 20 or 30 per cent reported resource problems. However, this was a higher rate than the 10 per cent or so at A level. The Advanced GNVQ students were more likely to report that these problems arose 'more than once a month'. Whether this was indicative of special demands placed on resources by Advanced GNVQ courses or the possibility that they took second place to A level courses, or some other explanation, is not known and may well vary from one institution to another. It is the feedback of this kind of information to the institutions that enables those who can interpret the data for their own situation to take the necessary steps, if given sufficient resources.

The rate at which equipment was reported *broken* or *in use* appeared to be half as great again for the Advanced GNVQ students as for A level students in each of the Advanced GNVQ courses.

Teaching and learning activities

The Perceived Learning Activities are described in other chapters. In interpreting them it must be recalled that Advanced GNVQ courses are equivalent in time commitment to two A level courses. Furthermore, the scale needs to be carefully observed as it is not an equal-interval one.

The use of IT was very substantially more on the Advanced GNVQ courses in 1995, being typically *about once a fortnight* in contrast to *about once a term* on the A level courses. Whether this was interpretable as a resource problem for A levels or the demands of the course may vary from one institution to another, but the feeding back of this information to schools and colleges at least raises the issue for discussion.

The finding with respect to IT use was certainly not peculiar to 1995. The 1994 datasets produced the graphs shown in Figures 3.6 (a) to (c) in which 'often' indicated *at least once a fortnight* and 'rarely' represented *about once a month* or *about once a term*. The data from the four Advanced GNVQ courses were combined and compared with three A levels: Accounting, Economics and Business Studies. The use of IT stood out, in this 1994 data, as the most dramatic difference, with large percentages reporting 'never' in the A level subjects and less than 10 per cent so reporting for Advanced GNVQ courses. It was puzzling to find that in A Level Accountancy substantial numbers of

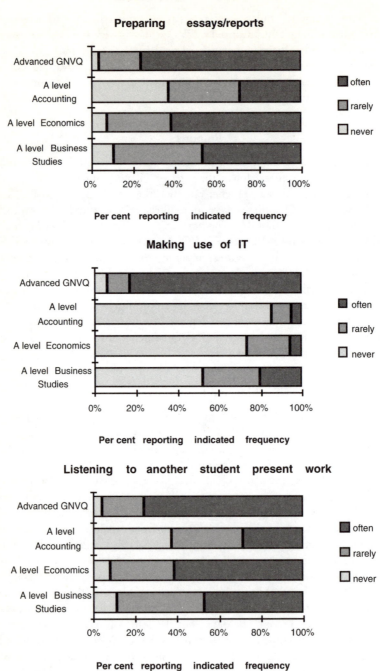

Figure 3.6 Reported teaching and learning activities in Advanced GNVQs and three related A levels

students (about 90 per cent) reported never using IT. One wonders whether outdated accountancy methods are being taught that do not employ spreadsheets, statistical or accounting packages. The frequency of use of IT in GNVQ Business in 1994 was reported, on average, to be close to every lesson or at least two or three times a week.

Students' levels of satisfaction with processes

Having considered how students reported that their courses had been conducted, we turn now to see how they independently reported their satisfaction or otherwise.

Lessons

Only a minority (about 30 per cent) of students on the Advanced GNVQ Business, Art & Design and Health & Social Care courses reported *looking forward to lessons*, whereas this indicator ran at a minimum of 45 per cent on the relevant A level courses and was up to 68 per cent for A level Art. It could be that 'lessons' were taken by Advanced GNVQ students as implying something different from the normal course activities, for other indicators of responses to the courses were not so relatively poor.

All Advanced GNVQ students seemed to have found their courses as *challenging* as did A level students, with the possible exception of Health & Social Care; but with the small numbers involved, the difference between 55 per cent and 71 per cent may not replicate.

Assessment

In view of the many critical comments about the assessment methods in GNVQs in general it was interesting to find, with regard to the question about *liking exams and tests*, that Advanced GNVQ students were generally more positive than A level students. On Advanced GNVQ Business, for example, 42 per cent reported that it was 'fairly true' or 'very true' that they liked exams and tests on the course as opposed to only 18 per cent of the A level Business Studies students. This very positive response may reflect an observation we have found in a number of datasets: that modular assessments are highly valued by students who like to receive ongoing feedback on their progress and to feel that they have accumulated some credit towards a final qualification. This modular approach, and the chance to resit, may account for the positive attitude of Advanced GNVQ students as opposed to the negative attitude to examinations and tests by A level students. End-tests in A levels are so decisive as to cause considerable anxiety.

The extent to which teachers, employers, admissions officers and others are content with the assessment methods may be quite different, for their concerns will be primarily on the validity and information-value of assessments. (Further discussion of assessment is postponed to later.)

General satisfaction in retrospect

The satisfaction levels were particularly positive in Advanced GNVQ Business with respect to '*I would advise others to take it*', with 67 per cent saying that was 'fairly' or 'very true' as opposed to only 42 per cent of A level Business students. However, those *regretting taking* Advanced GNVQ Business numbered 33 per cent as opposed to only 10 per cent regretting taking A level Business Studies. It seems there was some polarity of attitudes in Advanced GNVQ Business Studies or a wide variation from one institution to another. The polarity of attitudes is indicated in both Art & Design and Health & Social Care by neutral responses or worse to the items '*Would advise others to take it*' or '*Regretted taking subject*', thus indicating that students were both less positive and also less negative than A level students on those items. These polarised distributions may become less common as the delivery of courses is made more uniformly effective. Diversity is perhaps inevitable in a new set of courses, and variations in standards of delivery were noted in the FEFC reports. The rich data in ALIS suggested how complicated this picture is.

To complete the evidence on Perceived Learning Activities, Figure 3.7 was prepared from 1996 ALIS+ data. Advanced GNVQ Business is compared with A level Business Studies, and A level Accounting is also shown. The profile has been ordered by the frequency of use of Advanced GNVQ activities and the scale used was transformed to represent the probable number of lessons per course in which the activity was used.

The transformation used was:

1 = 1   Never or almost never
2 = 5   About once a term, as this was deemed to result in five lessons in the five terms that had taken place when the questionnaire was answered.
3 = 15 About once a month
4 = 30 About once a fortnight
5 = 60 About once or twice a week
6 = 120 About every lesson

Taking into account that the Advanced GNVQs should have twice the time allocation of A levels (as one Advanced GNVQ is deemed equivalent to two A levels), the A level profile would be one half as high as the Advanced GNVQ profile if A levels were taught in the same way. As usual, however, the A levels each followed a similar pattern that contrasted with the profile of the Advanced GNVQs. Moreover, the greater frequency of activities in A levels is clear and illustrates the point made by Nick Meagher with his concept of the lesson 'tempo' (Chapter 4).

Comparison of Teaching & Learning Styles

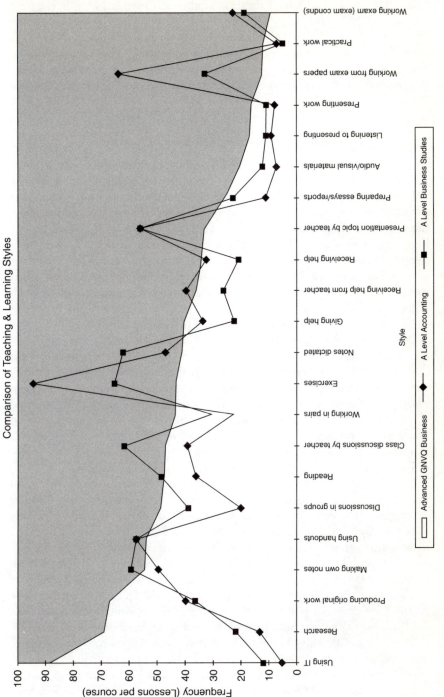

Figure 3.7 Perceived learning activities, 1996

It is noticeable that A level Business Studies was particularly different from Advanced GNVQ Business in having only a fraction of the use of IT and 'Research'. However, if we allow for the double-time of Advanced GNVQs, the A level rate of 'producing original work' was fairly close. The A level 'peaks' of considerably more frequent use related to Exercises and Dictated Notes, Presentation of the Topic by the Teacher and Working from Examination Papers.

Discussion of teaching and learning activities

The reports of various teaching and learning activities were generated by students filling out questionnaires under examination conditions. Students were not responding in groups but reporting independently, and not just in one school or college, but in many, widely spread across the country. Furthermore, they were not *comparing* their Advanced GNVQ courses with A level courses but simply reporting the frequency of use of various activities. The fact, then, that consistent differences emerged does suggest that Advanced GNVQ courses were delivered in a different manner from traditional A level courses, albeit within the range that is found in A levels. Although the average way in which A level is taught is pretty consistent from year to year and from subject to subject, there is nevertheless a wide range of practice at A level.

Previous work has shown that efforts to change teaching are often unproductive. For example, despite expectations of curriculum developers, there appear to be few differences between teaching activities in A level English Literature and English Language, as Frank Hardman reports in this volume, or between practically oriented science courses and more traditional courses (Tymms and Vincent 1994). Scarth and Hammersley (1988) found few differences between examination and non-examination classes with regard to the teaching methods adopted, and noted that 'our research does raise questions about the current orthodoxy that public examinations cause fact-transmission teaching'.

How is it that the delivery of GNVQ courses differed so consistently from the delivery of A Level courses, particularly in the use of active learning features? What gave teachers the signal to teach in a different way? Is this active learning style the way in which teachers preferred to teach? Do they, if freed from the demands of external exams, teach in this fashion, contradicting the findings of Scarth and Hammersley? Has the rhetoric altered practice? The research literature is rather pessimistic about changing teachers' traditional methods of teaching. Joyce and Showers (1984) suggest that in-service education has to be followed by extensive practice and coaching in the classroom. Such personal, in-class coaching has not been available to teachers of Advanced GNVQs. What, then, might explain this change from the traditional A level teaching, a change that was clearly and independently reported by hundreds of individual responses from Advanced GNVQ students? Is the change partly consequent upon changes earlier in GCSE work? Or was there pressure from the assessment methods used in Advanced GNVQs? The fact that a 'Distinction' requires that the student has worked on his or her own initiative may strongly encourage the adoption of active learning methods, with the students choosing activities. Another possible explanation may lie in the legacy of BTEC courses. Project work was *required* on BTEC courses, and projects were central to the philosophy of active learning. Are there considerable numbers of teachers of Advanced GNVQs who are implementing methods they had to develop to meet the demands of BTEC?

Although there is considerable variation from one classroom to another, consistent differences in teaching and learning activities seem to arise only when courses are substantially different in assessment practices. This difference seems to have been achieved in Advanced GNVQ courses and was also achieved in BTEC courses (Lacy 1993).

Another question that might be asked about these active learning activities relates to their intrinsic merit. By adopting active learning methods, were teachers taking time away from more routine and possibly more effective or efficient learning activities, or were they producing a different kind of learning? Was the same amount of learning accomplished but via a different route? Or were methods adopted that led to better retention of the learning? Comparability studies and long-term follow-ups are urgently needed to provide answers, but meanwhile other sources of argument and evidence can be considered.

If there is one rule that can be guaranteed with regard to learning, it is that people generally get better with practice. Consequently, if students 'present their work to the class' they are likely to become more skilled at presenting their work generally. Would this activity, then, be properly viewed as intrinsically valuable for the influence it will have on the skill of presenting work, even if it slowed down the coverage of the knowledge content? The skill of presenting work will, it could be argued, be an extremely valuable preparation for adult life, whether for work in industry, business or the public sector. Giving and receiving help must be good preparation for working collaboratively and for working in teams. In today's complex environment, teamwork, it can be argued, is an essential skill. Teaching teamwork probably requires getting students actually working in teams and giving them feedback on their effectiveness.

The point being made is that these active learning methods might well be excellent preparation for later vocational lives and are, therefore, appropriate in vocational courses. But are they in opposition to the more passive learning typical of some A level courses? We do not know. The simple supposition that such active learning would take time away from other activities is predicated on a view of time as an immutable dimension, whereas it seems to be rather a flexible yardstick. Given a short lesson, the pace is increased and there may be little effect on learning.

There is no strong evidence that the introduction of more active learning would be detrimental in more content-dependent, academic A-Level courses. In the ALIS 1994 A level Business Studies report, for example, two active learning methods ('Use of IT' and 'Researching a topic') were associated with better than expected Value Added if used moderately (monthly or termly). Although they *were* associated with negative Value Added *if used every week*, there were no other activities showing a negative influence on the Value Added.

Finally, a study from the Open University has implications. Adults who had obtained OU degrees some years previously were followed up, and it was found that the parts of the degree course that they remembered best were those parts that they had worked on in the context of project work (Cohen *et al.* 1992). Follow-up studies could be conducted to test this hypothesis in the case of Advanced GNVQ students.

PROGRESSION AND DESTINATION

Students were asked to indicate how likely certain destinations were. The responses do not necessarily add to 100 per cent since some students saw several possibilities as equally likely.

Jobs

Comparisons with the four A levels as described earlier, relating to course delivery, showed students' assessment of how likely various destinations were for them. Surprisingly, considering that they were taking 'vocational A levels', only in Health & Social Care were a substantial percentage expecting to start vocational training (33 per cent as opposed to 10 per cent in Social Biology). Otherwise the figures were generally less than 10 per cent.

Universities and further education

In the best-subscribed Advanced GNVQ, Business, 52 per cent reported that it was 'fairly likely' or 'most likely' that they would go to a university. The figure was 73 per cent for students who had taken A level Business Studies. A discrepancy of about 20 per cent in favour of A level students was also found in Art & Design and discrepancies of 30 and 50 per cent on Health & Social Care and Leisure & Tourism respectively. In short, the perception of university attendance was considerably lower for Advanced GNVQ courses than for A level courses.

Further education was the most likely destination for 74 per cent of students on the Advanced GNVQ Art course, with only 39 per cent expecting to go to a university as opposed to 62 per cent who had taken Art A level. On the other three Advanced GNVQs, between 30 and 50 per cent of students indicated that they were likely to go into further education.

Seeking employment

Some 43 per cent of Business students thought it 'fairly' or 'most likely' that they would get a *job with training*. This was not an expectation shared by high numbers on the other courses or by A level students. It would be interesting to know whether this perception was borne out in practice.

What could be called 'indicators of insecurity' were available from the percentage who thought it 'fairly' or 'most likely' that they would be *unemployed but trying to get a job*. This indicator reached 19 per cent, almost a fifth of students, on the Leisure & Tourism course as opposed to only 4 per cent for students taking A level Business Studies. Insecurity was also present among 13 per cent of those taking Health & Social Care as against only 3 per cent of those taking the relevant A level course, in this case Social Biology. Nine per cent of business students as opposed to 4 per cent of A level Business Studies students thought that unemployment might be a problem. Among the Art students, both those taking the Advanced GNVQ and those taking A level had a rate of 5 per cent thinking that unemployment was a likely scenario.

ACHIEVEMENT OUTCOMES AND THE ISSUE OF PARITY OF ESTEEM

Having students undertaking activities that are considered intrinsically or logically valuable and having students showing increasing levels of satisfaction are both important, but the question as to what successful Advanced GNVQ students 'know, understand and can do' is central to the esteem in which the qualification will be held.

The outcomes of a course can be reported in terms of raw scores, such as the per cent obtaining each qualification. Figure 3.8 shows that about 17 per cent obtained a distinction and about twice as many obtained the other two categories of awards: pass and merit. However, this data is difficult if not impossible to evaluate. It is simply a fact that much of the variation in outcomes can be predicted from a knowledge of students' prior levels of achievement.

Figure 3.9 shows that the GCSE average score for those obtaining a distinction was only slightly higher than those obtaining a pass or merit. This pattern results in low correlations between average GCSE and Advanced GNVQ awards, but

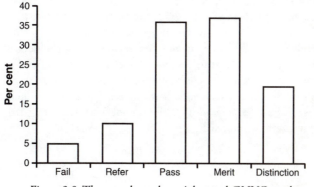

Figure 3.8 The awards made to Advanced GNVQ students

49

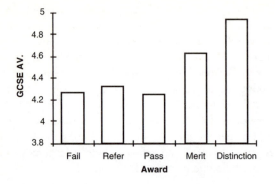

Figure 3.9 The GCSE average score of students with various awards

no lower than would be the case for A levels using the same restriction in range on the GCSE average score scale.

In the case of Advanced GNVQs there is an additional complication: due to the use of teacher assessments (even though moderated) there is some insecurity about the interpretation of the residuals as progress. They might be affected by severe or lenient grading, for example. There is a way to investigate this issue. In general, in the field of school effectiveness studies, variations between schools amount to about 10 to 20 per cent of pupil-level variance. The larger the variance, the more likely there is to be some problem with the data, such as teachers using more lenient or severe standards so that the standards from one school to another are not comparable. This issue can be addressed in a number of ways but we use here a multi-level modelling analysis to investigate this issue. If the variance accounted for by schools/colleges is larger than the usual 10 to 20 per cent, then there is the likelihood that standards are not comparable between institutions. The standards are not comparable, in this analysis, in that the institution that a student attends seems to matter more than is usually seen in studies of school effectiveness. The grades awarded do not relate to the intake characteristics of students in the way that is usually found.

The data presented in Table 3.8 suggested that there was a problem: standards did vary from institution to institution by more than usual. Some of this varia-tion might have been due to differences in effectiveness of the teaching, but even 20 per cent is high for such differences. It would seem to be more likely that the high dependence of students' grades on the school or college attended was due to differences in grading standards.

Table 3.8 Investigations of the per cent of variance in students' grades associated with the institution attended by the students

Outcome measure	Co-variate	Assessment largely external?	% of variance associated with institutions
Data from all students			
Average GCSE of all Advanced GNVQ candidates	none	YES	14.7
Grades on any of the four Advanced GNVQs	none	NO	27
Grades on any of the four Advanced GNVQs	Av. GCSE	NO	26
Data from Advanced GNVQ Business Students			
Average GCSE of Advanced GNVQ Business candidates	none	YES	17
Advanced GNVQ Business scores	none	NO	20
Advanced GNVQ Business scores	Av. GCSE	NO	26

Parity of esteem and standards

What is meant by 'standards' and why do they matter? The award of a qualification represents an item of public information that is widely used by employers and by those charged with offering places in further and higher education (i.e. admissions officers). The qualification provides two signals: that a certain content has been covered and that a certain level of accomplishment has been achieved in that content. In other words, a qualification signals *content covered* and *level of performance*. Employers, admissions officers and others all need to be accurately informed about the content covered and the level of accomplishment represented by certain grades and awards. The parity of esteem, which is an underlying theme in this book, will follow both from the presence of content and methods of teaching that are valued and also from levels of accomplishment (grading standards as opposed to content standards) that provide accurate signals.

Since the level of performance will depend to some extent on the developed abilities of the student, the award of a grade indirectly signals *levels of developed abilities*. If a student has 3 Bs at A level this signals a different level of achievement than 3 Es. Some of this difference will be attributable to effort but some will be attributable to developed abilities (*developed* not 'innate'). Some parts of these developed abilities could indeed be explicitly assessed as the 'core skills' component of a qualification.

A concern for standards is usually a concern for both aspects: the value of the content covered and the inferences from the level of performance.

The content covered is something that requires qualitative judgements and those kinds of investigations of what 'stakeholders' expect that have been conducted by staff of the National Council for Vocational Qualifications under their Fitness for Purpose studies (e.g. Coles and Matthews 1996; Coles 1996). This kind of standard setting, one responsive to the perceived needs of employers and higher education staff, must be on-going and is not absolute. Fitness for purpose in the 1990s was not the same as in the 1960s. Knowledge, technology, employment patterns and unemployment levels all changed drastically. Syllabuses and methods must surely change too in order to accommodate not only the changes in the technical and economic bases of society but also the ever larger proportions staying in education after the age of 16, in response to those changes.

This chapter could not tackle the issues concerned with the content covered, although the frequency of use of IT was an item of report and indicative of at least one aspect of skill acquisition. A content study would require an evaluation of the intended syllabus, its actual implementation and the coverage represented in the assessment procedures.

The data from ALIS+ could, however, be used to consider the levels of performance as indicated by the qualifications awarded. If it is accepted that levels of performance are related to developed abilities, then this perspective enables important questions to be considered regarding the 'equivalence' between A levels and Advanced GNVQs. What can employers and admissions officers deduce from the pass, merit or distinction awarded to a student who has followed an Advanced GNVQ course? How does this award compare with A level grades as an indicator of developed abilities?

The 50 per cent framework

It is an empirical fact that about 50 per cent of the variation in A level results can be predicted from a knowledge of the students' prior achievements at GCSE. This leaves room for considerable variation amongst individuals: from any given starting point, a wide range of outcomes is possible, as is shown each year in the Chances graphs produced in the ALIS project (Figure 3.10). Examining Chances graphs for A level Business Studies and A level Human Biology, we see that for students who all started the A levels from a position of low GCSE attainment (with GCSE average scores of about a D), the A level grades achieved covered the entire range. The grades with the highest chance, i.e. the most likely grade, were an E in both Business Studies and Human Biology, but there was about a 10 per cent chance of an A or B in Business Studies and a 5 per cent chance of an A or a B in Human Biology. Despite wide individual fluctuations, half the variation among students was predictable from their prior achievement. For groups, therefore, the expected average achievement can be quite well predicted yet individual students do not need to feel that their future is determined, for the chances graphs show that all grades are possible.

Whilst the Chances graphs show the spread of results from a given starting point, a regression line shows clearly the general trend across the range of prior

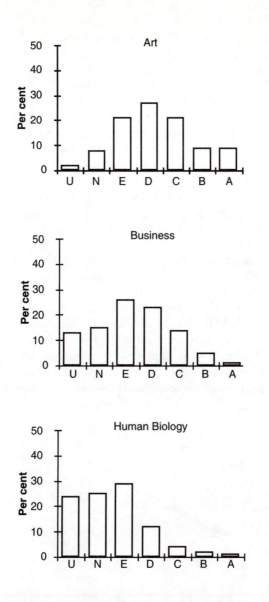

Figure 3.10 Chances graphs for A level Business Studies and Human Biology for students who had approximately a D average grade at GCSE

achievement. The regression lines can be regarded as indicating the grade achieved on average for each starting point (i.e. for each GCSE average points score (Figure 3.11). The Department for Education and Employment has recently accepted that the GCSE *average* score (as used in ALIS since 1983) is the best predictor of A level results (DfEE 1995) rather than the *total* score which the Department and others used until 1995. We can see from Figure 3.11 that A level Human Biology yielded lower grades than Business Studies for students at the same level of prior achievement. In this sense it was more difficult than Business Studies. The same approach can be used with the four Advanced GNVQ subjects under study, and the resulting regression lines are shown in Figure 3.12. (The correlation between GCSE average and Advanced GNVQs was of the order of 0.3 to 0.4, but this has to be viewed in the context of the restriction in range on the GCSE average scores. In other words, A levels also are not so well predicted *at the lower ranges of GCSE average scores*. Correlations between GCSE average and A level grades in these restricted ranges were only about 0.35, whereas in the whole range of A level entries the correlations are generally 0.6 or 0.7.)

Regression lines can also be used to investigate changes over time if there is an acceptable measure for the X-axis which has been given under the same conditions and not altered in its relationship to the Y-axis. In the ALIS project, the International Test of Developed Abilities has been given under standardised conditions since 1988. Studies of the A level Mathematics grades over these years show that, for the same score on the ITDA, grades awarded are now two grades higher. There is almost certain to be a temporal drift in standards and this drift was in the direction of meeting the National Training Targets, and so served a purpose. How it was brought about is an interesting question.

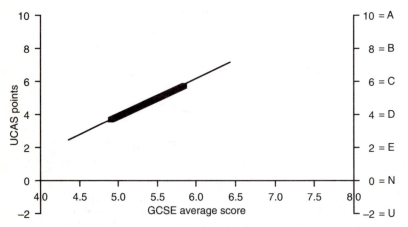

Figure 3.11a Regression line for A level Business Studies, 1994
Note: The thicker line shows the location of the middle half of the data,
i.e. the inter-quartile range.

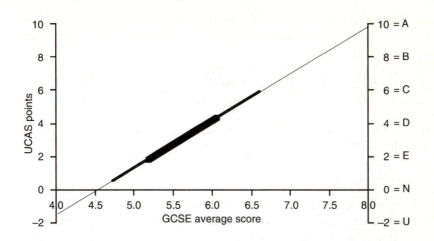

Example: Students with a C average at GCSE (i.e. GCSE average score = 5.0) entering A level Business Studies could be expected to achieve, on average, a 4 at A level, i.e. a grade D. Similar students entering for A level Human Biology could expect only an E or less on average.

Figure 3.11b Regression line for A level Human Biology, 1994
Note: The thicker line shows the location of the middle half of the data, i.e. the inter-quartile range.

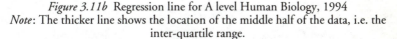

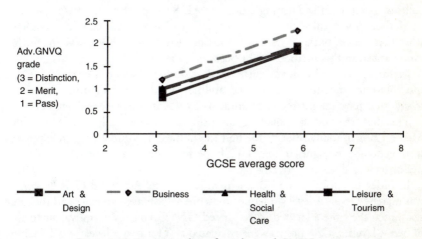

Figure 3.12 Regression lines for Advanced GNVQ courses

Equivalencies between Advanced GNVQs and A levels

The issue of the equivalence of Advanced GNVQs to A levels is similar to the issue of the differences in 'difficulty' of various A levels. It may be, for example, that Advanced GNVQ courses are equivalent to the easier A levels but not to the apparently more demanding ones such as Physics and Mathematics.

This concept of the 'difficulty' of a subject causes some concern. There is no accepted method to identify the *intrinsic* difficulty of a subject, but there *is* clear evidence that some subjects tend to yield lower grades (and therefore appear more difficult) than others. Whether this is due to severity of grading or inherent difficulty hardly matters. In a report for School Curriculum and Assessment Authority, Fitz-Gibbon and Vincent (1995) examined A level grades in different subjects by four methods:

A by comparing grades obtained by the *same students sitting different subjects*
B by comparing grades obtained by students *equated on prior achievement*
C by comparing grades obtained by students *equated on developed ability* as measured on the International Test of Developed Ability (ITDA), given as part of the ALIS project under carefully standardised conditions
D by comparing grades obtained on one subject with those obtained on all their other subjects using the *Relative Ratings approach* developed in Scotland (Kelly 1976; Fitz-Gibbon 1991)

Method D can be applied only if the outcomes are measured on the same scale. If Advanced GNVQs were given grades as per A levels, and if sufficient numbers of students took both an Advanced GNVQ and an A level, then correction factors could be worked out to determine the equivalencies between courses, as reported in Dearing citing the ALIS work (Dearing 1996: 94).

Method A was ruled out because of the small size of the sample of students who had taken both an A level and an Advanced GNVQ. With further modularisation this method might become more feasible.

Method C was ruled out because very few students had been given the ITDA, the voluntary measure of developed abilities. (The test is of most interest to *schools* that have taught the same students for GCSEs as well as A levels.)

This left method B, equating on prior achievement, i.e. GCSE results. Method B is in many respects the best method as the sample sizes are large and it is generally recognised that GCSE performance does predict subsequent performance, albeit imperfectly.

In order to apply method B, each student in the Advanced GNVQ sample was matched to an A level student of the same GCSE average score and the same sex. Since the time allocated to Advanced GNVQ courses is equivalent to that of two A levels, UCAS points were calculated as if for two A levels (e.g. by taking two-thirds of the total UCAS points if three A levels had been taken) and a regression equation was developed for UCAS points against GCSE average score.

Using the matched sample, the following equations were developed:

1994:
For students taking 2 A levels

UCAS points score = 2.35 * (GCSE average score) − 5.72

1995:
For students taking 2 A levels

UCAS points score = 1.88 * (GCSE average score) 3.63

Note: These equations apply only to students with the restricted range of GCSE scores that obtained in the sample of Advanced GNVQ students.

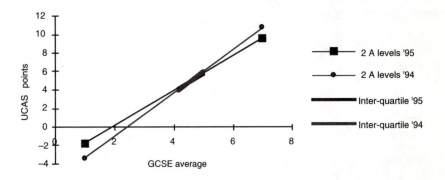

Figure 3.13 Equating Advanced GNVQs with A levels using the 50 per cent framework

Either by substituting values in the equations or by reading off the graphs, we see that if Advanced GNVQ students had taken 2 A levels, the expected total points for the middle 50 per cent of these students would likely have been between 4 and 6 (the end-points of the inter-quartile range), i.e. two E grades or one E and one D grade. These represent the 'tariff' value using the best available single predictor of both Advanced GNVQs and A levels: GCSE average scores. The equivalence suggested in the Interim Report for the *Review of 16–19 qualifications* (July 1995), namely that a distinction was equivalent to an A or a B at A level, did not seem justified by data from 1994 or 1995 Advanced GNVQs, as discussed in the next section.

Comparison with BTEC

It seems to have been the case that BTEC enrolled larger proportions of higher achieving students (it ran at a time when fewer students stayed in education post-16) and showed greater discrimination. The distinction was obtained by students whose GCSE average scores placed them firmly among the ordinary A level candidates on prior achievement, i.e. with GCSE average scores of about B.

Figure 3.14 shows the distribution of GCSE average scores for students who were awarded pass, merit and distinction in Advanced GNVQs and in BTEC National Diploma in Business.

In summary, the picture so far is one of courses enrolling students with predominantly Cs and Ds or lower averages. Students who obtained a distinction on their Advanced GNVQ courses tended to have had GCSE average scores of C (an average score of 4.90). This was lower than was found in a study of BTEC National Diploma Business courses in 1993, where distinctions were obtained by students with GCSE average grades of about 5.8 or nearly a B, and well within the normal range for A levels. At the time of that BTEC study far fewer students stayed on after the age of 16 and the A level grades were also probably more difficult to achieve.

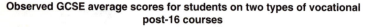

Observed GCSE average scores for students on two types of vocational post-16 courses

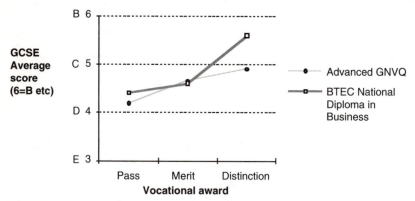

Figure 3.14 BTEC National Diploma awards compared with Advanced GNVQs

DISCUSSION

Assessment, grading and reporting

It would be helpful if there were set reporting dates at which time information had to be provided regarding the grades of completers and the status of non-completers such as 'continuing', 'left the course' or 'not known'. The transcript systems widely used in the US require that something is recorded at the end of the teaching on a course, such as 'withdrawn' or 'incomplete'. A subsequent completion of the course is recorded later as 'Incomplete removed'. In other words, transcripts showing the modules achieved at various standards would be easier to manage and the opportunity could still be made available for retakes.

The development of 'core skills' is an important part of Advanced GNVQ work. Since the skills are deemed highly important, it might be desirable if they were not regarded as simple 'pass' or 'fail' outcomes but were, rather, reported as being achieved at well differentiated levels. Variations in the quality of performance are inevitable in any complex activity, and employers and others need to know whether skills are highly honed or barely achieved. To leave the skills as pass/fail assessments is to encourage a minimum standards approach.

> In the majority of colleges inspected the development and assessment of core skills in GNVQ courses gave cause for concern. The inspectors identified a lack of planning and consistency and a lack of good practice as among the problems with the assessment of core skills.
> Sometimes the skills of Information Technology were developed separately from, and with no relevance to, the vocational area. The inspectors' views were that many of the difficulties with core skills arose from the lack of clarity in the criteria made available to teachers. Generally, the assessment of core skills was seen by teachers as difficult and often artificial.
>
> (FEFC 1995: 23)

Assessment, verification and grading were strongly criticised in the 1995 FEFC report. For example: 'The system remains too unwieldy to be either efficient or effective and further work is required' (FEFC 1995: 24).

It was notable that of the serious problems identified by the inspectors (pp. 34 and 35), six out of nine related to assessment procedures. One of the other three related to the need for staff development to enable teachers 'to come to grips with the problems inherent in offering these new qualifications' which could be seen as yet another problem arising from the unwieldy, inefficient assessment procedures that have been put in place.

Inspectors noted that some assessments were of such a general nature that they could have been passed by students who had not taken the course, whilst tests involving 'mathematical calculations or the application of formulae generally had low pass rates, as did those examining conceptual, abstract or specific knowledge which might not have been met in previous studies' (p. 28).

Why are there so many assessment problems in GNVQ work?

It is a possibility that many of the problems in assessment stem from the initial directions set some years ago and premissed on the use of criterion-referenced assessment (e.g. Jessup 1991). The systems resting on pass/fail judgements of highly specified competences were put forward without adequate trials or evidence and without citing any literature, for or against criterion-referenced testing. Had the literature been consulted, there were warnings available such as the following from one of the most highly respected US researchers:

> I am confident that the only sensible interpretations of data from assessment programs will be based solely on whether the rate of performance

goes up or down. Interpretations and decisions based on absolute levels of performance on exercises will be largely meaningless, since these absolute levels vary unaccountably with exercise content and difficulty, since judges will disagree wildly on the question of what consequences ought to ensue from the same absolute level of performance, and since there is no way to relate absolute levels of performance on exercises to success on the job, at higher levels of schooling or in life. Setting performance standards on tests and exercises by known methods is a waste of time or worse.

(Glass 1978: 259)

The problems with attempts to have criterion-referenced testing as opposed to assessing externally the relative performance of cohorts of candidates have been identified by Glass (1978), Wolf (1991) and Fitz-Gibbon (1991, 1996). A reason frequently put forward for the use of criterion-referenced testing is that it will be more motivating and better accepted by students and employers, but there has been no research to support this proposition.

It was perhaps inevitable that a newly developed vocational system would undergo considerable teething problems. And it will be of interest to watch the system develop to the point where students and staff find the coursework and the assessment methods reach acceptable levels of effectiveness and efficiency. The kind of monitoring provided by the ALIS+ work allows students' perceptions of the functioning of the vocational system to be monitored to a degree of precision and detail that will provide evidence in each school or college as to improvements, even if these are small and gradual, as well as evidence relating to the functioning of the entire system.

The certification role of Advanced GNVQs

The Advanced GNVQ is a qualification. As such it is meant to open doors, either to employment or to further study. This instrumental view of vocational qualifications is not mentioned here in order to distinguish Advanced GNVQs from A levels. There is considerable evidence that A levels themselves, although often enjoyed, are seen primarily in an instrumental way, as a means to higher education. The term 'vocational', however, emphasises these instrumental values. Advanced General National *Vocational* Qualifications are vocational in leading to jobs. (A levels lead to 'avocations' perhaps? A doubtful proposition, unless avocations are simply better paid jobs.)

As a qualification, GNVQ has to earn esteem (Edwards, Chapter 1). How does a qualification become valuable, recognised? It might seem logical to assert that only longitudinal studies can establish the value of a qualification, the esteem in which it should be held. However, life is never so tidy as logic, and admissions officers and employers have to take new qualifications on trust before such longitudinal studies have become available and in the absence of any 'clinical trials' as should be demanded of new procedures. There is, therefore, an imperative need to illuminate what it is that the Advanced GNVQ provides by way of assurance that the student is ready to proceed to a higher course or ready to be employed at some designated level.

This vocational readiness has two components, as suggested earlier. One is primarily a characteristic of the *student*: his or her *developed aptitudes* or core skills, the levels of which will influence the student's ability to profit from further, and presumably more difficult, content. The second is primarily a characteristic of the *course*: the *content*, i.e. the knowledge and skills acquired, on which subsequent work will build.

There has been, and continues to be, considerable reluctance to acknowledge the concept of 'aptitude', certainly if called 'ability' and even if prefixed carefully with the word 'developed'. Because of understandable concerns about labelling people and pretending to be assessing an immutable characteristic of the person, there has been a reluctance to acknowledge the considerable success of measures of general aptitudes as indicators of future performance. If this relevance is found to hold (a situation sometimes called 'validity generalisation', Hunter and Hunter 1984; Pearlman, Schmidt and Hunter 1980), then the issues of the equivalence of various qualifications can be easily established. It has been argued that these two functions of a qualification – to signal aptitude and to signal content covered – have to be separately considered and researched. The combination of the 50 per cent framework to take care of the aptitude signalling and the kind of evaluations of content exemplified by Coles and Matthews (1996) and Coles (1996) will, if combined with reliable and blind external marking of parts of Advanced GNVQs, create the conditions for fair parity of esteem judgements to become accepted. Separate but equal? Slightly different and equally useful seems an achievable goal, and they could all be called A levels.

4

CLASSROOM OBSERVATION IN ACADEMIC AND VOCATIONAL COURSES POST-16

Nick Meagher

Let observation with extensive view
Survey mankind from China to Peru;
Remark each anxious toil, each eager strife,
And watch the busy scenes of crowded life.
(Samuel Johnson, *The Vanity of
Human Wishes*, 1749)

INTRODUCTION

In a programme designed to detect differences in teaching and learning between academic and vocational courses, the observation of classroom practice is of central importance. It is, however, immediately evident that not every academic and vocational course can be studied, neither can every aspect of the complex human environment that constitutes a classroom. The first part of this chapter therefore raises and suggests answers to three deceptively simple questions in order to detect any differences that may exist:

- Which academic and vocational courses should be the subject of enquiry?
- Upon which aspects of classroom practice should observation focus?
- When the focus for observation is established, what methods are appropriate?

In the second part of the chapter results from two methods of classroom observation are examined, and interpretations are suggested which cast some light on the difference between academic and vocational learning.

WHICH ACADEMIC AND VOCATIONAL COURSES SHOULD BE THE SUBJECT OF ENQUIRY?

The original intention of this research, as expressed in the 1992 application to the Education and Social Research Council, was to investigate 'how teaching and learning are organised . . . across the A level/BTEC "boundary"', and subsequently to combine the results of this investigation with those obtained

62

from the A Level Information System (ALIS) data and its associated BTEC pilot project. Both these other projects rely on the collection of self-reported non-observational data in order to provide evidence about the effectiveness of different teaching and learning activities in terms of student satisfaction and examination results. The focus of the present study was on classroom observation.

In the initial design, 'academic' courses were to be selected from A levels, and 'vocational' courses from BTEC Nationals. By the time the research programme was developed in September 1993, however, the landscape of vocational education in England had been irrevocably altered by the introduction of General National Vocational Qualification (GNVQ) courses. GNVQ Level 3 courses were promoted as 'equivalent' to two A levels, and soon became known as Advanced GNVQs. In July 1993 John Patten, then Secretary of State for Education, used the term 'Vocational A levels', a phrase which I understand came as something of a surprise to NCVQ whose views on the appropriateness of this sobriquet had not been sought. Mr Patten claimed that the new name would 'help pupils, students, parents, teachers, higher education and employers to understand that these GNVQs require a level of achievement equivalent to two A levels' (quoted in *The Times Educational Supplement* 16 July 1993). The new term also conveniently glossed over the fact that the new qualification was in every other significant respect intended to be entirely different from traditional A levels. Nevertheless, this may have been an early signal that the government was prepared to countenance a new approach to links between education and training, and it is interesting to consider the significance of this name change in the context of Sir Ron Dearing's recommendation that GNVQs be called 'Applied A levels', because the present name 'is hardly memorable, and the qualification is not, strictly speaking, vocational' (Dearing 1996: 9.14). This accords closely with the view of Alan Smithers, a noted critic of the new qualification, that a stronger distinction between academic and vocational subjects is needed. 'A sensible separation would be if A levels were about subjects – like English, History or Geography which are ways of making sense of the world – and GNVQs should be about applied education' (quoted in *The Times Educational Supplement* 17 November 1995). Whether or not this will be a helpful distinction remains to be seen. GNVQ Science, for example, contains both 'subject' elements of knowledge and 'applied' elements of practice, and it is this breadth that has set it aside from traditional A level science courses. After the final draft of this chapter was complete, a very low-key government announcement by the Junior Education Minister revealed that the final aria in this production has not yet been heard, and may never be. The government has decided not to accept the recommended name, 'Applied A level', and intends to introduce 'external testing and academic rigour' to the qualification (*The Times Educational Supplement* 8 November 1996: 4). Confusion over the status of GNVQs therefore remains. Whilst on the one hand dropping the proposed A level label from its title, and simultaneously introducing elements associated with A level assessment (examinations set and marked externally) and curriculum (centrally determined content), GNVQs appear to have been consigned to an educational limbo inhabited by neither fish nor fowl.

The initial explosion of enthusiasm for GNVQs at Advanced level, far greater than anticipated by NCVQ, is well documented. It was not difficult for us to conclude that, our research having coincided with a major educational initiative, we should accept the opportunity and focus our study on comparing A levels and the new qualification. This decision had a direct bearing on the selection of subjects to be observed. The idea was to choose courses on both sides of the academic/vocational divide which commonsense suggested might be taught and learned in *similar* ways. If variations were detected, then it might be possible to argue that these were caused by the different requirements of A levels and GNVQs. The five GNVQ Advanced subjects available to us in 1994 were Health & Social Care, Leisure & Tourism, Business, Art & Design, and Manufacturing. Of these, the only one with a clear echo within traditional A levels was Business, and this was chosen together with A level Business Studies and A level Economics. Similarities and differences between these two A levels as perceived by HMI are referred to by Tony Edwards in Chapter 2. Conversely, it was necessary to select courses on the same side of the academic/vocational divide which commonsense suggested might be taught and learned in *different* ways. In these cases it might then be possible to argue that any similarities were the result of the nature of the qualifications. ALIS was able to provide a wealth of well-documented and detailed information about teaching and learning strategies in different A levels, and this is reported by Carol Taylor Fitz-Gibbon in Chapter 3. For Advanced GNVQ course comparisons, it was at this stage necessary to take whatever opportunities were available locally.

From this starting point a number of schools and colleges on Tyneside were invited to take part in the research programme. The subjects they felt able to offer for observation in addition to A level Business Studies and GNVQ Business (Advanced) were accepted with some negotiation and provided the essential evidence of similar and dissimilar work against which our findings could be set. A detailed research programme was established in twelve schools and four colleges of further education. The full classroom observation schedule involved forty-one different teachers teaching forty-three classes in fifteen subjects, as shown in Table 4.1. In addition, some lessons in A level French, English, Geography, History and Statistics were also observed. This represents a total observation time of around 400 hours. Towards the end of the data collection period in this ESRC project, NCVQ became interested in our methods and results, and a new contract was agreed with them to look at specific GNVQ courses in twenty-four centres in England, Wales and Northern Ireland. Data from this project comes from over 350 students and fifty staff in thirty Advanced GNVQ courses, including Hospitality & Catering (7), Business (11), Health & Social Care (5) and Science (7). This evidence is also drawn upon in what follows.

Table 4.1 Numbers of lessons observed in different subjects

Subject	Lessons observed	Subject	Lessons observed
GNVQ Advanced		A level	
Business	41	Business Studies	28
Health & Social Care	9	Economics	23
Science	6	Biology	10
		English	8
BTEC National		Physics	8
Business & Finance	14	Psychology	8
Engineering	5	Maths	5
Computing & Electronics	2	Chemistry	5
		Sociology	5
TOTAL:	77	TOTAL:	100

UPON WHICH ASPECTS OF CLASSROOM PRACTICE SHOULD OBSERVATION FOCUS?

Not wrung from speculation and subtleties, but from common sense and observation.

(Sir Thomas Browne, *Religio Medici*, 1643)

Having accepted that it is not possible to observe and record everything that happens during a lesson, an early judgement had to be made about the appropriate focus for this work. A number of issues were involved:

- avoidance of our own preconceptions about which activities 'ought' to be taking place
- the need to match results with those derived from ALIS student questionnaires
- the need to restrict the scale of observation to manageable proportions
- the relative merits of looking either at a restricted number of activities in greater detail, or at more activities in less detail
- the likely impact of the presence of an 'observer' (or several observers) in a classroom
- teacher or lecturer reaction to detailed scrutiny of their methods

After considerable discussion, a decision was made to focus the classroom observation on the students' learning experiences, rather in the way in which Neville Bennett's (Bennett *et al.* 1984) analysis of the nature of classroom tasks was used as evidence of the quality of the pupils' learning experience. In part this was to allow our findings to map consistently onto the ALIS results, but it was also to side-step some of the issues involved in starting from preconceptions about activities that 'ought' to characterise academic and vocational teaching and learning. There were two important consequences of this decision: firstly, the student focus led to illuminative work on the match between learning styles and course requirements, reported by Roy Haywood in Chapter 6, and secondly, classroom observation was linked very closely to the ALIS questionnaire. Responses to this questionnaire reveal the frequency of a number of classroom events, as perceived by the students themselves, and the results are statistically linked to student 'attitudes' and a Value Added analysis of examination successes. The questionnaire was already under revision to include activities appropriate for BTEC and GNVQ: for example, an additional category of activities 'outside the classroom' had been added.

The activities that students in the ALIS project report as having taken place more or less frequently are eminently observable, and formed the basis of the first observation schedule. They include:

Practical work	Presentation of a topic by the teacher
Exercises/working examples	Using/watching audio visual (AV) material
Reviewing previous work	Using IT/computers
Researching a new topic	Preparing essays/assignments/reports
Reading	Working in pairs/groups
Class discussion, teacher led	Presenting work/listening to presentations
Discussion in groups	Helping each other
Taking dictated notes	Getting personal help from the teacher
Making own notes	Getting help from business/industry
Receiving prepared notes	Producing original work

These descriptors were compiled twelve years ago in order to identify activities in A level classrooms, and we had some doubts about whether they would serve to distinguish between academic and vocational teaching and learning, even assuming that significant and generalisable differences exist. The nature of the pedagogic experience might be expected from curriculum debate to differ between academic and vocational classes in a number of additional respects, including:

- the nature of teacher/student discourse
- the extent to which activities are initiated, that is selected and formulated, either by the teacher or the student(s), or negotiated between them
- the extent to which activities are conducted on a 'whole class', 'small group' or 'individual' basis
- the use of 'worksheets' and other forms of direct transmission
- the importance of other activities such as work experience and role play.

It was also necessary to strike a balance between the need, on the one hand, to record activities in a large number of lessons in a way that would allow quantifiable analysis, and on the other to avoid obliterating some of the qualitative subtleties of discourse and interaction that reflect and signal how teacher and students perceive the pedagogic relationship. In Chapter 5 Frank Hardman challenges the belief that 'real' discussion lies at the heart of teaching and learning in A level English, and both he and Roy Haywood consider the significance of the transition from the more dependent status of 'pupil' to the more independent role of 'student'.

After piloting several different versions of an observation schedule drawn from the analysis of recently published ALIS results, together with a consideration of the consequences in practice of those assumptions about academic and vocational learning which Tony Edwards outlined in Chapter 2, the following thirty activities were selected:

Works on written assignment	General management/admin. by teacher
Reviews previous work	Works on problem solving investigation
Listens to teacher exposition	Spontaneously adds to another's response
Works on practical task	Spontaneously challenges another's response
Asks managerial question	Uses/watches audio visual (AV) material
Answers managerial question	Uses IT/computers
Reads or undertakes research	Receives individual help from teacher
Asks curriculum question	Makes own notes with teacher guidance
Answers curriculum question	Makes own notes without teacher guidance
Student discussion of work	Receives help from business/industry
Teacher-led discussion of work	Helps/receives help from another student
Initiates a contribution	Receives duplicated notes/handouts
Presents work/reports	Other task related activity (e.g. role play)
Takes dictated notes	Uses worksheets
Non-task related activity	Works on exercises/examples

To these activities were added, where appropriate, two sets of 'modifiers': firstly, whether they took place in the classroom, or out of the classroom, or off the site, and secondly, whether the answers and interjections were 'correct' – that is accepted by the teacher. The usefulness of some of these descriptors is still in question. 'Work on problem solving investigation', for example, taken from HMI accounts of 'good practice' (DES 1987a), is not a separate activity but a description that can apply to several of them. It also arguably requires too high a level of inference on the part of the observer to be reliable, and in fact was never used.

Concerns about student and teacher reactions to the presence of another adult in the teaching room proved unfounded. Although in the past most classroom interactions have been very private affairs, teachers and students, especially in GNVQ courses, are now very used to the presence of an inquisitive 'significant other' who may be there for any number of reasons. During my work in schools and colleges, for example, I met other colleagues engaged in course moderation and external verification, teacher appraisal, supervision of students and probationers, supporting SEN students, Ofsted and FEFC Inspection, LEA Adviser visits, and an Albanian college principal on a fact-finding visit.

WHAT METHODS OF CLASSROOM OBSERVATION ARE APPROPRIATE?

This question has taxed education researchers since the first codified systems for pupil observation were developed in America by W.C. Olsen in 1929. His sampling techniques recorded the amount of time spent on specific activities. The influence of that approach has remained visible in this research field ever since, with variations on perhaps the most popular of all, the Flanders Interaction Analysis System (Flanders 1963) being the most used. By 1970, Simon and Boyer were able to publish in America an account of seventy-nine 'Mirrors for Behaviour', mainly derived or adapted from Flanders, the essential characteristics of which were that they

> involve the presence of an observer in the classroom, the recording of events in a systematic manner as they happen, and the coding of the inter-actions in such a way as to make possible a subsequent analysis of . . . pupil behaviour.

> (Galton 1979: 109)

This closely describes our own intentions, and initial attempts to devise an observation schedule were based on a set of Flanders-style record sheets, using three- and subsequently five-second intervals. Some initial practice made it apparent that the method was inappropriate for the focus, subtlety and complexity of the required record. An attempt was therefore made to develop a computer assisted programme that could be used in the classroom. Coincidentally, a colleague in Behavioural Sciences had used Observer software (developed by Noldus Information in 1993) to record the feeding habits of antelope when hyenas are present. This software was investigated and found to be sufficiently adaptable to produce the type of record we were seeking.

The process of classroom observation is normally categorised either as 'unstructured' or as 'systematic'. 'Investigators using unstructured or flexible observation include social anthropologists and symbolic interactionists, who observe classroom events by immersing themselves in the classroom and joining in the lessons' (Dunkerton 1981). In this case the investigator must have no predetermined ideas about what to look for, and the record of events should be annotated and confirmed by explanations from the teacher and students rather than by the observer alone. Investigators using systematic methods have usually decided what they want to observe and how to collect the data before going into the classroom. Whilst this research project falls into the latter category and uses systematic methods, it is worth noting that the various amendments to the observation categories and their 'modifiers' were made as a result of the experience of observation, and the final categories are in that sense the result of 'immersion' in the classrooms. The ability of the observer to move between roles in this way is crucial to the successful development of the data collection process. A detailed review of the theory and practice of 'Coding

Classroom Interaction' may be found in Edwards and Westgate 1994 and Croll 1986, and a revised but powerful critique of systematic classroom observation is in Delamont and Hamilton 1984.

In practice, classroom observation requires two decisions to be made: firstly, what sampling strategy is appropriate (sampling determines which subjects are to be observed and when), and secondly, what recording method to use (recording determines how the behaviour is logged). Observer software allows a choice of three sampling and three recording methods. Inevitably, particular sampling and recording methods are inextricably linked, and this may have contributed to some of the confusion surrounding descriptions of these processes. The variables are shown in Table 4.2 with a tick to indicate normal associations.

Researchers involved in classroom observation have also tended to use their own individual phrases to describe similar sampling methods. To clarify matters, a simplified review of sampling and recording strategies follows. Scan sampling involves making observations at regular, predetermined intervals. The method of logging these observations then determines the nature of the record, and there are two ways of doing this. When associated with instantaneous recording, the researcher notes the current behavioural state of the subject(s) on the instant of each sample point. In the case of Flanders, for example, this may be at every three seconds. For our purposes, the problems of applying this recording system to a set of as many as twenty individual students, some of whom would form different sub-sets of small working groups from time to time, proved too complex and this method was not adopted. When associated with 'one–zero' recording, the researcher notes whether or not there has been an occurrence of each described behaviour during the preceding sample interval. Clearly the length of the sample interval is determined at least in part by the time taken to complete the record, and this presents a major drawback when, as in this case, there are a large number of descriptors and modifiers and potentially a large group of 'actors'. Under these circumstances, 'one–zero' sampling may well substantially underestimate the frequency of occurrence, whilst overestimating the amount of time spent on any particular activity (Dunkerton 1981: 149), and this method was not adopted. There are no systematic constraints attached to 'ad libitum' sampling, which involves the researcher making a record of whatever seems relevant at the time. It is used in conjunction with continuous recording. As we particularly required a systematic and therefore quantifiable observation record, this method was not adopted. Continuous recording, however, notes each

Table 4.2 The links between sampling and recording classroom observations

	Continuous recording	Instantaneous recording	One–zero recording
Focal sampling	✓		
Scan sampling		✓	✓
Ad libitum sampling	✓		

occurrence of a predetermined activity as and when it occurs, and when used in conjunction with 'focal' sampling produces an accurate log of events. This method was adopted, and the Observer programme modified, or 'configured', to include the thirty activities listed above. The configuration was downloaded onto a PC compatible lap-top computer, and used to make systematic records of over seventy-five hours out of the 400 hours of classroom activities observed in A level, BTEC National and Advanced GNVQ classes.

ADDITIONAL DATA SOURCES

The academic/vocational continuum

Our work on the match between learning styles and course requirements, reported by Roy Haywood, led to a further consideration of ways of recording student perceptions about the nature of their work. If student success depends at least in part on their being taught in ways that reflect their particular learning aptitudes, and if academic and vocational learning experiences are different, then it should be possible to describe a continuum, the extremes of which are associated with traditional 'academic' and 'vocational' practices, and within which selected learning experiences may be placed. Under 'Presentation of topics' for example, at one extreme all the necessary information will be given by the teacher, at the other it is researched by the students. In 'Core skills', explicit work may or may not be undertaken; coursework may or may not form part of 'Assessment strategies', and so on. Using this 'travellers' guide' to the academic/vocational landscape, it is possible to form a judgement about where in this context a course is located, based on activities observed in the classroom. The list of descriptors were taken from a number of sources. These include the concrete/abstract continuum which is at the heart of learning style theory, and discussions with practising teachers and within the research team. Six additional descriptors were taken from the ALIS research where results had shown these to be significantly different in 'academic' and 'vocational' courses (Table 4.3).

Table 4.3 ALIS descriptors showing significant differences between 'academic' and 'vocational' courses

ALIS descriptors	More in A level courses	More in BTEC Nationals
Using IT (and AV)		✓
Researching a topic		✓
Working exercises from past papers		✓
Group discussion		✓
Using handouts	✓	
Presenting work/listening to another student present work		✓

Finally, a consideration of different assessment evidence requirements and methods was added. The descriptors were re-expressed as short phrases grouped under separate headings in the form of a series of continua, and the result developed as a questionnaire. The categories are: presentation of topics, prescription of tasks, core skills, working as groups, problem solving and the application of knowledge and, finally, assessment strategies. The final version of this instrument is given in Table 4.4.

The original intention was that this instrument would be used by the observer during periods of classroom observation, and a judgement recorded using the seven-point scale on each line about the relative emphasis accorded within each continuum. When piloting the questionnaire, however, teacher and student interest was such that it was decided instead to ask them to record their views about the nature of the course as a whole, and an additional rephrased version was produced for students to complete. One advantage of this revised approach was the opportunity it provided to compare the views of students with those of their teachers. These results, reported in a later section of this chapter, have been of considerable interest to the schools and colleges taking part. Eventually, records were made by more than 350 students, and around forty were completed by teachers.

Questionnaires and interviews

Questionnaires and interviews were used with students, course teachers and leaders, and with senior curriculum co-ordinators. The main student questionnaire came from the ALIS project, and those results are reported by Carol Taylor Fitz-Gibbon in Chapter 3. Interviews with students and course teachers were conducted on an *ad hoc* basis as appropriate or when possible. Students and course teachers were also asked to complete a Kolb learning style questionnaire, and these results are reported by Roy Haywood. In the NCVQ project, course students and teachers were also asked to complete a questionnaire derived from ALIS asking about the frequency of a number of significant classroom activities. These results allow an interesting comparison between the views of teachers and students. Audio tape recordings were also made of some of the lessons observed.

As part of the later NCVQ project, systematic use was made of questionnaires for curriculum co-ordinators and managers. These were followed up by in-depth interviews, structured under the following headings:

Input

Courses offered	Student entry requirements
Student selection	Student induction
Local competition for students	Numbers of students enrolled
Combined class teaching	Student calibre
Staff qualifications	Staff additional qualifications
Profile of a 'good' GNVQ teacher	Staff/student contact time
Private study time	Availability of resources

Table 4.4 'Continuum questionnaire' for the balance of classroom activities

Presentation of topics

1	Information is given by the teacher	* * * * * *	Information is researched by students
2	Interpretation is given by the teacher	* * * * * *	Meaning is discovered by the students
3	The topics are not referenced to the world of work	* * * * * *	The topics are referenced to vocational contexts

Prescription of tasks

4	The task is closely defined by the teacher	* * * * * *	The task is closely defined by the student
5	The method is closely directed by the teacher	* * * * * *	The method is decided by the student
6	The pace of work is set by the teacher	* * * * * *	The pace of work is set by the student
7	Students work entirely in the classroom	* * * * * *	Students work outside the classroom
8	Students are engaged in the same activities at the same time	* * * * * *	Students are engaged in a variety of activities at any one time
9	Application of past learning to new topics is not necessary	* * * * * *	The application of past learning to new topics is necessary

Core skills

10	Students do not use IT	* * * * * *	Students use IT
11	Students do no explicit work on communication skills	* * * * * *	Students work explicitly on communication skills
12	Students do no explicit work on numeracy skills	* * * * * *	Students work explicitly on numeracy skills

Working as groups

13	Students work alone	* * * * * *	Students work as members of groups not just in the company of others
	Students do not present their work to the class		Students present their work to the class
14	a) Individually	* * * * * *	a) Individually
15	b) As groups	* * * * * *	b) As groups

Table 4.4 continued . . .

Problem solving/application of knowledge

16	The work does not require problem solving	* * * * *	The work requires problem solving
		If the work does require problem solving, go on to the next two statements: If not, go to line 19	
17	The work requires problem solving in an academic context	* * *	The work requires problem solving in a vocational ('real world') context
18	The work does not require problem posing	* * *	The work requires problem posing

Assessment strategies

19	Coursework does not form part of the final assessment	* * * * *	Coursework forms part of the final assessment
20	Students receive limited formative feedback	* * * * *	Students receive extensive formative feedback

Process

Delivery of units	Vocational relevance
Grading and assessment	Meeting deadlines
Work experience	Delivery of core skills
Choice of additional units	Choice of additional subjects

Outcomes

Completion rates	Destinations

Additional comments

Any other comments	Profile of successful GNVQ students

By consistently using this outline for interviews and transcriptions, not only could these important qualitative insights be linked to the results from classroom observation and questionnaires, but the views of colleagues in different centres could readily be summarised and compared.

RESULTS

Before considering any aggregation of the data derived from the Observer records, it is helpful to consider two examples which are in many ways typical of the records made. These examples also serve to illustrate the nature of the evidence and indicate the way in which it has been interpreted. Figure 4.1 reproduces the first ten minutes of an Observer record from an A level Economics class, with the coded labels expanded into full descriptors. The comments in *italic* font were typed into the record as the lesson progressed. This is a particularly helpful feature of the programme as it allows short notes or longer descriptive comments to be time coded and stored with the observation data. This allows records to be made of events outside the scope of the configuration being used, qualitative observations, and reminders to the researcher about where modifications to the programme would be advantageous. In this way a certain subjective interaction with the classroom events is made possible, and the record comes closer to the ideal – that it could be used to reconstruct an accurate picture of the lesson observed.

This information can then be summarised for each lesson as shown in Table 4.5. Left to stand alone this begins to look like a very blunt instrument indeed, and to confirm the worst fears of those who believe that quantitative analysis of the subtleties of classroom interaction is possible only at the cost of sacrificing the most important details. However, this is a tool designed primarily to detect differences between patterns of academic and vocational teaching and learning. When the same schedule is applied to the work in a BTEC National Diploma class, for example (in the same school), the results look very different (Table 4.6).

In the A level class the emphasis is very much on topic presentation by the teacher, followed by an intensive question and answer session with the proceedings dominated by one or two individuals. The pattern from the BTEC class is

{start} : 12.05

1	SS	General management and admin
		After a period of general management/admin the teacher gives out copies of The Economist *magazine to help class with revision*
187	SS	Teacher-led discussion
302	I1	Initiates contribution
322	I2	Initiates contribution
332	SS	Undertake research on a set task, in the classroom
366	SS	Listens to teacher exposition
383	SS	Reviewing previous work
442	I3	Answers a curriculum question
475	I4	Answers a curriculum question
488	I1	Answers a curriculum question
522	SS	Takes notes dictated by the teacher
567	I5	Answers a curriculum question
632	I6	Initiates contribution
		Topic is constructing retail price index
765	I1	Answers a curriculum question
771	I2	Answers a curriculum question
789	I6	Initiates contribution
814	I5	Answers a curriculum question
866	SS	Exercises, working examples, in the classroom
878	I1	Answers a curriculum question
		Teaching is 'spotting' future exam questions
966	I4	Answers a curriculum question
972	I2	Answers a curriculum question
994	I6	Asks a curriculum question
1185	I6	Seeks/receives help from teacher, in the classroom
		During this part of the lesson, students were working examples as individuals, but with help from the teacher and from each other, together with some discussion about the topic and general teacher-led question and answer

Note: Column 1 records the time elapsed in seconds, and Column 2 contains the entry code for each subject (in this case either individuals, e.g. I6, or the whole class, SS).

Figure 4.1 An Observer record of ten minutes from an A level Economics class

far more diffuse. The two most frequent activities are receiving individual help from the teacher, and spending time off task either in or out of the classroom. Other than this, a greater number of different activities are recorded, and they are spread more evenly between the students. Interestingly, although the lesson started with a brief presentation of a topic and a brisk question and answer session very similar to the pattern in the A level class, this information is contained in the full Observer record, and cannot be deduced from the summary diagram. This is a reminder of the dangers in aggregating data to the point where sequence and duration are lost.

These two examples were chosen to represent the many separate records made and for which there is no room in this present publication. They do, however,

Table 4.5 Observer record of an A level Economics lesson summarised

Activity	Students							
	2	4	6	7	8	9	10	All
Answers curriculum question	***	****	****	***	*****	****	***	
		***	****		****	**		
		****			*			
Asks curriculum question		**						
Topic presented by teacher								****
Adds to previous response		**	**					
Students make own notes								**
General management and admin.								*
Previous work reviewed								*
Dictated notes								*
Initiates contribution		*						
Corrects previous response		*						

Note: * = one occurrence

Table 4.6 Observer record of a BTEC National Diploma lesson summarised

Activity	Students									
	1	2	3	4	5	6	7	8	9	All
Individual help from the teacher	**	*	*	**	***	***	*	*	*	
					**					
Off task: in the classroom	*	*	*	*	*	**	**	**	**	
Off task: out of the classroom	*	****				**	*		*	
Works on examples	*	**				**	*		*	*
Answers curriculum question		***		**						
General management and admin.										**
Answers management question			**							
Asks curriculum question	**						*			
Gives and receives help	*	*								
Teacher-led discussion	*									
Asks management question			*							
Initiates contribution				*						
Topic presented by teacher										*
Handout notes used										*
Student-led discussion										*

Note: * = one occurrence

reveal the nature of the evidence from which generalisations have been drawn. Thus the spread of activities in Advanced GNVQ lessons is similar to that in A levels, and more restricted than in the BTEC data reported by Lacy and Fitz-Gibbon (1993). The next section of this chapter examines and compares the results from A level and GNVQ courses.

A level courses

An Observer record was made of thirty-two hours of A level classroom activities, using twenty-nine of the original categories: evidence of 'problem solving' was not recorded for reasons already noted. Four subjects were considered in some detail during a total of forty lessons: Biology (five hours), Business Studies (nine hours), Economics (eleven hours) and Psychology (seven hours). Totalling all the observed learning experiences in these subjects reveals that almost half of students' time (47 per cent) is spent in answering curriculum-related questions, as shown in Figure 4.2.

When all the interactions of discourse and questioning are aggregated, this figure rises to 73 per cent, almost three-quarters of the learning experience. The extent to which pedagogy is determined by the nature of the knowledge is discussed at some length by Frank Hardman in Chapter 5. Because these are aggregated numbers, it is reasonable to enquire whether the balance is different in the different subjects, and these results appear in Table 4.7. The 'discourse and questioning' activities aggregated here are:

Answer curriculum question	Initiate a contribution
Add to another's response	Ask curriculum question
Teacher-led discussion	Students discuss their work
Ask management question	Answer managerial question

It is interesting to note that in the lessons observed, Biology students lead the way in answering curriculum-based questions (152 replies in 240 minutes), and

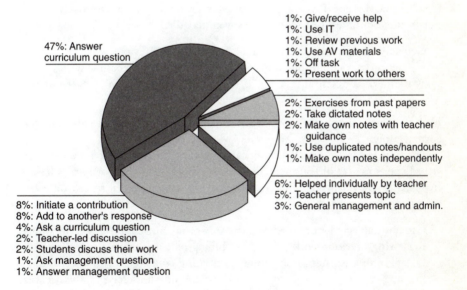

Figure 4.2 Percentage of time spent on various classroom activities for students on four A level courses

Table 4.7 Discourse and questioning activities in four A level subjects compared

Activity	Biology	Business	Economics	Psychology
Answering curriculum questions	62	45	40	47
All discourse and questioning interactions	70	77	77	64

Psychology students take part in rather less discourse and questioning inter-actions than the others. This suggests that the way in which a subject is taught may depend more on the pedagogic preferences of the teacher and less on the nature and content of the syllabus, a view further supported by analysis of the variety of learning activities in each of these subjects. Although twenty-seven learning experiences were identified, the 'average' number of different activities across the four subjects is eight. The range is from one to fifteen, these outliers being found in Economics classes where the 'one' activity was recorded in a lesson where a depleted group of students worked uninterruptedly with word processing IT programmes, and the 'fifteen' different activities came from a lesson where a lively revision session covering several different topics was under-taken.

Although the average length of recorded observations was just over forty-eight minutes, the range is between fifteen minutes and nearly two hours. As much variety of activity was observed in some of the shorter sessions as in some of the longer ones. In one Psychology lesson, for example, which effectively lasted ninety-three minutes, just six activities were recorded:

General management and admin.	Reviewing previous work
Answering curriculum-based questions	Adding to another student's response
Working on a practical task	Receiving individual help from the teacher

Here the practical task was group work constructing wall posters to illustrate the current topic.

The four lessons in which a significantly greater variety of activity took place were Economics (two), Business Studies and Biology. In the Economics lesson (referred to above), which effectively lasted fifty-two minutes, fifteen different activities were recorded:

General management and admin.	Answering curriculum-based questions
Reviewing previous work	Taking part in a teacher-led discussion
Listening to a teacher presentation	Initiating contributions to discussions
Helping each other	Working on an exercise in a past paper
Asking curriculum-based questions	Receiving individual help from the teacher
Taking dictated notes	

Making their own notes with	Adding to other students' responses
and without teacher guidance	Reading or researching

As well as the variety of learning experiences observed, the frequency with which each activity takes place is also an important variable. 'Answering a curriculum question' is one activity, but in a sixty minute Biology lesson it occurred sixty-three times, and fifty times in a fifty-eight minute Economics lesson. Taking all the different activities into consideration, an A level student could expect on average to encounter around thirty-nine 'acts' in a forty-eight minute session, representing an 'acts per minute' coefficient of 0.9. This measure is used to serve as an indication of the 'tempo' of a student's classroom experience: a coefficient of 1.0 occurs when a different 'act' happens on average once a minute. As may be expected, this varies between observed subjects, rising to 1.1 in Biology, and falling to 0.7 in Psychology. Within this range, the tempo of individual lessons in the same subject also varies, from a high of 2.9 in a particularly hectic Economics lesson when the overhead projector broke down, to a sedate 0.1 when three students sat in front of separate computers for three-quarters of an hour.

It is interesting to compare these observation results for different subjects. Because the observation periods varied in length, contingency tables have again been used. Simply standardising each record to a sixty minute norm would not do because there is no guarantee that a student who has received individual help from a teacher four times in thirty minutes will do so eight times in an hour. The appropriate table is shown (Table 4.8). This table suggests that the total frequency of classroom activities is higher in Biology and lower in Psychology than might have been expected, that the variety of activities in Business Studies is lower than in the other subjects, and that overall the tempo of the learning experience is slower in Psychology, and therefore possibly more reflective. The effect of a crowded curriculum and the pace at which content is delivered on opportunities for reflection and teacher control is referred to by Tony Edwards in Chapter 2.

Just as the various learning activities are not distributed equally between either the subjects or the lessons observed, so the volume of interactions varies between

Table 4.8 Frequency and range of classroom activities in four A level subjects compared

	Biology	Business studies	Economics	Psychology
Average duration of observations (in minutes)	48	39	48	60
Number of different activities taking place	7.8	7.3	8.0	8.0
Total frequency of classroom activities	49	30	43	36
Classroom activities per minute	1.1	0.8	1.0	0.7

individual students. Whilst it is not possible to aggregate and present this data in any meaningful way, a study of individual lesson records, such as that shown in Table 4.5, reveals a considerable variation in the extent to which each student participated in the lesson. Although the members of this A level Economics class were to all intents and purposes 'on task' for the whole of the observed time, individuals 2, 7 and 10 made very little contribution, speaking only when spoken to, and then only to answer a direct question on three occasions. Individual 4, on the other hand, wanted to answer every question regardless of to whom it was addressed. If others answered, this (male) student would add to what they had said or contradict them. He would ask questions, occasionally off the topic, during any lull in proceedings, and on one occasion started the class off on a new and unrelated topic. In this way the student was involved in the lesson, as an individual, on seventeen separate occasions. Where other students were involved as individuals in more than three exchanges it should be noticed that, in the great majority of cases, these involvements were to answer more curriculum questions.

Advanced GNVQ courses

An Observer record was made of thirty-seven hours of Advanced GNVQ lessons, using the same twenty-nine descriptors of classroom activities as were used for the A level observations. Four GNVQ courses were involved for a total of forty-two lessons: Business (twenty-one hours), Health & Social Care (four hours), Hospitality & Catering (four hours) and Science (eight hours).

Totalling the observed student learning experiences in these four subjects reveals that around a third of their time in class was spent either answering curriculum-based questions (19 per cent) or receiving individual help from the teacher (15 per cent). Figure 4.3 summarises the complete results. It is interesting to note that, even within a programme of work intended to appeal to the more practical students, verbal discourse occupies more than a third of their time (38 per cent), with 'answering curriculum questions' being the most frequent single activity (19 per cent). Practical work occupies around a quarter of the time, and around a third of this constitutes 'work on assignments'. Only two out of the twenty-seven activities recorded occupy students for more than 10 per cent of their time. They are 'answering curriculum questions' and 'receiving individual help from the teacher'.

Because these are aggregated numbers, it is reasonable to enquire whether the balance is different in different subjects. To answer that question the five most frequently observed activities in each subject are compared, and these results appear in Table 4.9. Because of the relatively large incidence of small numbers in this table, Chi-square analysis may not be appropriate; nevertheless, some of the differences in the frequency of activities recorded between these observed subjects are particularly striking. In Business, Hospitality & Catering and Science, for example, answering 'curriculum questions' was a frequent activity.

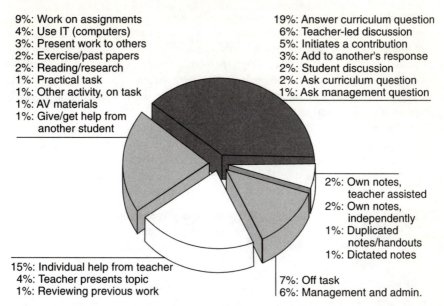

9%: Work on assignments
4%: Use IT (computers)
3%: Present work to others
2%: Exercise/past papers
2%: Reading/research
1%: Practical task
1%: Other activity, on task
1%: AV materials
1%: Give/get help from
    another student

19%: Answer curriculum question
6%: Teacher-led discussion
5%: Initiates a contribution
3%: Add to another's response
2%: Student discussion
2%: Ask curriculum question
1%: Ask management question

2%: Own notes,
    teacher assisted
2%: Own notes,
    independently
1%: Duplicated
    notes/handouts
1%: Dictated notes

15%: Individual help from teacher
4%: Teacher presents topic
1%: Reviewing previous work

7%: Off task
6%: Management and admin.

Figure 4.3 Percentage of time spent on various classroom activities for students on four Advanced GNVQ courses

Table 4.9 Five most frequent classroom activities in four Advanced GNVQ courses compared

Activity	Business	Health & Social Care	Hospitality & Catering	Science
Answers a curriculum question	20	0	23	20
Helped individually by the teacher	10	5	22	29
Work on assignments	8	32	6	4
Off task	8	8	4	4
General management & admin.	5	18	4	7
Teacher-led discussions	5	15	6	2
Teacher presents a topic	5	0	4	5
Make own notes, teacher guidance	2	0	0	6

In Health & Social Care, on the other hand, although 'teacher-led discussion' was strongly favoured, this was a complex interaction that did not include simple question and answer sessions. Students on this course in fact spent almost a third of their time working on their assignments, substantially more than in the other subjects observed. Students on Advanced GNVQ Science courses spend around half their time in curriculum-based question and answer sessions and receiving individual help from the teacher whilst involved in the practical work the course demands.

In these GNVQ lessons a total of twenty-seven different learning experiences were observed. The 'average' number of different activities across the four subjects is seven. The range is from one to twelve, both extremes occurring in Business: the 'one' activity was recorded in a lesson where, in the absence of a teacher, two students worked uninterruptedly on their assignments, and the 'twelve' different activities came from a lesson where the teacher presented a topic, followed by a question and answer session, some reading and research and finally individual work on assignments.

Although the average length of recorded observation was over fifty-two minutes, the range lies between fifteen minutes and nearly two hours. As great a variety of activity was observed in some of the shorter sessions as in some of the longer ones. In one Health & Social Care lesson, for example, which effectively lasted 112 minutes, just eight activities were recorded:

Work on assignments	General management and admin.
Off task	Teacher-led discussion
Initiating a contribution	Reviewing previous work
Student-led discussion	Receiving individual help from the teacher

The three lessons in which a significantly greater variety of activity took place were Science (two) and Business. In the Business lesson (referred to above), which effectively lasted fifty minutes, twelve different activities were recorded:

Working on assignments	Answering curriculum-based questions
Off task	General management and admin.
Teacher-led discussion	Adding to other students' responses
Initiating a contribution	Asking curriculum-based questions
Teacher presenting a topic	Using duplicated notes/handouts
Reading/research	Receiving individual help from the teacher

As well as the variety of learning experiences observed, the frequency with which each activity takes place continues to be an important variable. 'Receiving individual help from the teacher' is only one activity, but in an eighty-five minute Science lesson it occurred twenty-four times. Taking all the different activities into consideration, on average a GNVQ student could expect around twenty-three 'acts' to take place in a fifty-three minute session: an 'acts per minute' coefficient of 0.45. This measurement, used as an indication of the 'tempo' of a student's classroom experience, is remarkably consistent across the four subjects: 0.46 in Business, 0.41 in Science, marginally higher in Health & Social Care (0.54) and lower in Hospitality & Catering (0.34). Within this range, the tempo of individual lessons varies from a high of 1.2 in a concentrated question and answer session in a Business lesson, when the topic was 'how to deal with multiple-answer test papers', to 0.1 in another Business lesson when the students worked uninterruptedly on their assignments for forty-eight minutes.

It is interesting to compare the observation results for different subjects, and the results are shown in Table 4.10. This table suggests that the total frequency

Table 4.10 Frequency and range of classroom activities in four Advanced GNVQ courses compared

	Business	Health & Social Care	Hospitality & Catering	Science
Average duration of observations	46	108	71	53
Number of different activities	6.4	8.0	5.2	9.6
Total frequency of classroom activities	21	37	19	29
Classroom activities per minute	0.5	0.3	0.5	0.4

of classroom activities is higher in Science and lower in Hospitality & Catering than might have been expected, that the variety of activities in Hospitality & Catering is lower than in the other subjects, and that overall the tempo of the learning experience is much slower in Health & Social Care.

Just as the various learning activities are not distributed equally between either the subjects or the lessons observed, so the volume of interactions may vary between individual students. Whilst it is not possible to aggregate and present this data in any meaningful way, a study of individual lesson records, such as that shown in Table 4.11, reveals a very different pattern. In this GNVQ Science lesson, the smaller number of 'acts' are divided more evenly between the students, although the teacher gives more individual help to the boys than to the girls. Interestingly, group P1 comprised boys involved in a teacher-led discussion, and group P2 comprised girls working together at a computer. There is an issue here for classroom observation, and for any accurate description of group work: the students have to be actively involved in a collaborative effort, the successful outcome of which depends on their joint endeavour, not a group sitting together but working as individuals. Referring back to the original record, it is clear that whilst two of the boys were involved in making up electrical circuits, the girls' task was to record the results on the one computer terminal available in the classroom.

Table 4.11 Observer record of an Advanced GNVQ science lesson summarised

Activity	Students								Groups		All
	G1	G2	G3	G4	B1	B2	B4	B5	P1	P2	
General management and admin.											**
Work on assignments											*
Use IT (computers)		*	*	*					*		
Receive individual help from teacher	*				*	*	*	**			
Practical work/making something					*	*					
Off task	*										
Teacher-led discussion									*		

Note: * = one act

A level and GNVQ courses compared

First-hand observation records of this type may be used to compare the learning experiences of students following different courses and different subjects within them. The results for A level and GNVQ courses are shown in Table 4.12.

Although the variety of learning activities available to students is very similar, the nature of these activities is very different. Figure 4.2 above has shown that in the A level classes observed, almost half the time was spent in curriculum-related question and answer sessions, whilst in GNVQ classes (Figure 4.3) no single activity achieved anything like the same prominence. Here question and answer sessions were used for about 20 per cent of the time, slightly less than the time spent working on assignments and receiving individual help from the teacher. A significant difference is identified in the frequency with which the various activities occurred. In A level classes this is much higher than might have been expected. In GNVQs it is much lower, and the differences are clearly reflected in the 'tempo' figure of activities per minute. In the A level classroom things seem to happen almost twice as frequently as they do in GNVQ: question and answer sessions are conducted at a brisk rate, the work is compart-mentalised, and often delivered with little time for reflection or consolidation. When asked, teachers will say that the homework they set is designed to provide this opportunity. GNVQ students, on the other hand, tend to spend more time at each activity: after a topic has been presented, the assignment folders come out and students by and large settle down to the various tasks involved. In lessons where no teacher presentation is necessary, students either singly or in small groups will be reading and researching the topic, discussing it with each other and the teacher, using a word processor to copy up their notes (or directly from their sources), and sometimes doing nothing at all related to the work in hand.

There are a number of issues raised here that extend beyond the evidence being reported, but which relate to some critical dimensions of GNVQ learning. For example, how do teachers deal with the problem of 'teacher assistance' when this may exclude students from higher grades? How can students best be encouraged to remain on task in what has to be a highly self-directed learning environment? How important is the use of IT if this is restricted to using a word processor for neat presentation of passages copied from source materials?

Table 4.12 Frequency and range of classroom activities in A levels and Advanced GNVQ courses compared

	A levels	GNVQs
Average duration of observations	48	53
Number of different activities taking place	7.8	6.9
Total frequency of classroom activities	39	23
Classroom activities per minute	0.9	0.5

And, although learning to 'work with others' is both an intended outcome of GNVQ courses and a teaching strategy to encourage learning to take place, how much attention is paid to the very clear difference between working collaboratively as opposed to working individually whilst sitting together at the same table? Perhaps in this context pedagogy is determined more by the nature of the assessment criteria than the curriculum, and teachers may sometimes struggle to find a satisfactory replacement for their tried and tested methods. This is borne out in a recent study by Harkin and Davis (1996) which suggests that 'the communication styles of teachers on GNVQ programmes are different to those of teachers on BTEC or A level programmes, being perceived by learners as higher in leadership and warm/understanding behaviours'. There is little evidence to suggest that these friendly behaviours have a positive effect on retention rates.

Subject comparisons

If A levels and Advanced GNVQs are indeed taught differently, then these differences ought to appear in a comparison of subjects that might otherwise be expected to show similarities, and similarities ought to appear in a comparison of subjects that might otherwise be expected to show differences. If the students' learning experiences depend on curriculum content, then similarities might reasonably be expected between Advanced GNVQ Business and A level subjects such as Business Studies and Economics.

I now turn to a comparative analysis of recorded observations of lessons in these subjects, the results of which are shown in Table 4.13. These results are drawn from an observation of twenty-seven GNVQ lessons, and twenty-six A level lessons (thirteen of which were Economics). Although the number of different activities experienced in each subject is similar, there are many more 'acts' involved in the A levels than in the GNVQ, and many more than would have been expected. This is reflected in the 'tempo' coefficient, which is substantially higher in the A level classes. However, taking the most popular activities, the number of those activities that make up just over half the classroom experience in each case is very different, as shown in Figure 4.4.

Table 4.13 Frequency and range of classroom activities in A level Business, A level Economics and Advanced GNVQ Business compared

	A level Business & Economics	Advanced GNVQ Business
Average duration of observations	44	47
Number of different activities taking place	7.7	6.7
Total frequency of classroom activities	37	22
Classroom activities per minute	0.91	0.46

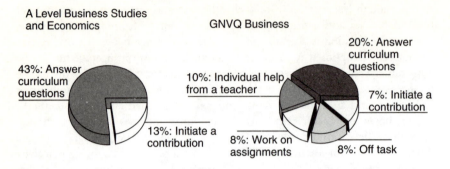

Figure 4.4 Comparison of classroom activities for A level and Advanced
GNVQ classes

It becomes clear therefore that whilst the A level students spend most
time frequently repeating a small number of activities, in this case the discursive
business of answering curriculum questions and initiating contributions, GNVQ
students undertake a wider range of activities in the same proportion of time.
Here, as well as answering curriculum questions and initiating contributions,
they also work on assignments, receive individual help from the teacher, and
spend around 8 per cent of their time off task.

School/college comparisons

There is a view held by teachers in schools that learning experiences in colleges
are organised differently, and vice versa. There is a familiar image of colleges
providing a freer, more adult and less formal learning environment, and this
image is often significant in students deciding to transfer from schools to
colleges, 'Where they treat you like grown-ups'. Harkin and Davis (1996) refer
to the tensions this can cause 'between treating people as responsible adults and
displaying strong leadership' (p. 101), and mention the use of first names
between staff and students. To the extent that this is an indicator of a 'freer,
more adult learning environment', it was never observed in any of the schools
visited as part of this project. When raised in conversation with teachers in
schools, the most common explanation was that younger pupils might become
aware of this informality and take advantage of it in a way damaging to discipline and good order. When raised in conversation with teachers in colleges,
they would often refer to the presence of adults in large numbers in the college
and the impracticality of trying to adopt one protocol for 16 year olds and
another for the adults. There is of course a discernible irony in college teachers
whose employment arrangements are bound by a considerable and very formal
bureaucracy creating a much more informal environment for the students, and
it is fair to say that tensions may arise as a result of this.

During the course of this project no systematic evidence was collected about the different student experience in one type of centre as opposed to another. However, the classroom observation data does allow comparisons to be made for both courses and subjects. As an example, a comparison of school and college approaches to GNVQ Business is shown in Table 4.14. It would seem that in the colleges GNVQ Business students experienced a slightly greater variety of learning experiences, rather more of them, and a correspondingly higher 'tempo' coefficient. Significant differences were observed in the type of activity favoured. Taking the 'top four' activities, accounting in each case for around half the student experience, a very different pattern emerges:

In colleges	*In schools*
15% Individual teacher help	27% Answer curriculum questions
14% Presenting work to others	8% Working on assignments
13% Initiating a contribution	8% Off task
10% Add to another's response	7% Individual teacher help
Total : 52 per cent	Total : 50 per cent

Table 4.14 Frequency and range of classroom activities in Advanced GNVQ Business in schools and colleges compared

	Schools GNVQ Business	Colleges GNVQ Business
Average duration of observations	51	36
Number of different activities	6.4	7.4
Total frequency of classroom activities	21	24
Classroom activities per minute	0.4	0.6

An observation record of A level Business Studies was also made in schools and colleges, although the duration of the recorded observations was restricted to just under six hours, and confidence in the transferability of the results is therefore low. Whilst the 'tempo' coefficient was very similar, 0.8 in schools and colleges, students in schools experienced a greater variety of learning activities, but fewer of them, and college students experienced fewer different activities, but many more of them. Significant differences were observed in the type of activity favoured, and once again the 'top four' activities reveal a very different pattern:

In colleges	*In schools*
58% Answer curriculum question	36% Answer curriculum questions
20% Initiate a contribution	10% Teacher presents a topic
8% Add to another's response	8% General management and admin.
5% Teacher presents a topic	8% Add to another's response
Total : 91 per cent	Total : 62 per cent

It would seem that more traditional 'lecturing' goes on in schools, and more interactive discourse in colleges.

A comparison of all the GNVQ courses observed in schools (sixteen hours recorded) with those in colleges (twenty-two hours recorded) reveals marked similarities. Contingency table analysis shows virtually no significant differences either in the number of different activities undertaken, or the frequency of these activities, or the 'tempo' coefficient. Interestingly, the same is true of all the A levels observed (fifteen hours recorded in colleges and nineteen hours in schools), with the possible exception of slightly fewer different activities recorded in colleges than might have been expected, and a correspondingly marginal reduction in 'tempo'.

Results from the academic/vocational continuum

The way in which this instrument was designed and used has already been described, and the staff version included (Table 4.4). Each continuum consists of a row of seven asterisks which, for purposes of data entry and analysis, were converted to a seven-point scale numbered from left to right. For example, under 'Presentation of topics' row one becomes:

Information is given by   1 2 3 4 5 6 7   Information is researched
the teacher   by students

Scores along each continuum are then presented as horizontal bars to either side of a central axis, as shown in Figure 4.5. These results are from a group of a dozen A level students in a comprehensive school sixth form taking a variety of subjects. In this chart the length of each bar indicates the strength of agreement with that descriptor; to save space only the 'academic' descriptors have been used, in summary form. The complete list may be referred to in Table 4.4. The classroom experience shared by these A level students is clearly defined by them. Having given the students information and interpreted its meaning, the teacher then tells them what to do and how and when to do it. Students do their work mainly in the classroom, and are engaged in the same activities at the same time, generally working alone. They are not required to make presentations of their work. This group of students report working on communication and numeracy skills, but not IT. They believe that the application of past learning to new topics is necessary, that their work requires problem solving, and that they receive plenty of formative feedback from their teacher.

The picture from GNVQ classes can be very different. Figure 4.6 shows the results from sixty-six students in Advanced Health & Social Care. The classroom experience for these GNVQ students and their teachers is some distance away from traditional concepts. The students research their own information, and to some extent also discover what it means. They define their own tasks, decide how to do the work and when to do it. Much of their time is spent working outside the classroom, on a variety of different tasks, and they recognise explicit

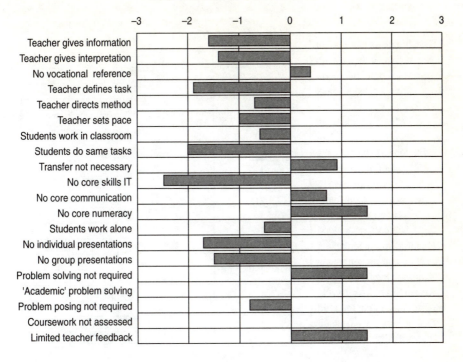

Figure 4.5 Balance of classroom activities as perceived by A level students in one school

core skills work in IT, communication and numeracy. They undertake group rather than individual presentations, problem solving in a vocational context, and receive considerable formative feedback from their teacher.

Although the A level data was collected during lessons in four specific subjects (Business Studies, Economics, Physics and Psychology), and from ninety-one A level students, virtually all of them were taking three A levels. It is probably not wise therefore to assume that the results apply only to those lessons. These young people were informed by a joint experience of over 250 permutations of some twenty-five A level subjects between them, and under these circumstances their collective view probably gives a very accurate picture of the nature of their learning experiences. GNVQ Data was collected from 316 students following Advanced courses in Business, Health & Social Care, Hospitality & Catering and Science. No one was taking more than one GNVQ. Amalgamating their results is also likely to give an accurate picture of their learning experiences. The combined results for A level and GNVQ courses are graphed together in Figure 4.7.

At first glance the two sets of results look very different, with GNVQ subjects tending strongly away from the traditional 'academic' norms. In some cases the results are diametrically opposed to each other: the extent to which

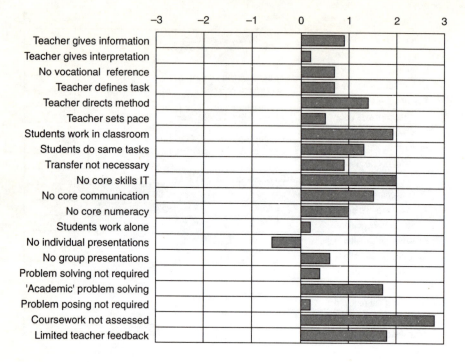

Figure 4.6 Balance of classroom activities as perceived by Advanced GNVQ Health &
Social Care students

information is given by the teacher or researched by the student; the extent to
which the method of working is determined by either the teacher or the
student; who sets the pace of work; whether students all work on the same task
or are engaged in a variety of activities; the use of IT. But these are only five
occasions out of twenty, and where the 'origin of information' is concerned,
there is in fact little difference between the two positions. I suggest that the
remaining four are central to any understanding of the difference between the
student experience of A levels and GNVQs. The remaining fifteen descriptors
are all paired on one side or the other of the continuum. Careful examination,
however, reveals that the differences between some of these pairs is as great as
the differences between those diametrically opposed. These include the extent
to which interpretation of meaning is given by the teacher; the extent to which
tasks are defined by either the teacher or the student; the amount of explicit
work undertaken on communication skills; and the extent to which students
make individual presentations of their work. Added to the other four, a set of
eight descriptions of variance between A level and Advanced GNVQ emerges.
Of equal interest are the similarities that occur, revealed where pairs of results
in Figure 4.7 are very close to each other. This occurs particularly in five

90

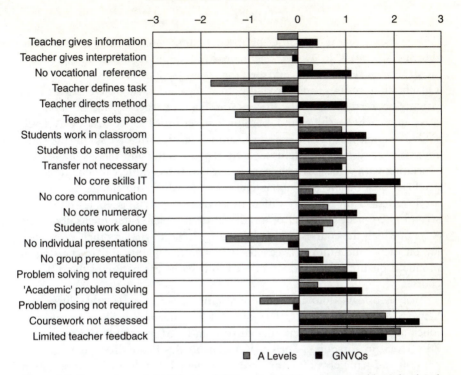

Figure 4.7 Comparison of the balance of classroom activities as perceived by A level and Advanced GNVQ students

instances: the extent to which the application of past learning to new topics is necessary; the frequency with which students work together as members of small groups and undertake group presentations of their work; the extent to which their work requires 'problem solving' activities; and the extensive formative feedback both sets of students receive from their teachers. Looking at Figure 4.7, what may be surprising is not that the results from GNVQ courses tend towards activities associated with 'vocational' education, but that the results from A level courses are so evenly divided between those activities associated with 'academic' education and those on the other side of the traditional 'divide'. That said, the pedagogic thrust in A level teaching remains firmly with the teachers in the key areas of presentation of topics and prescription of tasks. Students may be expected to undertake a certain amount of research, but having obtained information the A level teacher will interpret its meaning, closely define the tasks, direct the method and set the pace of work.

CONCLUSIONS

The purposes of the two lines of investigation reported here are, firstly, to describe the ways in which classroom learning is organised in traditional 'academic' A level work and in the new General National Vocational Qualification courses, and, secondly, to determine what differences exist in practice between the resulting student learning experiences. Evidence about the ways in which 'teaching and learning are organised . . . across the A level/ BTEC boundary' is drawn from two sources. Firstly, extensive systematic classroom observation was made using a lap-top computer and Observer software. Operating with a focal sampling and continuous recording configuration, this produces quantifiable data about the extent to which individuals and groups are involved in up to thirty different activities as part of their learning. The second instrument consisted of a series of twenty paired statements about the ways in which the courses were delivered. By indicating where their experience lay on each continuum between the statements, students and teachers again produced quantifiable information used to describe the nature of the different courses.

Analysis of data from classroom observation reveals considerable differences between A level and GNVQ learning. A level students are likely to spend as much as half their time answering curriculum-based questions, and more than 70 per cent in 'discourse'. For GNVQ students this figure drops to around 37 per cent and represents the occasional short sharp burst of teacher presentation followed by a question and answer session to introduce a topic. There is little consistency between the activities observed in different lessons within the same subject. In A level Economics the range was from one to fifteen; in GNVQ Business it was from one to twelve. It is hard to escape the conclusion that these teachers were driven by their own pedagogic preferences rather than the demands of the subject. Although the classroom activities observed in A level and GNVQ subjects were very different, the number employed, about seven or eight, was very similar. However, the frequency with which they were employed varied considerably, and was consistently higher in A level teaching and learning. The frequency record was used to produce a 'tempo' coefficient in which 1.0 represents one activity per minute. The average for A level lessons is 0.9 and for GNVQ lessons 0.45. Student participation in lessons is very variable. GNVQ students spend more time obviously off task. This is very much to do with the structure of the lessons: the absence of whole-class activities, the prevalence of small groups of students sitting together, the need for self-motivation, the slower tempo requiring more time to be spent on each activity and therefore a longer attention span, the constraints on the extent to which teachers are able specifically to direct the work and so on. A level students give every appearance of being more focused and spending very little time off task. Closer analysis, however, shows that it is common for a small number of students, often male, to monopolise the traditional exchanges and interactions, and for other students to take virtually no part in the proceedings unless deliberately targeted by the teacher. The extent to which these students are off task is difficult to ascertain: some of them sit and think, and some of them just sit. These differences are reflected in comparisons between subjects which it might have been thought would be taught in similar ways. Taking A level Business Studies and Economics together, they are delivered using an average of 7.7 different activities at a tempo of .91. GNVQ Business, on the other hand, uses fewer activities (6.7) at about half the pace (0.46). The A level courses devote half their time to only two activities frequently repeated, both discursive. The GNVQ course devotes the same proportion of time to five different activities.

There are also differences between the experiences of GNVQ Business students taught in schools and those taught in colleges. College courses operate at a slightly higher tempo, and students get more individual help from their teachers. In schools, curriculum-based question and answer sessions are more predominant, and it is possible in these two approaches to detect echoes of custom and practice – from BTEC in colleges and from traditional pedagogy in schools. Differences between schools and colleges also exist in the delivery of A level Business Studies. In schools, teachers spend more time presenting a topic and less time discussing it; in colleges the opposite is true. It would seem that, in this subject at least, more traditional 'lecturing' goes on in schools, and more interactive discourse in colleges.

Other similarities and differences between A level and GNVQ work are clarified by the 'academic/vocational' continuum results. Although the results from GNVQ courses are strongly associated with descriptors of 'vocational' education, the results from A level courses are evenly divided between both sides of the 'academic/vocational divide'. That said, the pedagogic thrust in A level remains with the teachers who interpret meaning, and retain control over what work is appropriate and how and when it is to be done. In A level courses, although students may sometimes sit together in groups, they are likely all to be doing the same thing rather than working collaboratively, and very little use is ever made of IT. In GNVQ courses, topics are habitually referenced to vocational contexts, and students have much more control over their methods of working. They sit together in groups most of the time, often work collaboratively and frequently use low level IT skills. Students undertake regular core skills work in communication and the use of number, their work requires problem solving skills applied in a vocational context, and they receive extensive formative assistance from their teachers. Although the assessment of coursework is an important component in some A level subjects, assessment is by a formal end of course examination, set and marked externally, referenced to part of the work covered, and which up to 20 per cent of students may expect to fail. The final GNVQ grade depends entirely on the contents of a portfolio of work completed during the course, assessed internally and verified externally, and the extent to which the student has received outside assistance in completing the work. The award is conditional on the candidate having passed a series of 'end of unit' tests, set and marked externally.

This chapter set out to identify differences between the learning experiences of GNVQ and A level students, and the results may finally be summarised as profiles of a 'typical' student following each course.

An A level student:

- spends about 70 per cent of his or her time in classroom discourse with the teacher, who supplies information and explains what it means, defines the work to be done, directs the method and sets the pace
- is required to participate in seven or eight different tasks during the course, some of them, like answering curriculum questions, repeatedly. The tasks will have been selected by the teacher more on the basis of pedagogical preference than on the curriculum content
- will normally be working on the same task as all the other students in the group who, even though they may be sitting together round a table, will rarely be required to work collaboratively. Some work will take place outside the classroom
- will rarely use IT applications
- recognises that the work requires problem solving skills, and the application of past learning to new topics
- is rarely seen to be off task during lessons
- receives extensive formative feedback from the teacher
- may have some coursework assessed, but sits an external examination.

A GNVQ student:

- spends about a third of his or her time in classroom discourse with the teacher
- will participate in seven or eight different tasks during the course, some of them, like working on assignments for his or her portfolio, for long periods of time. The tasks will have been selected to fulfil course requirements, often in negotiation with the teacher, and they will be referenced to vocational contexts
- decides how to complete each task, and makes extensive use of low level IT skills. Core communication and numeracy work are built into the assignments
- is probably working collaboratively with one or two others, but on a different task from the other people. This may be either in the classroom, or in another room, or off site
- recognises that work requires the application of problem solving skills, again in a vocational or 'real world' context, and the application of past learning to new topics

- is regularly seen to be off task during lessons
- receives extensive formative feedback from the teacher
- is required to pass external 'end of unit' tests, but is graded on a portfolio of coursework assessed internally and verified externally.

5

A LEVEL ENGLISH LANGUAGE AND ENGLISH LITERATURE

Contrasts in teaching and learning

Frank Hardman

INTRODUCTION

This chapter will explore methods of teaching and learning in the A level English curriculum consisting of both the traditional A level English Literature and the more recent arrival of A level English Language. It draws on two empirical studies: an extensive survey of students' perceptions of the instructional practices employed by English teachers, carried out by the well-established A Level Information Service (ALIS) project at Newcastle University (Tymms and Vincent 1995) (see Chapters 3 and 7), and a small-scale, intensive study investigating the teaching styles of ten teachers who taught across the two A level English subjects. In the second I used a descriptive system adapted from the study of discourse analysis (Sinclair and Coulthard 1992) to examine the structural complexity or patterning of classroom discourse between teachers and students, in order for comparisons to be made of teaching styles across the two English subjects. The findings of both studies suggest that teachers do not vary their teaching styles, as many commentators suggest.

In much of the recent literature on post-16 teaching and learning, as discussed in other chapters, it is assumed that there are differences in learning experience between the academic and vocational alternatives. Therefore A level is seen as requiring a high level of reading and writing skills and the ability to think analytically, whereas vocational alternatives are presented as being more suited to the less academic, being more practical, less deskbound, more collaborative in modes of learning and concerned with the application of skills and knowledge. They are therefore seen as representing very different ways of organising, valuing, transmitting and assessing knowledge.

As Tony Edwards argues in Chapter 2, however, such shifts from teaching to learning that are said to characterise vocational alternatives, and that supposedly differentiate Advanced GNVQ from its academic alternative, have also been a feature of recent developments in A level syllabus design and assessment, particularly in the A level English curriculum. Spours (1993) suggests that the period from 1985 to 1990 saw noticeable experimentation within the academic track through the development of GCSE, the impact of Technical and Vocational Education Initiative (TVEI) curriculum development projects, a growth of modular A levels and AS and a slow but marked increase in the coursework component of many A levels. Such developments were also seen as a major feature of 'alternative' A level English Literature syllabuses which allowed up to 50 per cent coursework assessment (Greenwell 1988).

Through such developments at A and AS level, it was hoped that the narrowness of the subject matter could be broadened to create greater breadth and that a wider range of teaching styles beyond didactic instruction would allow students to take considerable responsibility for their own learning, to do more of their own thinking and to develop problem solving skills and self-reliance. This would involve less teacher direction and more student initiative, thereby creating opportunities for students to 'engage in extended conversation and discussion' (DES 1988: 29). Such innovations were also seen as bridging the 'academic–vocational' divide by enabling students to take modules from equivalent vocational qualifications, such as the links between BTEC and A/AS levels, thereby promoting common learning processes across the two tracks. Many commentators claim that this is reflected in 'alternative' A level English Literature syllabuses (e.g. McCulloch *et al.* 1993; Canwell and Ogborn 1994) and particularly in the English Language syllabuses (e.g. Scott 1989; Whiteley 1990; Blue 1995) which have been influenced by the language and practices normally associated with the design of vocational A level courses.

Until the mid-1980s, A level English had mainly consisted of the study of literary texts selected from a traditional canon of English literature, and the explicit study of the nature and functions of language had not been a major feature in the curriculum. Therefore the introduction of an A level in English Language was seen as a major innovation. Not only was the new subject considered as being different in content, drawing upon the study of linguistics, it was also seen to differ in its teaching and assessment methods by encouraging investigational, independent and collaborative forms of learning normally associated with vocational alternatives to A level.

According to Scott (1989), it was the first A level connected with English to allow a substantial element of practical work or to require study of its own theoretical position. It did so by laying great stress on the relationship between theory and practice and defining the subject largely in terms of its application. There were claims of a strong vocational element because it looked at knowledge about language and the uses of English, and because by such means students would increase their competences in its uses. Such attempts to bridge the academic–vocational divide and create an alternative version of post-16 English are seen even more conspicuously in the study of communication studies and media studies at A level, and in the prominence of the communication strand in the core skills in GNVQ.

It is therefore generally assumed in commentaries on A level English teaching that English Language is taught differently from English Literature. There is, however, surprisingly little empirical evidence about how students are taught and how they learn in different courses. Commentators can, therefore, do little more than assume or infer pedagogic distinctiveness.

The widest evidence comes from HMI, though it has little theoretical or empirical justification, and is limited to the teaching of English Literature. In their account of how the subject is taught, HMI found that students often had a passive role because of teaching preoccupied with the requirements of the final examination. They therefore found 'a considerable amount of teacher-monologue in evidence' and questioning techniques that 'were sometimes narrow or obscure, with a preconceived notion of the "correct" answer' (DES 1986: 8). This, they report, often resulted in teacher domination of the class-room discourse, with little interactional space for students and a narrow range of written work with little opportunity for wider reading. Their account seems to describe the style of teaching that A level English Language was intended to challenge. However, it was the lack of comparative evidence that prompted me further into investigating how the two subjects are taught.

PERCEIVED LEARNING ACTIVITIES IN A LEVEL ENGLISH TEACHING

Extensive statistical data on students' perception of the instructional practices employed by teachers, referred to as Perceived Learning Activities (PLAs), were collected by means of a questionnaire as part of the ALIS performance indicator project (Tymms and Vincent 1995). The data for the analysis came from the 1993 ALIS survey in which twelve subjects were studied in all (Art, Biology, Chemistry, Economics, English Language, French, English Literature, Geography, History, Mathematics, Further Mathematics, Physics). The sample size for both A level English subjects was the highest for any of the subject areas (English Literature n = 6,690, English Language n = 6,523). The questionnaire on instructional practices made use of a six-point scale in estimating the frequency with which twenty-two learning activities were employed by A level teachers (see Nick Meagher's Chapter 4 for details of PLAs).

When the students' perceptions of the instructional practices employed within all twelve subjects were compared to see if there was a differentiation of classroom practices between subjects, differences in teaching and learning activities were revealed, although with little (if any) variation across syllabuses within subjects. Some of the most dramatic differences can be seen between English Literature and Mathematics in Figure 5.1. Mathematics teaching at A level appears to be dominated by teacher presentation, exercises, dictated notes and working previous examination questions. English Literature, by contrast, was more characterised by class discussion, making own notes and reading. Such findings lead Fitz-Gibbon and Wright (1995a: 7) to conclude that 'how you teach depends on what you teach'. However, Hodgson (1994) suggests that the

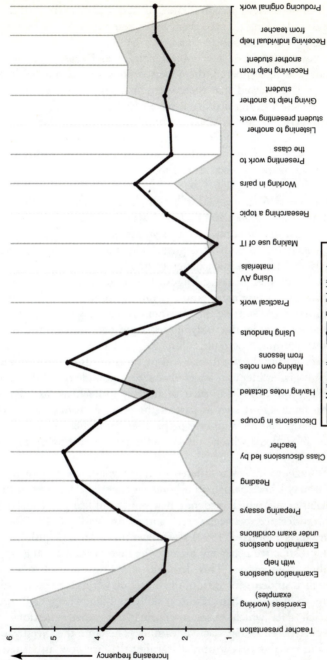

Figure 5.1 Students' perceptions of learning activities in A level Mathematics and English Literature lessons

pedagogic differences between subjects as revealed in the ALIS data may be tactical variations on didactic teaching rather than a departure from it, depending on the kinds of learning that are perceived as being effective by teachers and students within the different subject areas.

When the pattern of PLAs for 'subject pairs' like English Language and English Literature were compared, there were striking similarities, as shown in Figure 5.2. The data showed that there was remarkably little variation in the employment of each learning activity between English Language and English Literature, and between the syllabuses within each subject. Such a finding conflicts with the assumption discussed earlier, that the two subjects are taught differently because they draw on different subject disciplines with their own established content, working practices and modes of discourse which mark them off from each other.

English Language at A level is said to have its own academic identity because it draws on linguistics rather than English Literature and adopts methods of study and assessment that not only have a vocational aspect but also embody new academic approaches to the study of language. The study of English Language is therefore seen as fundamentally challenging the ideology of English Literature because it removes its special status: English Literature is studied as a language variety, one discourse among many, and any form of spoken or written form of discourse from the world outside the classroom is seen as worthy of study and analysis. It therefore includes the study of media and non-literary texts as well as the students' own writing. As a result, A level English Language is said to go some way towards recognising the vocational and personal needs of students because of its concern for giving them the tools to analyse and understand the manipulation of language and to develop their proficiency in language use. Therefore A level English Language is seen as part of the post-16 curriculum, serving a wider range of ability and not simply as preparation for higher education serving a tiny minority of students who go on to read degrees with English as a major component.

Scott (1989) suggests that clear differences in pedagogy are emerging from the English Language syllabuses which go beyond the superficial changes in English Literature syllabuses and which recognise new notions of text and context along with important differences between speech and writing and questions about the value of literary texts. Goddard (1993) also argues that A level English Language brings with it a distinctive pedagogy because the investigation of language is at the core of the whole course. This demands adopting more of a 'scientific' approach, in which students focus from the outset on what investigation means, allowing them to develop their research skills and knowledge by regularly working on rich data which raises interesting and varied questions about language and thereby encourages active learning. Therefore the investigational, independent and collaborative forms of learning that are now associated with GNVQ courses were also seen as underpinning the teaching of A level English Language.

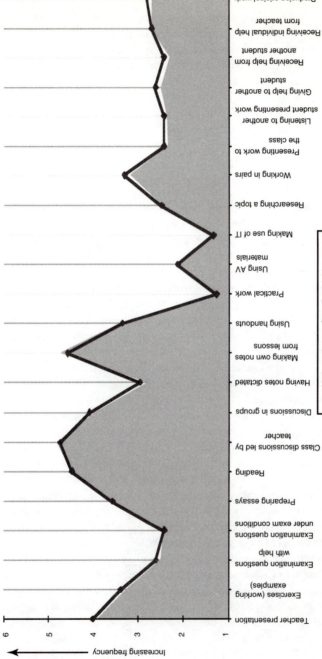

Figure 5.2 Students' perceptions of learning activities in A level English Literature and English Language

Given the numbers involved in the ALIS data, however, the picture of teaching and learning activities was necessarily derived from students' perceptions rather than from observations. Another limitation of the ALIS statistical evidence is that the PLAs do not include the combination of teacher presentation and teacher-directed question and answer that research suggests constitutes the 'pedagogic recitation' that has dominated classroom practice (Edwards and Westgate 1994). In order to address some of these limitations, and to investigate further the hypothesis that teachers do perceive and teach the two subjects differently, I decided to carry out an intensive study of the teaching styles of ten teachers who teach across the two A level English subjects.

ANALYSIS OF TEACHING STYLES

In order to investigate the teaching styles, I looked at the patterning of the classroom interaction displayed in classroom discourse. Stubbs (1983) argues that classroom dialogue between teachers and students is the educational process. Therefore it is important to see the relationships between participants in the classroom as social ones; learning is not simply a cognitive or psychological process, it depends largely upon social interaction between teachers and students, and language is central to this interaction. Similarly, Wiemann and Giles (1992: 220) suggest that 'much of our social behaviour is manifest linguistically' and Semin and Fiedler (1992: 1) argue that 'language provides the medium in which social knowledge in general and knowledge about interpersonal relations in particular are mapped'. Therefore it is argued that underlying relations between teachers and their students can be seen in the way in which interactions are maintained and developed.

The study adapted Sinclair and Coulthard's (1992) discourse analysis as a framework for analysing the teaching styles of an opportunity sample of ten A level English teachers from the Tyneside area who taught across both subjects and whose profiles are given in Table 5.1. At the time of the data collection for the study (i.e. January 1993 till December 1994), all of the teachers were teaching the NEAB English Language syllabus with 50 per cent coursework, except for Teacher C who was following the London Board syllabus with 30 per cent coursework. Seven of the ten teachers were also teaching an English Literature syllabus with 50 per cent coursework.

Since the late 1980s, coursework moderation had become immensely popular, especially amongst English teachers at both GCSE and A level. However, following the ferocity of the educational Right's attack on coursework moderation (North 1987; Norcross 1990), which was blamed for undermining academic standards, the government imposed a 20 per cent restriction on all A/AS syllabuses so as to ensure a return to traditional forms of assessment for first examination in 1996. Coursework assessment was seen by the educational Right as reflecting a progressive–egalitarian position with a distaste for real learning,

Table 5.1 Profile of teachers

Teacher	Gender	Years in teaching	Type of school
A	Male	27	11–18 all-girls comprehensive
B	Male	23	13–18 suburban high
C	Male	9	11–18 urban comprehensive
D	Male	32	13–18 suburban high
E	Male	11	11–18 urban comprehensive
F	Male	17	Sixth form college
G	Male	24	11–18 urban comprehensive
H	Female	2	11–18 suburban comprehensive
I	Female	6	Sixth form college
J	Male	4	13–18 rural high

whereas A level as the 'gold standard', assessed through traditional examinations, was seen as a way of preserving 'traditional learning' taught through subjects by teachers who are an 'authority with knowledge to impart to uneducated minds' (O'Hear 1991: 8).

The teachers' perceptions of teaching the two subjects in terms of differences in subject paradigms (i.e. aims, objectives, content, ideology, boundaries) and subject pedagogies were also sought using semi-structured interviews which were audio recorded and transcribed for analysis. The interviews were carried out prior to the collection and analysis of the classroom data. Following the analysis of the classroom data, the teachers were asked about their reactions to the findings in follow-up interviews.

In order to compare the teaching styles used in both subjects, inclusive classroom data were collected through video recording each of the ten teachers teaching a complete English Language and English Literature lesson (twenty lessons in total making up over twenty-two hours of video tape). This allowed for a comprehensive analysis of the teacher/student interactions and the teaching and learning activities in each of the lessons, which were transcribed and coded according to the system of analysis devised by Sinclair and Coulthard (1992).

FRAMEWORK OF THE ANALYSIS

The descriptive apparatus for spoken discourse developed by Sinclair and Coultard (1992) proposes that lessons can be analysed as having five *ranks*: lesson, transaction, exchange, move, act. A lesson consists of one or more *trans-actions*, which consist of one or more *exchanges*, which consist of one or more *moves*, which consist of one or more *acts*. My own analysis focused on the patterning of the teacher/student interaction at the rank of the exchange, as it is here that Sinclair and Coulthard are confident that the system is most reliable as it draws on linguistic considerations in describing what is going on. I also thought it appropriate that the study should focus on teaching exchanges to compare teaching styles, as they are seen by many commentators (see Edwards and Westgate 1994) as the basic unit of interaction in which a distinctive structure has been identified in much teaching.

In its prototypical form, this discourse format consists of three moves: an *initiation*, usually in the form of a teacher question; a *response*, in which a student attempts to answer the question; and a follow-up move, in which the teacher provides some form of *feedback* (very often in the form of an evaluation) to the student's response. This 'I-R-F format' (the variant 'I-R-E' is preferred by some writers because of the high level of evaluation, and for the purposes of the present chapter it will be denoted by I-R-F/E) is therefore seen as the essential teaching exchange. The frequency of the exchange, and the overwhelming tendency of teachers to make the first and third move, is what makes classroom discourse so distinctive. The third move, which is usually an evaluation of the student's comment, is seen as being the most critical in the exchange in order for the teacher to retain interactional and semantic control over the discourse.

Sinclair and Coulthard identify eleven sub-categories of teaching exchanges with specific functions and unique structures. Of the eleven sub-categories six are *free* exchanges and five are *bound*. The function of bound exchanges is fixed because they are not initiating move, whereas the free exchanges can be initiated by the teacher or, as in two cases, by the students. The four main functions of exchanges are informing, directing, eliciting and checking. The *teacher inform* exchange is used for passing on facts, opinions, ideas and new information to the students, and usually there is no verbal response to the initiation, as in the following example from Teacher G's English Language lesson where he is explaining his criteria for a mini-language project (the *moves*, initiation, response, feedback, that make up the three-part teaching exchange are in turn made up of *acts*: acc = accept; ack = acknowledge; ch = check; cl = clue; com = comment; con = conclusion; d = direct; e = evaluate; el = elicitation; i = inform; l = loop; m = marker; ms = metastatement; n = nomination; p = prompt; rea = react; rep = reply; s = starter; z = aside. Different stages in lessons are signalled by *boundary* exchanges consisting of two *moves*: *framing* (Fr) and *focusing* (Fs), both of which can occur together):

Exchanges			Moves	Acts
Boundary	T	right	Fr	m
Teaching	T	you seem to have a clear idea of where you're going	I	s
		try to remember that your work is largely descriptive that is don't worry about discovering some earth moving conclusion that no one's ever seen before don't worry about that what you need to exhibit are these		i

> things in a good project you need to be
> methodical hence the reason for talking about
> the method you need to be methodical you
> need to be open minded and you need to
> record honestly what you find don't set out
> looking for things you think might be there
> just look and record what you do find open
> mindedness and method and thoroughness
> so leave no stone unturned eventually

The *teacher direct* is designed to get the students to do but not say something, whereas the *teacher elicit* is designed to get a verbal contribution from the students. The teacher elicit exchange which occurs inside the classroom has a different function from most questions in everyday life because the teacher usually knows the answer to the question that is being asked. This accounts for the feedback move being an essential element in an eliciting exchange inside the classroom, because the students, having given their answer, want to know if it was correct. Both teaching exchanges are illustrated in the following extract from Teacher D's English Language lesson where he is working with a group of students on how language is used to establish points about Jimmy's character from *Look Back in Anger*. The *teacher elicit* is illustrated by Exchanges 1 and 6 and *teacher direct* by Exchanges 5 and 9:

Exchanges			Moves	Acts
Teaching	T	let me just pull this together with a few final questions because they're touching the same ground over there I would suggest	I	s
		what do you think of Jimmy here		el
2	S	he's bigoted as well	R	rep
3	T	go on evidence	I	el
4	S	well he just writes off anything that you're saying and he thinks he's always right all the time	R	rep
5	T	put that down Mark	I	d
6	T	any other words to err to attach to Jimmy	I	el
7	S	pretentious	R	rep
8	T	pretentious	F	e
9	T	put that one down as well	I	d

Although *student elicit* is listed as one of the free exchanges, Sinclair and Coulthard acknowledge that inside the classroom students rarely ask questions and if they do they are usually of a procedural nature. The crucial difference between teacher and student elicits is that students usually provide no feedback, as evaluation of a teacher's reply would normally be seen as deviant. A *student elicit* is illustrated in the following extract (Exchange 1) from Teacher J's English Language lesson where the students had been asked to discuss a series of statements on standard English:

Exchanges			Moves	Acts
Teaching	S	do you have to write down what you say	I	el
2	T	yeah you have to write down whether you agree or disagree	R	rep
3	T	(To whole class) can I just remind everybody that I want you to put down whether you agree or disagree or somewhere in between and then put down the question but don't sit around and worry about it it's no good putting down the question until you've answered the query about it	I	d

Occasionally students offer information that they think is relevant or interesting, and they usually receive an evaluation and comment on its worth, as in the following example from Teacher G's English Literature lesson where a student has been asked to do a presentation on the character of Autolycus from *A Winter's Tale*:

Exchanges			Moves	Acts
Teaching	S	if he didn't go to the sheep shearing festival then nothing that would be the end of the play wouldn't it because then you there wouldn't the Shepherd and the Clown go to Sicilia and the father wouldn't be presented before Leontes and then the reconciliation between his daughter wouldn't happen	I	i
	T	umm that's very true isn't it as far as the direction of the plot is concerned Autolycus plays a very important part there	F	e com

The final free exchange is the *check* which teachers will use to check on how well students are getting on, whether they are following the lesson and whether they can hear; feedback to such questions is not essential as they are real questions to which the teacher does not know the answer. This is illustrated in the following example from Teacher H's English Literature lesson where the teacher is paraphrasing line by line an extract from Chaucer's *The Pardoner's Tale*:

Exchanges			Moves	Acts
Teaching	T	the next one brothels and *tavernes* same meaning inns pubs	I	i
	T	ok you all keeping up this won't take long just a few words to fit in	I	m ch

Of the five types of bound exchanges, four are bound to teacher elicits and one to teacher direct. With a *reinitiation* exchange, of which there are two sub-categories (for the purposes of the research the two sub-categories for reinitiation were subsumed and quantified under the one heading), if the teacher gets no response to an elicitation he or she can rephrase a question or use a prompt (p), nomination (n) or clue (cl) to get a reply to the original question (reinitiation i). Alternatively, if the teacher gets a wrong answer, the choice can be to stay with the same student and try by Socratic method to work round to the right answer, or to stay with the same question and move on to another student (reinitiation ii). Here feedback does occur in the exchange. Both types of reinitiation are demonstrated in the following extract from Teacher E's English Language lesson where he uses reinitiation (ii) (Exchanges 8, 10 and 12) and re-initation (i) (Exchange 14) to move the students towards the 'correct' answer in response to his question about the stages of children's lexical development:

Exchanges			Moves	Acts
Boundary	T	which brings us on to just about where we ended up last term	Fs	ms
2	T	which is the third stage called	I	el
3	S	semantics	R	rep
4	T	no that's the third element of language acquisition	F	e
5	T	we divided up phonology grammar semantics we said that the early in looking at grammatical development we said there are three stages in grammatical development one word holophrastic two word and then	I	el
		Rose has got a crib list (inaudible)		n
6	S	do you call it stage three or something	R	rep
7	T	stage three no	F	e
8	S	telegraph	I	rep
9	T	telegraph good guess not quite there	F	e
10	S	telephone	I	rep
11	T	mm closer	F	e
12	S	telephonic	I	rep
13	T	telephonic (laughs)	F	e
14	T	Sarah has actually found her file and is going to tell us the answer	I	n/p
15	S	telegraphic	R	rep
16	T	telegraphic	F	e
		the third stage called the telegraphic stage		com
17	S	what's the middle one called then	I	el
18	T	two word one word holophrastic and the third stage telegraphic	R	rep

If the teacher withholds an evaluation until two or three answers have been provided, such an exchange is categorised as a *listing*, as in the following extract, also from Teacher E's English Language lesson, where he is looking for the part of speech known as a determiner in answer to his question (Exchanges 10, 11 and 12):

Exchanges			Moves	Acts
Teaching	T	I'm interested in this is a certain type of	I	s
		well what does this tell you about the milk		el
2	S	adverbial	R	rep
3	T	NV	F	e
4	S	adjective	I	rep
5	T	no adjective would say oh it's milky milk it's creamy milk it's sour milk	F	e
		that would be an adjective wouldn't it		com
6	T	it tells you something about the amount or the extent doesn't it or the number yeah	I	s
		now the type there is a term which will explain what those types of words are		el
7	S	(inaudible)	R	rep
8	T	I'm going to do something easier I'm going to play hangman soon (laughter)	F	z
9	T	you do know	I	el
		it begins with *d*		cl
10	S	*di*	R	rep
11	S	*du do da* (laughter)	R	rep
12	S	*de*	R	rep
13	T	oh you've got another letter	F	e
14	T	well these types of words determine oh I've just said it that determines the amount doesn't it a milk some milk any milk yeah so therefore determiners		com

In situations when someone does not hear or where the teacher has heard but wants the reply repeated for some reason, the exchange is classified as a *repeat*. This is illustrated in the following example from Teacher B's English Language lesson where the students are considering and translating a pastiche of *A Clockwork Orange* written by one of the students; here the teacher asks the student to repeat the answer (Exchange 7):

Exchanges			Moves	Acts
Teaching	T	one I liked this bit	I	s
		one drippy day		el
2	S	one rainy day	R	rep
3	T	one rainy day	I	el
4	S	yeah	R	rep
5	T	Julie go on	I	el/n
6	S	he saw a man walking with a a cow	R	rep
7	T	with a what	I	l
8	T	a black and white beef is a cow a frinesian cow	F	com
		alright		e

Finally, in the bound exchange there is a *reinforce* which very occasionally follows a teacher direct when a teacher has told the class to do something and one student is slow or reluctant or has not fully understood. This exchange was not used by any of the teachers in the study.

THE PATTERNING OF TEACHER EXCHANGES

The framework of analysis I adopted provided a clear and systematic basis for analysing the patterning of the teaching exchanges in all twenty lessons, because for the majority of the time the teachers were exerting maximum control over the discourse. The lessons were therefore coded and the frequency of each of the ten teaching exchanges quantified, so that a comparison could be made of the patterning of the exchanges used by each of the ten teachers as they taught across the two subjects. Results of the quantification of the teaching exchanges were converted into percentages to allow comparison of discrete data from unequally sized distributions of exchanges between lessons. Figure 5.3 shows the patterning of the teaching exchanges based on the percentage scores for all ten teachers teaching across the two A level English subjects.

The data from my study, when transcribed, coded and set out according to Sinclair and Coulthard's conventions for presenting analysed texts, amounted to 563 pages of documentation. For the purposes of the current chapter, a selective choice of transcripts has been made that reflects the whole of the data and illustrates common patterns in the teaching exchanges.

My findings suggest that there was little overall variation in the patterning of the teacher exchanges across the two subjects, and that teacher-directed question and answer dominated most of the classroom discourse in all twenty lessons. They therefore support the extensive ALIS data on Perceived Learning Activities (PLAs) which suggests that teachers do not vary their teaching styles when teaching across the two A levels in English. But they contradict the general conclusion arising from the ALIS data that what you teach determines how you teach it, at least to the extent that English Language and English Literature can be seen as different kinds of knowledge (Fitz-Gibbon and Wright 1995a).

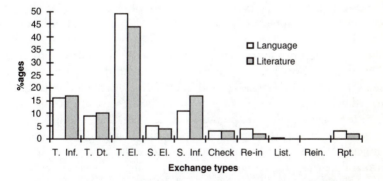

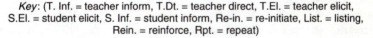

Key: (T. Inf. = teacher inform, T.Dt. = teacher direct, T.El. = teacher elicit, S.El. = student elicit, S. Inf. = student inform, Re-in. = re-initiate, List. = listing, Rein. = reinforce, Rpt. = repeat)

Figure 5.3 Patterning of teaching exchanges for ten teachers of A level English Literature and English Language

The analysis of the lessons also supports the ALIS findings on students' perceptions of the instructional practices employed by their English teachers which show that, after 'class discussion', the more common activities were 'making own notes' and 'reading': in all twenty lessons, written texts were a central focus of the work which frequently included reading activities and the making of notes on the texts being studied. However, the findings from the discourse analysis did suggest that the students were interpreting teacher-led 'recitation' as 'class discussion'.

Because the nature of classroom discourse in A level English teaching has received little attention in research, commentators assume that 'discussion' is a regular classroom activity. Such an assumption, as discussed by Tony Edwards in Chapter 2, goes back to the already nostalgic image of the 'intellectual discipleship' of the Crowther Report (1959), where 'subject-minded' students are introduced to scholarship through the mediating influence of a specialist teacher's knowledge. In such rhetoric, it is assumed that on the route to 'mastery' of an academic craft there must be increasing opportunities for students to display a growing acquisition of the skills in specialised speech and writing, and to demonstrate them without close direction from the teacher.

It is also assumed that there is a developing mastery that carries with it the right to question as students acquire some of the working practices of the subject. Therefore the ideal English lesson at A level is often conceived as being a 'seminar' in which the teacher is no more than a leading participant in a process of discovery. However, the findings from the discourse analysis suggest that 'real' discussion, as defined by Dillon (1994), in which there is the exploration of a topic or issue and interchange of ideas with no predetermined answer, rarely occurred. In other words, teacher-directed interrogation of students' knowledge and understanding was the most common form of teacher/student interaction, with teacher questioning rarely going beyond the recall and clarification of information.

There was therefore little evidence in the twenty English lessons of a less asymmetrical relation between teacher and taught developing, and of the students interpreting, evaluating and speculating on the information being presented, which, according to a social constructivist view of learning, is associated with higher cognitive responses in discussion (Barnes and Todd 1995). This social constructivist perspective on learning suggests that knowledge is constructed by the individual through an interaction between what is already known and new experience, and that understanding is therefore not so much a state as a process and is helped by social interaction. Learning and teaching are seen as collaborative and involving the social and cultural perceptions of all participants, and talk is central to this process as it is the primary medium of interaction which enables learners to make explicit what they know, understand and can do.

My findings also question the idealised notion of A level teaching that has a large component of independent study and a developing 'intellectual discipleship' that bestows some right to question. This right to challenge is thought to be particularly appropriate at A level, where students are seen as 'cultural apprentices' who are progressively socialised into the working practices of their chosen subject. The study, however, showed little variation in teaching styles across the two year groups at A level and so no obvious progression to more independent learning.

The following example from an A level English Language lesson taught by Teacher A, in which he is reviewing a topic on taboo in language with a year 12 group, is typical of the patterning of teacher recitation that dominated all twenty lessons:

Exchanges			Moves	Acts
Teaching	T	do you remember we dealt with this briefly when we were going over language and gender erm we said that there are some areas where erm in lexis where you can identify the main areas of taboo language	I	s
		what are they		el
		can you remember that for bad language		el
2	T	go on under examples	I	s
		first title animals		s
		come on		p
		do you remember some of the words we got out of that for bad language		el
		like we say well your mother says eeh you shouldn't call her that you shouldn't call her a		cl
3	S	bitch	R	rep
4	T	bitch animal language	F	e
5	T	well yes quite I mean in his book Trudgill goes into the question as to why it's wrong to call someone a bitch and say oh you rotten kangaroo	I	s
		I mean what's wrong with kangaroo (laughter)		el
		why can't you use kangaroo		el
		I mean toad is a bit nasty but it's not as I suppose it's greasy nasty one but bitch has got horrible overtones it's got animal and sexual overtones to it		com
		any other words in the animal area		el
6	S	cow	R	rep
7	T	yes bitch and cow quite	F	e
		we're back to that you see how it all links up again to language and gender language and society		com
8	T	but you've got another couple of areas which I think are obvious ones	I	el
9	S	food	R	rep

10	T	now hold on a minute under taboo language let's get this clear	F	e com
11	S	I know tart	I	i
12	T	oh right	F	e
13	T	now is it taboo	I	s
		I know I must ask the question because I'm starting off with the assumption that I know and perhaps I don't		s
		would your mother say to you that's bad language you can't call her a tart		el
14	S	no	R	rep
15	T	mince pie yes but not a tart (laughter)	F	z
		no I think that it's a bit strong		e
		yes it's close to it but I can't think of any food words which actually enter the area quite of taboo I think it gets close to it but not quite		com
		it's mind boggling isn't it erm but I don't think so		e
16	T	is there anything else	I	s
		oh you jelly you you liquorice comfort you		s
		no it's not quite right is it		el
17	S	(non-verbal reaction)	R	rea

This extract shows clearly the teacher's use of the three-part exchange that characterises recitation, and the elaborate and predictable nature of many of his sequences of elicits. This is seen in the way in which the teacher often uses starter acts as a matter of routine in opening moves, where he provides advance warning that a question is imminent and some clues as to how to answer it. We also see him reformulating his questions throughout the sequence in an attempt to arrive at the answer he desires by simplifying and building into its restatement some of the information needed for the acceptable answer. It also shows the way in which teacher-directed talk of this kind creates the impression of knowledge and understanding being elicited from the students rather than being imposed by the teacher, whereas in fact all that is expected from the students is a brief response showing a high level of simple recall. Similarly, the students' responses are usually evaluated and commented upon by the teacher, who has the right to determine what is relevant within his pedagogic agenda. Therefore, the students are expected to respond within the teacher's epistemological frame of reference, and as the 'expert' passing down infor-mation, the very fullness of his exposition generally excludes the possibility of alternative frames of reference.

It is also interesting to note how, in the above extract, the teacher deals with the rare example of a student attempting to introduce an alternative frame (Exchanges 9–15) with the suggestion that the language of food can be included under taboo. Following the teacher's questioning of this suggestion, the student supports her suggestion with the 'tart' example, thereby drawing upon her everyday knowledge. Although the teacher pauses for a moment to think it over, and acknowledges that he may not know the answer, the opportunity for further exploration as to the sexual connotations of the word 'tart', and for handing over the mantle of the expert to the students, is not taken up and the lesson is quickly brought back to his frame of reference by an elicit exchange (16).

A similar patterning of teacher-directed question and answer exchanges also dominates the classroom discourse in his English Literature lesson with a year 13 class, as the following extract illustrates. Here Teacher A is considering Blake's use of repetition of *Tyger, Tyger*:

Exchanges				Moves	Acts
Teaching	T	now I reckon that despite that you can't start off generally a poem about a creature by repeating the name of the creature twice he does it here and gets away with it		I	s
		why			el
		if you start off something in this fashion what is he doing			el
		he isn't saying I've got a poem here about a tiger I'd better tell them what the poem is about and give them the word twice in the first line overwise they'll forget it that's not the point of it is it			el
		why do you have tyger tyger			el
		have a look at the little arrow that comes off the tiger			cl
		why repetition when do you hear repetition			el
2	T	if you go home tonight Alison and you are met by your mother and your mother says Alison Alison (laughter) you say hey that reminds me of a poem (laughter)		I	s
		no what is her frame of mind			el
		what's her approach			el
3	S	something is wrong		R	rep
4	T	something is wrong		F	e
5	T	why does she repeat it		I	s
		I mean why do you say to her oh come on mother you know me you don't have to remind me you don't have to tell me twice you don't have to go on through that rigmarole do you but come on			s
					p
		or if teacher comes into class and says Emma Emma what's she trying to do			el
6	S	(inaudible)		R	rep
7	T	be boring and repetitive like all teachers I suppose		F	z
		yeah			e
8	T	erm no what's teacher trying to do		I	s
		Emma Emma			s
		why repeat			el
		emphasis yes more than that though			p

9	S	find out something on you find out why you done (inaudible) get to us	R	rep
10	T	it is trying to get you to respond	F	e
	T	but why is it that people when they are addressing you might might feel obliged to I don't know to use that tone of voice	I	el
		I mean it's not Emma Emma (laughter)		cl
11	S	that's your mother	R	rep
12	T	precisely	F	e
		that means come here because I want you to do something isn't it		com
13	T	we're back to the language area quite you go into the room you go into the house and you hear the voice upstairs Emma Emma then you know she's not going to break into poetry erm it means that you've forgotten to clean the budgie's cage out or something	I	s
		but if she confronts you in the hall and says Emma Emma what's her feeling what does she feel like		el
14	S	disgust distressed	R	rep
15	T	oh no I know why she's saying that Emma Emma (laughter)	I	s
		how does she feel Emma Emma		el
16	S	distressed	R	rep
17	T	yeah she feels distressed in despair	F	e
18	T	certainly there's a lot of strong feeling going through her	I	s
		she is in		s
		what's she trying to do		el
		erm I mean what's she trying to come to terms with perhaps		el
19	S	confusion	R	rep
20	T	yes	F	e
21	T	something you do that she cannot com	I	cl
22	S	comprehend	R	rep
23	T	comprehend precisely	F	e

Again, as in the first extract from the English Language lesson, Teacher A tightly controls the turn taking and topic by working rigidly within an I-R-F/E framework. Therefore the students are given little opportunity to initiate and contribute ideas beyond their utterances in response to the teacher's questions. This is reflected in the very low level of student initiations in both lessons.

Overall, the analysis of the patterning of the teaching exchanges for both lessons, as shown in Figure 5.4, shows little variation. The similarity of the patterning of the teaching exchanges reveals the extent to which teacher presentation and teacher-directed question and answer dominate both lessons: the teacher's eliciting and informing exchanges account for 82 per cent and 78 per cent of the exchanges in the English Literature and English Language lessons respectively.

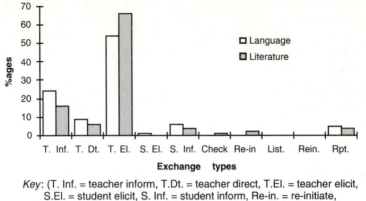

Figure 5.4 Patterning of teaching exchanges for Teacher A

When asked prior to being filmed about whether he perceived any differences in subject paradigms and in pedagogy, however, Teacher A described clear differences. He reported that many of the differences arose from the fact that A level English Language drew from the field of linguistics, thereby allowing for the study of a much wider range of texts in the classroom of which English Literature is only one variety. It therefore removed the privileged status that English Literature was still accorded in the traditional literature syllabus that he taught (NEAB, syllabus B). He also thought that English Language had more of a 'vocational' orientation because of its emphasis on communication skills, and for this reason attracted less academic students who would not normally be accepted onto an A level English Literature course. As a result of this, he perceived that there were distinctive pedagogic differences in the way he approached the teaching of the two subjects:

> Looking at the practical arrangements in class I find that in Literature, despite what I say about going into the social background and philo-sophical factors, I spend probably a lot more time actually interpreting texts to the whole group of students. I don't know whether this is because I take a traditional approach to it. I think partly because that is necessary, they need that input especially when you're dealing with you know texts as old as Shakespeare so they need that assistance in interpretation and it must be done in a group to a great extent. So there's a lot more time spent on whole class activities.

Therefore, although he reported that he frequently used discussion in his English Literature lessons to encourage a 'personal response' to texts from his students, he thought that there was a greater tendency for the work to be teacher-directed because of the need to provide interpretations so as to ensure that they used the specialist language of the literary critic. However, in his English Language lessons, he felt that there were more opportunities for investigative and collaborative work in which students could draw on their everyday knowledge and undertake and report on a small-scale study of an aspect of language in everyday use:

> In Language what we are increasingly doing in lower sixth at this very moment is asking the students, having sampled over two terms of the course again a lot of theory in the first two terms, there has to be, but at this stage we ask them to prepare a mini-project which will allow them for a start to conduct some research of their own in preparation for the main project in upper sixth. But it also involves a change of teaching style, they are very diverse topics and so as a result each I advise . . . have you read this, have you seen this? I can stop them all occasionally and say of course when you're approaching research first of all you must go through this form. They all have a pack, a hand-out pack, in which the basic approach is explained but I'll stop them every so often and reinterpret things and then they'll go back to doing what they are doing. It's always very difficult to know in trying to balance the type of input you have for lessons because you can get it too heavily weighted towards the didactic approach and then all of a sudden they can be researching themselves where they're very much more independent.

He therefore reported that he used much more of a 'student-centred' approach in his A level English Language teaching, where the students were expected to take considerable responsibility for their own learning through the use of individual research projects or investigations, in contrast to a more didactic approach in his English Literature lessons. Similar views, explicitly justifying a different approach to A level English Language in terms of its subject paradigm and pedagogy, were also expressed by the other nine teachers in the study, whose analysis of the discourse also showed a mismatch between their perceptions of how they teach the two A level English subjects and their classroom practice. These findings, and the teachers' reactions to them, will be returned to later in the chapter.

As discussed earlier, the overall patterning of the teaching exchanges for all ten teachers shows that they work within an I-R-F/E format and suggests little pedagogic distinctiveness between the two A level English subjects. Some variation in the patterning of the teaching exchanges did occur, however, in the level of student informing exchanges in the case of four of the teachers (Teachers G, H, I and J). All four teachers appeared to provide more opportunities for the students to report back on their ideas. This can be seen in the patterning of the teaching exchanges from Teacher J's lessons (Figure 5.5), where student informs constitute the second highest percentage of exchange types in each lesson (31 per cent in English Literature and 22 per cent in English Language). This suggests that the students were given more opportunities to make contributions than is normally the case within an I-R-F/E format.

116

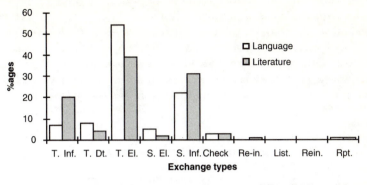

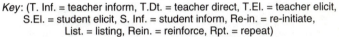

Key: (T. Inf. = teacher inform, T.Dt. = teacher direct, T.El. = teacher elicit,
S.El. = student elicit, S. Inf. = student inform, Re-in. = re-initiate,
List. = listing, Rein. = reinforce, Rpt. = repeat)

Figure 5.5 Patterning of teaching exchanges for Teacher J

This conclusion is illustrated in the following extract from the early stages
of Teacher J's English Language lesson in which he is exploring with a group of
students the view that standard English should be considered as a dialect:

Exchanges			Moves	Acts
Teaching	T	erm anything else that you can think of that would be perhaps against the idea that a standard English is not a dialect it's perhaps a more purer language	I	el
2	S	if it was a pure language it would be like a lot more people who'd speak it you know like sort of so with all the dialects and stuff like that not one of them's right and one of them's wrong	R	rep
3	T	right ok	F	acc
4	S	if one was right then it would be sort of enforced on you	I	i
5	S	yeah there would be more like people speaking it like you know the upper classes all of them would speak standard English	I	i
6	S	and I think err everyone would err you'd have to be able to speak if it was the proper language you'd have to speak that dialect that just to get anywhere	I	i
7	T	right so you're saying there that standard English has a kind of special status almost	F	e com
8	S	well it does but it would have more it would be more so if that was the proper language	I	i
9	T	oh I see what you mean yeah using this idea that it's somehow other than a dialect something more than a dialect	F	e com

117

Here, unusually, the teacher allows time and space within the I-R-F/E exchange for the students to contribute their ideas through informing exchanges that build on previous contributions (Exchanges 4, 5, 6 and 8). A similar patterning of exchanges can also be seen in Teacher J's English Literature lesson when he is working with a pair of students. It is taken from the early stages of the lesson when the students have been asked to compare Lockwood's language to that of the other characters in an extract from *Wuthering Heights*:

Exchanges			Moves	Acts
Teaching	T	so give us an example of the forcefulness of the characters	I	el
2	S	well on the very first one where he always says erm (reads) 'What the devil is the matter' he's not it doesn't seem he's asking a question he's almost telling the person off for what he's doing or feeling the what he does	R	rep
3	T	it's a violent aggressive phrase isn't it	I	el
4	S	yeah (inaudible)	R	rep
5	S	that one where Hareton's saying 'Sit down! . . . He'll be in soon' it's like ordering him (inaudible)	I	i
6	S	and he's supposed to be a guest and like you know how you obviously he's doing what he's supposed to do he's offering him a chair and stuff he doesn't really do it in the kind of friendly manner that you expect I think	I	i
7	T	yeah	F	e
		there's no courtesy there's no formality no politeness is there so you know Hareton is just like giving a command sit down		com
8	S	everything they say is like that	I	i
9	S	they're all commands	I	i
10	S	and at the end as well	I	i
11	T	right	F	e
12	S	the forcefulness	I	i
13	S	(reads) 'My name is Hareton Earnshaw, and I'd counsel you to respect it'	I	i
14	S	they expect to get they expect to get	I	i

Again the teacher builds on the student's contribution by incorporating his answer into a subsequent question (Exchange 3) and in his feedback (Exchange 7) to a further contribution. In both extracts therefore it seems that the students are given the opportunity to contribute their ideas. However, while there seems to be more extended contributions from the students, the discourse does not take on a conversation-like quality, with teacher and students taking more equitable turns in speaking, because the teacher is still controlling the discourse by asserting his 'right' as the 'expert' to control the frame of reference through his questioning and evaluation of the students' answers and contributions.

Despite the many concerns expressed (see Edwards and Westgate 1994) about the potentially stifling effect of adult talk in educational settings, recent studies (Nystrand and Gamoran 1991; Mercer 1992; Geekie and Raban 1993; Wells 1993) have returned to the I-R-F/E structure and suggested that it can be functionally effective. Wells (1993), for example, calls into question what he sees as the over-simplified acount of the three-part I-R-F sequence, and suggests that in the hands of different teachers it can lead to very different levels of student participation and engagement. He argues that many of the critics of the I-R-F structure have treated triadic dialogue in an undifferentiated manner and that such a homogeneity does not exist. Drawing on evidence from a small case study, he suggests that it can be used by the same teacher, in different contexts, to achieve very different educational purposes. He therefore proposes that there are different 'discourse genres' within the same basic discourse format which make different use of the *feedback* move: on some occasions the dominant function of the third move was evaluative, where the teacher was checking the student's knowledge; on other occasions the third move functioned much more as an opportunity to extend the student's answer, to draw out its significance, or to make connections with other parts of the student's total experience during lesson topics, which created a greater equality of participation for all the students. Wells (1993: 35) therefore argues that teachers can provide extending rather than evaluating feedback, so that 'it is in this third step in the *co-construction* of meaning that the next cycle of the learning-and-teaching spiral has its point of departure'. This would seem particularly appropriate at A level where, because of the relative expertise of the students, a more symmetrical relationship between teacher and taught should be possible, with the students taking over some of the functions of the third move.

The analysis of the A level English lessons shows, however, that even where there appeared to be a higher level of student participation through student informing exchanges, the discourse and frames of reference were still tightly controlled by the teacher's questioning and by the third move being used in most cases to evaluate rather than to extend the student's contribution. The findings, therefore, do not support the suggestion that in the hands of different teachers the same basic discourse format can be used for different purposes, and can lead to less constrained forms of classroom discourse with very different levels of student participation and engagement.

Because of the domination of teacher-led recitation in all of the twenty lessons, challenges to the teacher's frame of reference were very rare. The following two examples, both from Teacher J's English Literature lesson, stand out because of their unusual nature. Both arise in response to the teacher's attempts to introduce a new theoretical position in order to move the students away from a Leavisite perspective of seeing the characters in *Wuthering Heights* as real people who develop throughout the novel, so as to get them to focus on the stylistic choices being made by the writer. After a long explanation of this point, he asks the students if they agree with this view; this is challenged, however, by one of the students in reply to the teacher's question:

Exchanges			Moves	Acts
Teaching	T	does everyone get what I'm saying there about this kind of narrative trick going on	I	s
		do you see what I'm saying		el
2	S	yeah I do I just don't know whether I agree with you	R	rep
3	T	don't know whether you agree with me	F	e
4	T	well I think what I'm trying to do is throw the emphasis slightly away from character and more towards the kind of techniques that the author is employing	I	s
		erm I mean I agree with what you've said that within the character and within the fiction itself it's all you know all of what you've said makes perfect sense and yes I agree that it's likely that the moors would have had a dramatic impact on Lockwood and would kind of strip away some of this veneer of culture that he's got I agree with that but I think also it's Emily Brontë at work kind of driving the narrative forward		i

Here the student's challenge (Exchange 2) is brought back to Teacher J's |frame of reference through an informing exchange (Exchange 4) in which he elaborates on his view and effectively closes down the challenge before moving on to explore another extract from the novel. However, later in the lesson, the student is given the opportunity to return to the topic and once again challenges the teacher's view on character development. Following her presentation, the teacher asks if she has got anything else to add:

Exchanges			Moves	Acts
Teaching	T	anything else to add	I	el
2	S	erm well I find it quite erm Emily Brontë's made a narrative and made quite a lot of the story erm and the first one beginning although she's saying things to people throughout the novel she's interpreting people entirely we can see the change in them from erm the beginning of the novel even though it's set in the present time as she's talking to Mr Lockwood she's still creates the atmosphere the feeling of her background and where she came from at the beginning (inaudible) and then she erm paragraph number six it basically shows how the transformation of Heathcliffe Wuthering Height and Thrushcross Grange and how	R	rep

> she's sort of erm maybe influenced them
> through erm I mean she's quite young at the
> beginning but she's now growing up she'll be
> an adult then and she'll probably be better
> educated and it'll influence what she says
> through the direct language

3	T	right	F	e
		I think you make some very very good points		com
		there I think particularly the one about the		
		different many different voices that Nelly		
		Dean has		
4	T	erm you know she does have all these different	I	i
		voices for different occasions for different parts		
		of the story erm again though you're tending		
		to suggest that tell me if I'm wrong but you're		
		suggesting that Nelly Dean actually changes		
		during the novel I mean I'm not denying		
		that but you're saying her narration changes		
		because she's learning and because she's		
		growing through the novel no it's just		
5	S	she does she changes from being a teenager	I	i
		to an err old lady throughout the novel and I		
		can see that transformation in the language		
6	T	absolutely I would agree with that	F	e
7	T	but the problem with that when we come down	I	s
		to it is this idea that of course she's we're		
		supposed to believe that she's actually telling		
		the story to Lockwood in a couple of sessions		
		or you know three or four sessions		
		erm so surely then she's not skilful enough		
		perhaps she is as a narrator to imitate her own		
		voice as it was when she was younger not to		
		mention all the voices of all the other		
		characters and her own voice as it kind of		
		grows more sophisticated from her experience		
8	S	perhaps it's that's a technique Emily Bronte	I	i
		wanted to put in I don't know I kind of		
9	T	yeah yeah	F	e
		I mean I think I'm kind of being unkind in		
		a way because I keep kind of throwing it back		
		to the point of view of the novelist but I agree		
		entirely with you what you said about erm		
		Nelly Dean and about the different voices		
		involved		

Here the student is given a rare opportunity, within a response slot, to elaborate at length on her views on character development, which was denied her earlier in the lesson (Exchange 2); and for a time, because the teacher responds to the challenge on its own terms, a less asymmetrical pedagogic relationship develops. Eventually, though, the teacher asserts his 'right' as the 'expert' to reformulate her answer so that it fits in with his earlier frame of

121

reference on narrative style (Exchange 4). However, the student does not accept this and challenges his interpretation through two further student informing exchanges (Exchanges 5 and 8). Eventually, however, he suggests a 'compromise' (Exchange 9) by acknowledging the worth of her contribution, while at the same time re-emphasising his 'authoritative' answer, before moving on to another topic and sequence of questions. Overall, though, such challenges to the teacher's frame of reference are rare, mainly because of his control over the I-R-E/F structure, so that the students' contribution is usually restricted to the response slot, with little opportunity for them to initiate challenges through questions.

CONCLUSIONS AND IMPLICATIONS

The general findings of the two very different kinds of investigation discussed in this chapter show no evidence of differences in pedagogy between the two A level English subjects, despite the assertions of the various commentators discussed earlier. Within Bernstein's (1990) theoretical framework, discussed in more detail by Tony Edwards in Chapter 2, the discourse analysis shows that A level English Language is no less strongly defined (or classified) as an academic subject than English Literature, which leads to a hierarchical (or strongly framed) relationship between teacher and taught.

Therefore, although A level English Language is seen by many as being a 'hybrid' subject and therefore more vocational in its orientation, it seems that it is still represented in traditional academic terms rather than being 'regionalised' into 'areas of application' (Bernstein 1990: 63). In other words, it draws upon the academic study of linguistics in higher education in the same way that A level English Literature draws upon the study of an established literary canon, with all its specialist working practices. This is despite its stated aim of encouraging investigational, independent and collaborative forms of learning and assessment normally associated with vocational alternatives, and its concern with the study of language and its uses so as to increase students' language competence.

Conservative fears (e.g. O'Hear 1991; Pilkington 1991) that a 'hybrid' subject like English Language will undermine the teacher's authority in an established body of knowledge, and therefore the 'proper' relationship of teacher and taught, because it is not disciplined by the rules and practices of an established academic tradition, are not borne out by the research evidence. The ubiquity of the three-part exchange structure in all twenty A level English lessons meant that both English Language and English Literature lessons were predominantly conducted within the teacher's frame of reference. Because of the teacher's claim to prior knowledge of the subject content and right to control the pacing and sequencing of its transmission, students rarely managed to impose their own relevance outside the teacher's frame of reference. This is particularly reflected in the very low level of student questions. The teacher was therefore often seen retaining control over the direction and pace of the lesson and the lines of knowledge that were to be pursued.

Such findings on the lack of differences in teaching styles revealed in both studies, and on the nature of classroom discussion in A level English lessons, came as a surprise to the ten teachers involved in the study in follow-up interviews. They believed that they did teach the two subjects differently and that they created opportunities for more exploratory forms of discussion so as to allow for an interchange of ideas and the right to question and challenge which is thought appropriate at this level of the educational process. In particular, they were disturbed to find that they were using a style of teaching that they perceived as reducing the students to a passive role.

Many offered familiar explanations for these departures from how things ought to be. Like HMI (DES 1986, 1987a), Harrison and Mountford (1992) and Macfarlane (1993), they thought that teachers were constrained towards didacticism by examinations that are narrow in what they test (more so since the reduction in coursework) and high in the rewards they carry as passports to prestigious universities, degree programmes and 'middle-class' employment achieved through such specialised academic study. They also reported that the stakes are getting higher with the publication of league tables. Similarly, they felt that the pressures to get through the syllabus and cover the required material often meant that they over-employed teacher-directed methods at the expense of creating opportunties for students to take more responsibility for their own learning. As Macfarlane (1993) suggests, it seemed that all of the teachers appreciated the benefits of tempering didactic methods, but for pragmatic reasons they were forced into limiting opportunities for 'open' discussion because it could lead to distracting diversions in which the teacher loses control over the pedagogic agenda and so fails to cover the syllabus.

Many also felt that there was a 'subject culture', which they themselves had been inculcated into at school and university, by which traditional practices were perpetuated, and they were conscious of having to prepare their students for similar modes of study in order to secure a place in higher education. As Leach (1992) suggests, teachers of A level English Literature are themselves examples of students who have successfully achieved the qualifications and surmounted the hurdles provided by the British education system. They therefore have been inculcated into ways of seeing, understanding and teaching English Literature and feel constrained to teach it in the same way that they themselves were taught, thereby creating a subject culture. The teachers in the present study certainly thought this to be the case. This, argues Leach, encourages a 'traditional' range of classroom techniques which includes: students at desks, teacher at the front in the position of power and purveyor of wisdom, knowledge and information, line-by-line examination and explication of the text involving complex explanation of words and phrases, followed by essays that are expected to take on acceptable critical stances.

As a result of the findings, all of the ten teachers thought that there was a need for more classroom observation and analysis of their teaching. They were therefore interested in follow-up studies in order to develop alternative discourse strategies to recitation, through which they could encourage student discussion so as to give them more opportunities for input and control over the discourse.

Clearly the findings of the study have implications for the range of roles students can play in the classroom discourse and for their linguistic and cognitive development. The social constructivist view of learning, which Barnes and Todd (1995) take to be widely accepted amongst educationists, indicates that our most important learning does not take place through the addition of discrete facts to an existing store but by relating new information, new experiences, new ways of understanding to an existing understanding of the matter in hand. One of the most important ways of working on this understanding is through talk, particularly group talk, in which students are given the opportunity to assume greater control over their own learning by initiating ideas and responses and consequently promote wider communicative options and higher order thinking (i.e. describing, explaining, predicting, arguing, critiquing, explicating, defining) which Ohlsson (1995) suggests can be exercised only through spoken discourse and written texts.

This theory of learning therefore emphasises the need for the exploration and researching of alternative teaching and learning strategies that will help to raise the quality of teachers' interactions with their students and promote wider communicative (and hence more cognitively demanding) options to those in which students are often mere listeners or respondents within an I-R-F/E mode. The need to create such opportunities for students to interact in such a way as to exercise their cognitive and communicative competence to maximum effect has led to alternative strategies to a recitation format being advocated (e.g. Dillon's (1994) use of statements, signals, silences, student question; Nystrand and Gamoran's (1991) 'high-level evaluation'; Wells' (1993) 'extending feedback'; and Wood's (1992) 'low control' moves) that aim to break the I-R-F/E cycle and enable a wider range of discourse moves by students. There is, however, a pressing need for more systematic research into the effectiveness of such teaching strategies, which aim to develop positive kinds of teacher-involved discourse that move from recitation to a more conversational style of interaction and enable a wider range of discourse moves for students.

If such alternative strategies are to have any real impact on the classroom to bring about a change in the status quo, there is a need for more powerful teacher education programmes that get novice and experienced teachers to challenge their beliefs and practices through critical reflection so as to make this 'invisible pedagogy' (Bernstein 1990) more visible, or as Edwards and Westgate (1994: 98) suggest, 'making the familiar strange'. Monitoring and self-evaluation will therefore need to become a regular part of initial and in-service training, as advocated by Joyce and Showers (1988). Similarly, Dillon (1994) and Westgate and Hughes (forthcoming) suggest that talk-analysis feedback may be a useful tool whereby sympathetic discussion by groups of teachers of data (recordings and transcriptions) derived from their own classrooms could be an effective starting point for professional development.

Barnes and Todd (1995: 105) also argue that research, as in the present study, will need to go hand-in-hand with professional development for teachers, since 'beginning to set up opportunities for students to learn through collaborative talk is much more than a change in their perception of their own roles and those of students in the process of teaching and learning'. As the evidence discussed in this and the other chapters suggests, it is a challenging agenda requiring 'hard' evidence from classroom contexts to be analysed by qualitative approaches and markers of 'quality' that do justice to the contextual complexities of the classroom.

6

LINKS BETWEEN LEARNING STYLES, TEACHING METHODS AND COURSE REQUIREMENTS IN GNVQ AND A LEVEL

Roy Haywood

INTRODUCTION

This chapter takes up some of the themes outlined by Tony Edwards and revisits them from a different perspective. The main emphasis is to explore some of the potential and real links between learning styles, teaching methods and course requirements in the post-16 GNVQ and A level courses. Learning styles are defined here as the teachers' and students' preferred ways of perceiving and of processing incoming information and their experience for engaging with particular learning activities and tasks. The concept of learning style preferences is based on the premiss that individuals prefer to learn in different ways, and that given a choice they will tend to approach learning tasks in a relatively consistent manner. Yet empirical work on learning styles in the 16–19 stage seems to be a neglected area, especially when compared with the number of studies focusing on the higher education stage. Therefore, early on in this project, it was decided to build out from the extensive datasets of the ALIS project, which included post-16 students reporting on their experiences of the ways in which they have been taught. The new features were to incorporate a well-known measure of learning styles (Kolb's Learning Style Inventory, 1976) and extensive classroom observations of teaching and learning.

At the age of 16 it is commonly assumed that, after eleven years of schooling, pupils have matured sufficiently to have been transformed into students. Those who elect to stay on have already been differentiated for their grasp of knowledge, understanding and skills in the National Curriculum subjects by the GCSE assessment system. The schools and colleges, with an eye on the funding implications, are anxious to retain or recruit them for their post-16 A level or Advanced GNVQ courses (Anderson and Haywood 1996). Both the schools and colleges and their potential students use the GCSE results as strong (reliable) performance indicators of suitability about which track to follow. The students bring an apparently objective measure of current performance which is

126

then used to assess potential performance in a new course of study. Generally, though not exclusively, potential students with 'good' grades (conventionally set at 5 or more A-C grades) tend to be offered and accept the A level track to the pursuit of a subject *specialist* form of education in which 'pure' knowledge is supposed to play a dominant part. Teachers assured us that such students have demonstrated that in the basic curriculum they have acquired a body of content knowledge on which to build, that they have an understanding of what a specific subject is about, and also have the necessary skills to go on further and study more deeply. Other potential students, with less good GCSE grades (in the 1994 ALIS sample only 2.5 per cent of GNVQ enrolments were in the top quartile, while 75 per cent were in the bottom quartile), who for a variety of reasons elect to stay on, are often steered onto the GNVQ track heading towards 'applied' knowledge and a vocationally oriented form of *general* education. These students have demonstrated that, in Gillian Shephard's words, 'they do not respond best to a purely academic curriculum'. In their teachers' eyes, although considered to have some knowledge of subject content, they have relatively lower levels of understanding and the requisite skills appropriate for developing further subject knowledge. What happens subsequently in the teaching and learning process to these young people, and how it is linked to the 'separate but equal' course requirements, provides the focus for this chapter.

The chapter is divided into two parts – the theoretical background of the main themes and the empirical findings. It begins by highlighting some of the current policy issues because I assume that 'a truth universally acknowledged' is that policy, theory and practice are all tainted with 'pride and prejudice'. Certainly engaging with them produces a remarkable sense of *déja vu*. This is followed by a theoretical examination of the philosophical and pragmatic orientations that underpin, but are often neglected in, the current debates. Then the focus moves to teaching and learning, with an emphasis on learning that entails reviewing recent work on students' conceptions of learning and also their preferred styles of engaging with learning. The second half of the chapter is based on our empirical work and is shaped by looking at five questions about students' learning style derived from the previous sections. These are:

1 Do learning styles differ across the academic and vocational domains?
2 Are they associated with particular subject bases?
3 Do they assist in transfer of learning?
4 Are they appropriately used to achieve the 'shift from teaching to learning' referred to in Chapter 2?
5 Do teachers' learning styles affect the teaching/learning process?

POST-16 CURRICULUM: POLICY, PHILOSOPHY AND PRAGMATISM

For policymakers the current challenge in 16–19 education and training is 'to produce an education system which can provide access, increase participation and promote learning experiences which will contribute to economic regeneration and at the same time preserve A levels in all their "rigour"' (Higham *et al.* 1996: 153). On the other hand, the current challenges for practitioners are, firstly, to make sense of the issues which have to be tempered by the structural constraints (legal and budgetary) and restraints (teaching staff and student clientele) erected on the shifting sands of policy. Then they have to try to resolve these as best they can as they realise that in the current preoccupation with 'standards' the only point that seems to matter is that standards are never high enough. Faced with such problems, is it any wonder that the teachers have engaged in a protracted period of guerrilla warfare and have been forced to use the strategies of 'selective negligence', 'creative insubordination' and 'planned delinquency' just to cope and survive?

It is appropriate here to quote at length a succinct and illuminating commentary on the curriculum development process. Over twenty years ago, Mauritz Johnson stated:

> Mechanisms and procedures for educational planning differ in regard to the thoroughness with which needs are identified, alternatives considered, and solutions tested, as well as in regard to the extensiveness with which various sections of the professional education community are consulted before a decision is taken. Very possibly, the more efficiently decisions can be arrived at the less effectively they can be implemented. A decision taken at a level other than that at which it is to be implemented can be promulgated, but the willingness and capacity to implement cannot. . . . When many forces simultaneously tend in the same direction, decisions can be quickly reached and efficiently put into operation. But when forces work against each other, disagreements, uncertainties, and resistances arise to forestall and retard progress.
>
> (Johnson 1974: 12–13)

For schools and colleges, dealing with post-16 students who have opted for a period of 'deferred vocationalism' by taking A levels or who have embarked on the occupationally oriented GNVQ courses, there's the rub. And it's not just a recent phenomenon. Their problems are of long standing and were once seen as solutions. To take just one example, the Norwood Report (Board of Education 1943) is often cited for its justification of the divisive three 'types of mind' ('intellectual', 'technical' and 'concrete') and with their associated curricula and future occupational prospects. However, protagonists of this 'separate but equal' position seem to ignore the early sections of the Report which are peculiarly apposite to current policy of the continuing gold–silver–bronze view of the social hierarchy.

As secondary education attracts more children, the needs to be met grow more numerous and diverse . . . Criticism against the curriculum is not really directed against the curriculum itself but against its suitability for many of the pupils in the extended Secondary Schools of the country.

(Board of Education 1943: 12)

Norwood maintained that the pre-war secondary school curriculum was 'traditional' because it 'rests upon a conception of a liberal education which is outmoded, . . . a liberal education is now held to include vocational education'. The curriculum was unsuitable because there was a 'lack of flexibility' in a congested timetable of 'too many subjects' leading to 'meaningless congeries', in which 'too much is being attempted and too little performed'. Subjects were 'handled rigidly with little contact with each other or with life or with reality or future occupations or interests'. Furthermore, because 'examination require-ments cast their shadow over all; the acquisition of information is given undue importance; a premium is put on memorisation; power of judgement remains untrained; second-hand opinions pass for knowledge' (Board of Education 1943: 10).

The pick-and-mix mentality has prevailed in education and training policy and currently, according to Brown and Lauder (1995), incorporates elements of Fordism (mass production, standardisation of product, moving along peda-gogical assembly lines whilst picking up gobbets of pre-specified knowledge that reduce complex tasks to their most elementary form) with neo-Fordism (a shift to the flexible accumulation of accredited qualifications in order to create a flexible workforce engaged in low skilled, low wage, temporary and part-time employment) and post-Fordism (a shift to high value customised production of a multi-skilled and high waged workforce). However, the work of the curriculum theorists and philosophers Lawrence Stenhouse and Paul Hirst have made important and influential contributions to clarifying the resulting problems.

Stenhouse's seminal work on curriculum development and research proposed that 'education as we know it in schools necessarily comprises of [sic] at least four different processes' (1975: 80) – first, *training* (acquisition of skills resulting in performance); second, *instruction* (learning information resulting in retention); third, *initiation* (familiarisation with norms and values, often through the 'hidden' curriculum, resulting in interpretation and potential indoctrination); and fourth, *induction* (introduction to thought systems resulting in understand-ing and making judgements). The first three of Stenhouse's categories are often associated with behavioural objectives and a 'product' model of curriculum. This he consistently attacked in favour of the 'process' model which he saw as aligned with the fourth process and as constituting 'the raw material for thinking'. Continued support for focusing on Stenhouse's induction process in the post-16 arena of 'cognitive apprenticeship' in 'situated learning' is seen as the process of enculturation into an expert community and as part of the promotion of higher-order thinking skills, which shapes learning interaction from teacher-oriented episodes to goal-oriented problem solving between teacher and pupil (Collins *et al.* 1989). Thus, Stenhouse distinguished between the mundane, and by implication the profane, knowledge and learning that critics of GNVQ use to damn it, and the sacred knowledge and learning encapsulated in the kind of intellectual discipleship that, as Edwards argues, the cultural restorationists currently seek to defend.

Paul Hirst (1993) is more direct. He regards the epistemological roots of education and training as conforming either to the 'rationalist view' or the 'practical experience view'. 'The rationalist approach to the curriculum thus holds that the curriculum is first about understanding, then about skills and attitudes, and then about getting on with life' (p. 33). This knowledge for its own sake is part of the classical-humanist ideology of the elite academic curriculum, and is in direct contrast to 'opposing views which differ radically in their account of what is fundamental in education' (p. 35), and is a view that reverses the order of priority of the rationalist's position.

> People must get on with their lives, whether fundamental areas of knowledge are there to assist or not, and the most significant knowledge we live by . . . has come in practical activities and pursuits, by trial and error . . . living as a human being or developing as a person, does not come from learning and applying abstract subject knowledge. It comes from practical experience . . . and sees the best practices of living as foundational to which subjects are adjuncts and of secondary significance.
>
> (Hirst 1993: 34)

Such sentiments appear to fall in with the instrumental ideology that comes through in pronouncements of Gilbert Jessup, regarded by many as the arch-mover or even architect of the 'shift from an input-led system to an outcome-led system' (Jessup 1991: 11) which is the model of learning associated with NVQs, and which influenced its adaptation into a school- and college-based GNVQ.

The familiar distinction between 'knowing how' and 'knowing that', or between practical knowledge and theoretical knowledge, seem to place GNVQs on the practical experience side of the line. Practical knowledge, usually referred to as procedural knowledge or 'knowing how', is concerned with observable outcomes measured against pre-specified competencies (effective goal attainment). Procedural knowledge, Ohlsson (1995) contends, follows a set of general methods (means–end analysis, analogical reasoning, heuristic searching). The medium is action and learning to do. The novice is presented with an unfamiliar task, provided with opportunities to perform the task, and then performance is measured on successive attempts before recording the before–after changes in performance. The cognitive mechanisms for acquiring competence incorporate a sequence of actions that requires making choices and decisions, from a set of multiple options, about what to do and about what is specifically required in the particular case under consideration. In doing so the students are expected to adapt and learn from their errors by creating new rules derived from one context and using them as templates for applying to a new context. The 'knowledge problem' here is about developing a conceptual understanding that enables new problems to be resolved – if not solved – or for new tasks to be completed as rigorously as is possible. The analogical reasoning that this incorporates means that 'transfer of learning' becomes a key component of learning, and it is maintained that this causes behaviour that can be empirically validated – the student can or cannot do the task. 'Successful performance proves the existence of practical knowledge and (consistent) failure its absence. However, in the case of abstract knowledge, these relations do not hold . . . because understanding is a state of mind, not a process' (Ohlsson 1995: 48).

In contrast, or by comparison, A level is more readily associated with Hirst's rational view. Propositional knowledge, or 'knowing that', leads to learning for understanding, which implies having the wherewithal and motivation to acquire facts and relate them to prior knowledge in order to turn them into 'concepts, principles and ideas that do not refer to particular objects or events but to universal features of reality' (Ohlsson 1995: 46). The 'knowledge problem' here is that understanding is employed not so much in action as in generating symbols via discourse in a series of epistemic tasks (describing, explaining, predicting, arguing, critiquing, evaluating, explicating, defining). Constructing meaning by thinking through 'situated practices' is a 'discursive process' because 'thinking, to a large extent, is achieved through talk'. Thinking is what goes on in the head and is based on cognitive structures that are built around prior experience, concept maps and mental models. Obviously, the students' existing schematic models may contain prior mistaken misconceptions, as well as correct or appropriate structures, which are open to change in the same ways as Newton needed Kepler and Einstein needed Newton to develop new knowledge from old. However, a problem in measuring understanding is the lack of reliable indicators. Understanding is not directly observable. Failure to produce competent behaviour does not imply lack of understanding. We all know that attendance at an exotic ski-school will cover the essential concepts of weight-transfer; but the number of skiers on crutches getting off the plane when they return home is undeniable evidence of the gap between human understanding and action. As Ohlsson points out, 'the most powerful methodology for discovering and expressing regularities is quantification and discourse is more difficult to quantify than action' (1995: 52).

The above discussion and different conceptions of knowing and knowledge have implications for what sort of curriculum is on offer to post-16 students, and for how it is delivered and received. Socialised students proceed from the earlier grounding in the (common) National Curriculum and continue to engage in that unified 'holy trinity' (or should it be troika, with the implied potential for pulling in different directions?) of knowledge, understanding and skills, along the A level or GNVQ tracks.

LEARNING STYLES: CONCEPTIONS AND MODELS

In the literature on learning models there is general agreement that, particularly for 'students' rather than 'pupils', an individual's approach to learning is a complex combination of intellectual ability and prior knowledge, personal motivation and preferred cognitive learning styles (Schmeck 1988; Corno and Snow 1986). For post-16 students, intellectual ability as well as prior knowledge have been assessed through their GCSE grades. These grades also serve as proxy or indirect measures of other desirable personal attributes, such as motivation, conscientiousness and the degree of self-regulation and control that the student possesses. Such components, drawn from an extensive research literature, feature in a model of epistemological orientations developed by Brody (1995), which is particularly relevant to the post-16 debate (Figure 6.1). Furthermore, it allows us to highlight our own choice of research stance.

Now it may be argued that the *transmission* orientation could be broadly aligned with the theory and practice of the GCSE framework; the *transaction* orientation to the GNVQ pattern; and the *transformation* orientation to A level aspirations and practices. Whilst, as other contributions to this book show, there are clear divisions and differences between the 'pure' academic A levels and 'applied' vocational approaches of GNVQ, there is 'increasing convergence in the middle reaches of what must by now surely be accepted as more like a continuum than two separate areas' (Committee of Vice-Chancellors 1995). Additionally, both GNVQ and A level classrooms exhibit both transaction and transformation characteristics, and will contain episodes that are purely transmissional, since traditional 'instruction' – in its sequentially ordered form of tell, show, imitate and then practise – is a necessary condition of some features of 'good learning' in both GNVQ and A level teaching. It is, therefore, our expectation that it will be the proportion and the quality of didactic or expository teaching that will be significant.

Brody's general epistemological scheme can be related to post-16 teaching and learning by incorporating De Corte's (1995) research findings that 'good learning' has six inter-related characteristics. De Corte found that 'good learning' was constructive, cumulative, self-regulated, goal oriented, situated and collaborative. These six characteristics can be incorporated in developing a theoretical model that can be used later to gain some empirical purchase on the connections between teachers' and students' conceptions of learning (understanding) and their preferred styles for undertaking it (dispositional skills) as both parties learn to learn (metacognition).

De Corte's six features constantly occur and reoccur in the classrooms observed and create patterns of learning resembling Brody's transmission, transaction and transformation modes across *both* A level and GNVQ courses. Their occurrence is now illustrated in a series of vignettes selected from both A level and GNVQ.

The transmission mode at GNVQ occurred in a welding lesson that mirrored all the features that De Corte reported. The teacher explained a welding

Transmission	Epistemological Orientation Transaction	Transformation
	The nature of knowledge and knowing	
Knowledge is transmitted from the teacher or text to the student. Knowledge is static and objective and knowing is seen as closed linear paradigms. Quantity and breadth are emphasised.	Knowledge is gained through the interaction between the learner and his/her environment. Knowledge is dynamic and alive. Knowing is based on learning strategies. Quality of learning is emphasised instead of quantity.	Knowledge is dynamic, changing and it is constructed by the learner. Knowing is contextual. Formal and informal discourse are essential when building the community of learners.
	Sense of authority	
Teacher centred. Teaching is emphasised and the learner dependent on the teacher. Teacher is also responsible for the learning outcomes and the design of the learning environment.	Student centred. Learners are responsible for their own learning with the teacher. Teacher has the control of the situation but he/she is not authoritarian. Strong intrinsic motivation is empowered.	Community of learners. Visible authority does not exist. Teacher uses the power of the environment and the community when new knowledge is created/transformed. Complexity, openness and creativity are emphasised.
	Conceptions of learning	
Learning is transferring knowledge and skills from teacher to learner. Effectiveness of learning is tested in achievement tests and mastery of the content is emphasised. Learning is understood as a linear and simple action.	Learning is empowered through cooperative activities, problem solving and higher order thinking. Productive talk and positive interdependence among the students are essential characteristics of the learning process.	Learning is a change in the learner's experiences and values and the constructive, self-regulative and cooperative processes are emphasised. Learning is seen as a construction of the community of learners.

Figure 6.1 Model of three epistemological orientations

technique, demonstrated how to do it, and the students individually tried, under supervision, to do it whilst receiving feedback on whether their product was successful or not. Here the students had a goal pre-specified for them (externally regulated), in an artificial context, which did not require them to build on their existing knowledge and construct different meanings. The collaborative aspect was lacking since the teacher offered the same advice and repeated demonstrations to the students, who obviously had paid insufficient attention to the initial demonstration, and who seemed unreflective about what they were doing and why they were not doing it very well. The students, when questioned at the end of the session, regarded this form of learning as quite appropriate. They said that they had to learn this for their exam and that their teacher was teaching them new things which, given more practice, they would eventually master. Similarly, in an A level Mathematics lesson on Hooke's Law, the students received the necessary formulae and diagrams from the blackboard and the textbook and wrote them down; then the teacher rehearsed these with them by an oral question and answer session in which selected students recited the appropriate responses which were reviewed by the teacher for correctness; finally the students replicated these in the last ten minutes as they were invited to complete a further six examples from the textbook with the teacher advising, checking and clarifying individual students' work and interrupting the class to draw everyone's attention to particular points before requiring them to 'finish the examples for homework'. The students confirmed later in interview that this was a typical lesson and an acceptable approach appropriate to the subject: 'In Maths the teacher gives us examples to do and we do them because Maths is about learning rules and applying them. . . . Often you don't understand at first but then it comes – sometimes straightaway.'

In the transaction mode, a GNVQ Science lesson and an A level Business Studies lesson were observed. The GNVQ Science lesson required individual students to appear as expert witnesses in a fictitious murder trial and give scientific evidence. Each presented their evidence to the whole group (jury) and the teacher (judge) on such things as analysis of paint fragments from the car using chromatographic techniques, illustrating the material evidence as graphs on the overhead projector, stating clearly and without jargon what they set out to show and why such evidence was valid. In the A level lesson, the Business Studies students watched a BBC training video on marketing different companies' images, before going into groups to work on a number of specific questions for each group which related to the particular case study they were currently engaged with and which the teacher had written and published as part of Northumberland's Self-Supported Study Units. The students used flipcharts to present their interpretations and suggestions to the whole group. In both these lessons the agenda was set by the teachers but the case study knowledge was there to be worked on in a collaborative and co-operative way, as the Business Studies teacher said 'to get the students to do research on my research'.

In the transformation mode, a GNVQ Science and an A level English lesson can be cited. During the Science lesson the students were given the problem of solving the representation and measurement of the transfer of energy. They decided to do this by making a series of 'cars' with varying materials at the front and run them down a variable incline to crash into a fixed ramp. The whole process was filmed on video which was to be presented as evidence for their BTEC course. The teacher assessed the project, and although offered, advice was recessive throughout. In the A level English class the teacher was more than recessive. She was absent, but had got the students to work on a co-operative critical analysis of two of Dylan Thomas' poems, which fitted well into all of De Corte's criteria for good learning in the transformation mode and also for autonomous learning.

From the perspectives illustrated above it seemed appropriate to develop our own theoretical model of the teachers' and students' shifting conceptions of teaching and learning (Figure 6.2). In this model, Berliner's (1988) novices and advanced beginners could be deemed to be at GCSE level. There is some controversy over whether successful GCSE pupils have been mainly passive participants in a form of cognitive apprenticeship and following a transmission

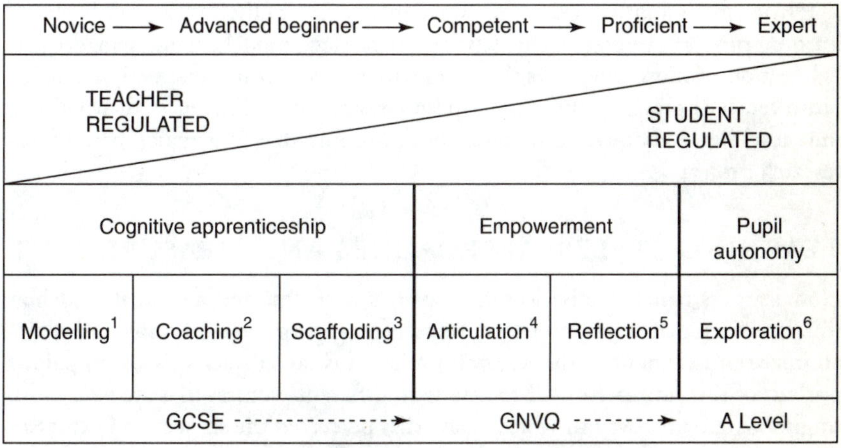

Novice ⟶ Advanced beginner ⟶ Competent ⟶ Proficient ⟶ Expert

TEACHER REGULATED					STUDENT REGULATED
Cognitive apprenticeship			Empowerment		Pupil autonomy
Modelling[1]	Coaching[2]	Scaffolding[3]	Articulation[4]	Reflection[5]	Exploration[6]
GCSE - - - - - - - - - ⟶			GNVQ - - - - - - ⟶		A Level

Figure 6.2 The shifting teaching and learning process

Notes:
1 Teacher does task, pupil observes and builds own attempts to replicate
2 Teacher observes pupil doing, and offers help and guidance (hints, reminders, feedback)
3 Teacher directly supports pupil (makes suggestions, does the bit the pupil cannot do)
4 Teacher gets pupil to articulate own knowledge and reasoning, problem solving processes (questions, talking through, criticism)
5 Teacher gets pupil to compare own processes with those of others and transfer appropriately
6 Teacher pushes students to find interesting and useful tasks, do them, understand and learn from them

regime, or whether they have been exposed to a pervasive progressivism. At this level the learners are required to observe and model themselves on what experts (teachers) do and say, relying on them for guidance (coaching and scaffolding). As they progress, the more advanced students are encouraged to engage in or find conducive problem solving tasks (reflection) and control their own problem solving strategies (articulation), in a shift to a kind of progressive learner-centred pedagogy corresponding to the transactional orientation that pervades, for example, Chorlton's advice to potential GNVQ students (Chorlton 1994: 88). Even more advanced students are encouraged to emulate the expert through the process of intellectual discipleship and to define, formulate and develop their own questions, problems and solutions in the specific domains and tracks of the academic A level courses.

The model attempts to explicate the nature of the process strategies that different students follow. In doing this, it covers the ways in which teachers organise, present and control the content and processes of learning. It encompasses both expository teaching (pre-specified outcomes determine what is and how information is received, rehearsed, recited, reviewed and replicated) and experiential learning (either in the form of open-ended self-directed discovery or as developing cultivated intelligence through guided discovery).

Obviously, as argued earlier, this conceptualisation of the shifting teaching and learning process exhibits all the deficiencies of stage models, namely inadequate delineation of those categories that are neither invariant nor distinctly exclusive. However, it is precisely this variation and degree of exclusiveness of what goes into teaching and learning in post-16 classrooms that is a major part of our research project.

LEARNING STYLES: APPROACHES AND MEASUREMENT

How learners conceptualise learning both as a process and as a goal, and how this is reflected in their preferred ways of engaging with learning tasks, was an important element in the research project. Just as various artists who paint a portrait of the same person all end up with different pictures that are clearly distinguishable by the way in which each artist perceived the subject and expressed these perceptions in the finished picture, so too it might be expected that individual students respond differently to similar as well as different teaching regimes and course requirements. The previous sections have tried to indicate the complex nature of learning styles and hinted at the difficulties of engaging with it as an area for empirical research. I now outline issues that helped to shape some of our research questions and how we tried to answer them.

Style is a stable but permeable trait (Messick 1984). What causes an individual to cling stubbornly to a way of approaching and dealing with a particular task – even if feedback shows it to be inappropriate – is hard to ascertain. That an individual's strategies may change over time because of the demands of different kinds of task is obvious; but is this done randomly or idiosyncratically, or might there be a pattern or cycle that underlies the individual's conception and execution? Messick also asserted that learning style cuts across curriculum subjects and students' ability because it is a controlling and organising mechanism that regulates impulsivity and thought when an individual is faced with responding to uncertainty and the unconventional. The potential for looking at this with the post-16 cohort is clear. Do the schools and colleges follow the rhetoric of 'separate but equal' in the way in which they screen, recruit and prepare students for the different courses and for the different subjects in those courses, and do they pay any attention to the preferred learning styles of their students – which is what GNVQ publicity seems to require? The match and mis-match between teachers' and students' learning styles can act not only as a stimulus but also as a stumbling-block to effective learning in the classroom. But do the teachers and students recognise this for what it is, and what do they do about it if they do? Do students break out of the 'learned-helplessness trap' into which they might have fallen during their previous schooling and use their learning style as a strength to be capitalised on or as a weakness that can, with sympathetic guidance, be compensated for in the new learning milieu? Also, learning styles can be linked with the recent work on mental models and the constructivist cognitive paradigm. How students incorporate their existing knowledge base into their thinking and use it to build a meaningful structure of their own that goes beyond merely copying or reproducing an externally given structure, may be linked to the novice/expert processes of retrieving appropriate knowledge, modifying it, accommodating it and then integrating it into a new schema. Although it has long been recognised that sixth-form students say that they like working independently, they find it most difficult actually to become autonomous students (Schools Council 1970). Is this because in the reality of classroom life expository teaching takes precedence over guided discovery? Do the students prefer to remain with the ready-made and undemanding conceptual model of authorised and authoritatively presented material, or do they prefer to 'risk grades for performance' and venture to engage with Brody's transformation mode? These questions helped to shape the way in which the research was planned and carried out.

To operationalise these concerns meant taking some practical matters into account. Since the research required the co-operation of schools and colleges, our methods had to be acceptable to them. We were also aware of the 'law of the instrument', which states that 'Give a small boy a hammer and he will find everything he encounters needs pounding' (Kaplan 1964: 28), and that basic fact of all research that any method we chose would provide some evidence but exclude other evidence.

Of the many instruments for measuring learning styles (for a quick review see Kyriacou *et al.* 1996), we tried out those of Gregorc, Honey and Mumford, and Riding. Ultimately, despite several reservations noted in the literature (e.g. Newstead 1992; Willcoxson and Prosser 1996), we came to agree with the view that 'Kolb's work, or work derived from it, is likely to remain at the centre of attempts to explore and develop the application of learning styles to the circumstances and context of education pre- and post-16' (Fielding 1994: 401).

Kolb's (1984) theoretical approach was developed from earlier work (Kolb and Fry 1975; Kolb *et al.* 1974) and stresses the importance of experiential learning, which is defined as 'the process whereby knowledge is created through the transmission of experience' (Kolb 1984: 38). The theory is incorporated in Kolb's (1976) Learning Styles Inventory (LSI) and draws extensively on the work of Lewin, Dewey, Jung and Piaget. Using research on left and right hemisphere dominance in the brain, Kolb maintains that knowledge comes from the ways in which individuals *perceive* or grasp experience (either concretely or abstractly) and then the ways in which individuals attempt to understand the new experience by *processing* and transforming it (either actively or reflectively). Using these two dimensions, Kolb constructed a bi-polar scale of the individual's propensities or predilections for learning in a dialectic relationship of Concrete Experience (CE) opposed to Abstract Conceptualisation (AC); Active Experimentation (AE) opposed to Reflective Observation (RO) (Figure 6.3). These concepts have often been seen, in commonsense terms, to apply to the ways in which post-16 learning is viewed across the academic–vocational divide – albeit perhaps crudely and as stereotypes. A levels are commonly represented as entailing the acquisition of lots of abstract concepts, all of which require careful observation and reflective thought to transform these into understanding. On the other hand, GNVQs have often been represented as concerned with actual 'real' experiences (Norwood's 'concrete' experiences) and using them to do or make things.

According to Kolb, effective learning follows a cyclical process (CE $\rightarrow$ RO $\rightarrow$ AC $\rightarrow$ AE). However, he maintains that it is not always necessary to start at the beginning of the cycle. Individuals may start at any point in the cycle and indeed meander between stages. What is not conceded is that effective learning requires the learner to encompass *all* of the four inter-related stages, because each offers particular demands and opportunities that continue upwards in a spiral developmental process. Even if an individual's preferred style of working favours a particular stage, it is incumbent on that individual to incorporate the others at some point for effective learning to take place.

Kolb's LSI, in which the learners rank a series of adjectives, measures the emphasis an individual places on each mode (CE, RO, AC, AE), as well as two combined scores indicating their stress on abstractness over concrete (AC – CE) and action over reflection (AE – RO). These latter scores, plotted as a single point on the two axes, indicate the individual's preferred learning style (Diverger, Assimilator, Converger, Accommodator). Kolb indicates the strengths and weaknesses of the particular attributes that are associated with each stage or sector of the learning cycle (see Fielding 1994 for lists of descriptors of these), and the teacher and learner should be aware of these for effective learning to take place. When reporting back to schools and their pupils about preferred learning

Knowledge results from gaining and transforming experiences

1   Gaining experience

    Through immediate   ⟵—————⟶   Through indirect
    Concrete Experience   *Abstract* Conceptualisation

2   Transforming gained experience

    Through *Active*   ⟵—————⟶   Through *Reflective*,
    Experimentation   thoughtful Observation

3   'Learning styles' are shown as a combination of preferences on these two axes:

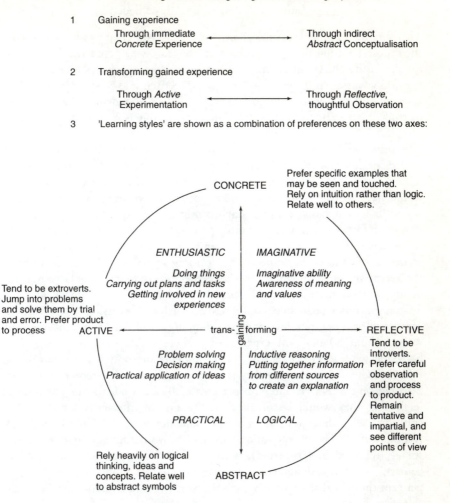

Figure 6.3 Kolb summarised

styles, we translated the above results and converted Kolb's descriptors into more commonly used terms, so that Kolb's 'Accommodators' became 'Enthusiasts'; 'Convergers' became 'Practical'; 'Assimilators' became 'Logical'; and Divergers became 'Imaginative'.

LEARNING STYLES AND PREFERENCES

It was with the issues raised earlier that we approached the series of related research questions listed at the beginning of the chapter, to which we now turn.

Are students' preferred learning styles associated with whether they are pursuing a GNVQ or an A level course?

This section examines empirical evidence of, first, what students expected their post-16 education would be like; second, what students reported it is like using ALIS questionnaires and also questionnaires derived from the ALIS work; third, what we saw pupils getting and what they and their teachers said they were getting; and finally, how the evidence above is linked to students' preferred learning styles, in so far as this is measured by the Kolb LSI.

A survey of 759 students going on to a tertiary college showed widespread agreement that they expected that their post-16 studies would be more informal, relaxed but harder (Bloomer and Morgan 1993). They anticipated that they would have to take more responsibility for their own learning, because there would be an emphasis on independent study, group work and discussion, and that the BTEC courses would be more practical. The study found a statistically significant difference between those going on to A levels and those to BTEC courses over whether they expected the learning activities of the courses to be in the 'receptive' mode (instructed by the teacher, dictation, learning facts, remembering, repetition, revision and being lectured rather than taught), and the 'interactive' mode (experimentation, research, debate, discussion, interpretation, exercise of own opinion, own analysis, 'thinking for ourselves' and independent work). About 50 per cent expected that there would be a combination of both; but while 21.5 per cent of A level students and only 6.8 per cent of the BTEC students thought that they would be subjected to a 'receptive' regime, 29.3 per cent of A level and 42.3 per cent of BTEC students thought it more likely that they would be involved in the sort of interactive activities that coincided with those learning strategies laid down in the BTEC handbook (BTEC 1993). These expectations are in line with findings from the ALIS survey (reported in Chapter 3), where of 1,856 students following GNVQ courses, 84 per cent thought that the courses would be more interesting and 54 per cent thought that they were not good at exams and that coursework would suit them better.

ALIS questionnaire results provide the largest database of reported teaching and learning experiences and clearly show that the students' perceptions of their learning experiences differ in the following respects. In GNVQ classes the students report that their lessons rely heavily on making use of IT (computers); using teacher-prepared handouts, working in pairs or small groups; working on assignments by making notes and preparing reports; engaging in discussion – either as a class or as a group; researching individual aspects of the prescribed unit; and deciding for themselves what to do, how to do it and when to do it. They report that they do very little practical work (using apparatus or making things), producing original work or receiving help from business or industry. Using Brody's classification, these GNVQ students do seem to conform broadly, if perhaps somewhat weakly, to the 'transaction' mode. Students from A level classes report that they all work on the same thing at the same time, and are told by the teacher what to do, how to do it and when to do it. They rarely use IT or present work to the class. (There are, however, differences between A level subject practices which are reported later.) Here the A level students appear to be saying that they do not fit in with Brody's 'transformation' mode and that they work in classes where the 'transmission' procedures previously criticised by several HMI reports still hold sway.

To the extent that these responses represent vocational and academic courses, they indicate differences between A level and GNVQ classrooms, particularly in respect of developing core skills through using IT; presenting work to the class; and the prescription of tasks, and how and when these are carried out. There are similarities over teacher feedback on individual progress, and how this relates to the assessment requirements.

Classroom observation, from the Noldus Observer programme developed by Nick Meagher (Chapter 4) and from retrospectively coding less structured observational records, show a high frequency of apparently didactic methods in *both* A level and GNVQ classes (Figures 6.4 and 6.5). They also indicate, however, some educationally significant differences. IT was used far more frequently in GNVQ classes, as was students' presentation of work to their fellows. A level students were likely to be working on the same topic at the same time, and to have the nature and timing of the task closely prescribed. GNVQ students were likely to be working on different topics and to have more control over pacing of their work. In A level classes, the relatively restricted range of learning activities was dominated by teacher exposition, teacher-directed question and answer exchanges, and student note taking (again, teacher directed). The much wider range of activities engaged in by GNVQ students included, with greatest frequency, being 'helped' by the teacher either individually or in a group; working on individual assignments, often in a group though more rarely as a group, and using IT; and being off task, both in and out of the classroom. GNVQ classes often included short bursts of formal teaching similar to that more frequently employed in A level. They were used to introduce a new unit and the criteria for assessing it, to cover the information needed for the end-tests of underpinning knowledge, to satisfy the teacher that 'real' learning was taking place, or to remind students that they were still working within a framework of disciplined learning.

It is worth taking this last point, about 'classroom teaching in GNVQ lessons', further. Meagher's observations of a series of classes taking Advanced GNVQ Business Year 13, suggested that two distinctive patterns were present, both sometimes appearing in the same lesson. Pattern A was where the teacher 'teaches a lesson' and knowledge is 'transmitted' to 'receptive' students. Pattern B was where the students 'work on their assignments' to produce evidence for assessment, and are involved in a more 'transactional' or 'interactive' mode.

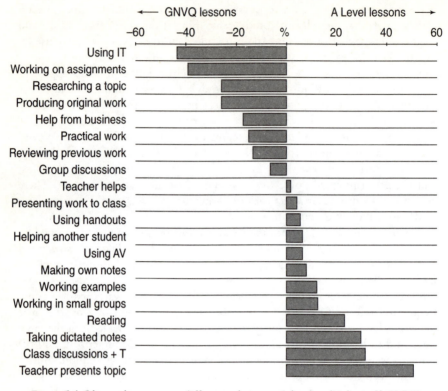

Figure 6.4 Observed percentage differences between A level and Advanced GNVQ
activities

Pattern A involved the presentation of a topic by the teacher and some follow-up work for students to complete in class. None of De Corte's features of 'good learning' seemed to be present. The teacher presentation usually showed a marked absence of the question and answer session normally associated with teacher presentations. Completing work in the class was a commonly observed feature of GNVQ work. Whether this was a feature of the students having access to IT only in class time, or whether it was an expectation of teachers and students that work, and therefore learning, took place only in classrooms, and by implication under supervision, is open to speculation. What is not speculative is that completing work on their own, in their own time, was a commonly accepted expectation observed and reported by A level students. Whether this implied that A level students were expected to work independently and develop by 'transformation' their intellectual skills, or whether this was a way of coping with an overloaded content and a shortage of time (A level students usually follow three subjects, whilst GNVQ students follow one course, representing the equivalent of two A levels) is open to speculation. But the principle was fully accepted by the students.

A Level subjects

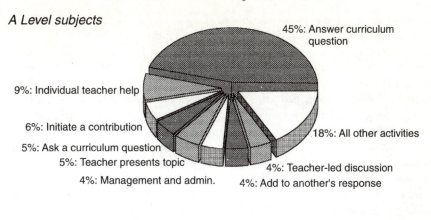

45%: Answer curriculum question

9%: Individual teacher help

6%: Initiate a contribution

5%: Ask a curriculum question

5%: Teacher presents topic

4%: Management and admin.

18%: All other activities

4%: Teacher-led discussion

4%: Add to another's response

GNVQ subjects

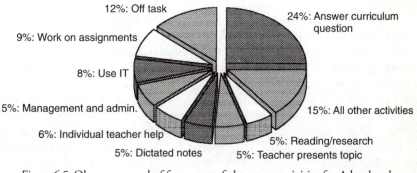

12%: Off task

9%: Work on assignments

8%: Use IT

5%: Management and admin.

6%: Individual teacher help

5%: Dictated notes

24%: Answer curriculum question

15%: All other activities

5%: Reading/research

5%: Teacher presents topic

Figure 6.5 Observer record of frequency of classroom activities for A level and Advanced GNVQ subjects

We come to school to socialise – to meet friends and have a good laugh – and we do most of our work at home in the evenings. They (GNVQ students) come to school to work. They are always sitting at their computers. We never do that.

(A level student)

Pattern B, where the students work independently on their assignments, usually meant they spontaneously formed loose aggregates or small groups, with the teacher spending more or less equal time with each group. Meagher observed the extent to which group members worked collaboratively on task in groups or worked in groups but as individuals. For many classes, it has to be said, the social emphasis outweighed the focus on work, and a different version of De Corte's collaborative learning occurred more frequently in GNVQ classes. Another activity of particular importance in the GNVQ rhetoric is about the presentation

143

of work by small groups of students to the rest of the class, because it should benefit the motivation and Value Added outcomes for the students doing it. Observation of the GNVQ class mentioned above revealed that even Year 13 students do not automatically make good teachers. Although the process of collaboratively preparing a presentation may well produce the intended outcomes noted above, delivering it can present a considerable strain on both the presenters and the audience. Both have strategies in place to mitigate the more negative effects. Particularly fearful presenters turned up without their notes or, in the case of one student, did not turn up at all. The audience, in some cases perhaps mindful that they themselves would soon be presenters, tended to be acquiescent. Students who had already made their presentations and could be inclined to mischief were often controlled more by peer pressure than teacher intervention. The role of the teacher during presentations was particularly interesting. The opportunity to act as 'benign expert' or even 'mentor' to absolute beginners is one that, although frequently wished for, comes very rarely to a busy classroom teacher. With the audience in self-regulatory mode, these sessions can be extremely and sometimes surprisingly rewarding for the teacher.

I turn now to the students' preferred learning styles. Those surveyed by Bloomer and Morgan stated an overall preference for interactive activities (50 per cent) far more frequently than they did for receptive activities (21 per cent), with 29 per cent preferring a combination of both. There was, however, no statistically significant difference between the preferences expressed by intending A level students and their BTEC counterparts. However, when compared with their expectations, both groups of students' preferences were stronger for interactive (transactional and transforming) learning opportunities, particularly so for the A level students; and whilst the proportion of intending A level students' preferences matched the proportion who expected receptive learning activities, there was a significant number of BTEC students who preferred receptive (transmission) teaching. It is interesting to record that the results from the Kolb Learning Style Inventory given to 214 GNVQ and 187 A level students support Bloomer and Morgan's findings, and are presented in Figure 6.6.

The graphs appear to indicate that individual preferences are widely dispersed, but there is a discernible difference between the preferences of those A level and GNVQ students in our overall sample. When individual class preferences were plotted, there was a more striking difference, as is shown for the A level Physics and the GNVQ Business classes shown in Figure 6.7. Whether this difference is associated with different courses or with different subjects requires deeper and more extensive attention than we were able to bring to it.

The four sectors of the main charts were also plotted separately as bar charts to bring out the proportional differences in how the A level and GNVQ students responded to Kolb's main constructs of gaining and handling information (Figure 6.8). Although both groups prefer to obtain information more

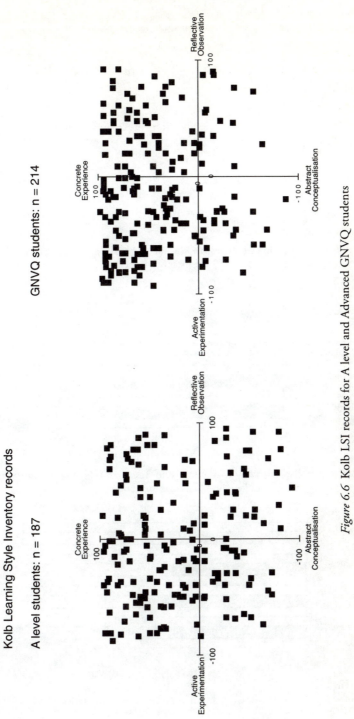

Figure 6.6 Kolb LSI records for A level and Advanced GNVQ students

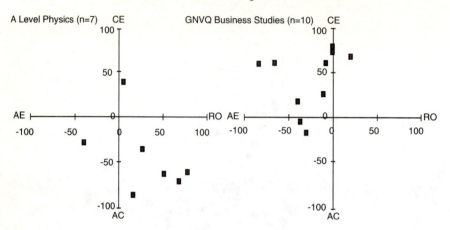

Figure 6.7 Kolb LSI records for an A level Physics and an Advanced
GNVQ Business Studies class

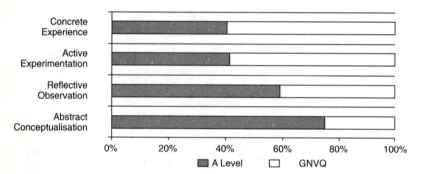

Figure 6.8 Bar charts showing how A level and Advanced GNVQ students prefer to
gain and handle information

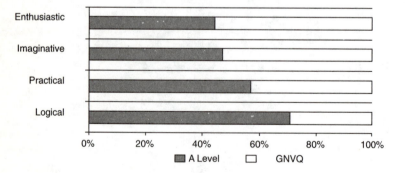

Figure 6.9 Bar charts showing different preferred learning styles of A level and
Advanced GNVQ students

146

through Concrete Experience than Abstract Conceptualisation, GNVQ students seemed to dislike the latter, and so may be unlikely to benefit from being asked to undertake individual research. A level students who would are not required to. This is an important interpretation of the data, which is further substantiated in a later section of the chapter.

Both groups are fairly evenly balanced between Imaginative and Practical learners, with a slight tendency to the Imaginative. A level students, however, tend more to Logical learning preferences, whilst GNVQ students tend towards the Enthusiastic dimension. A level students appear to enjoy planning, creating mental models, defining problems and developing theories – although in many A level lessons these are not required for assessment purposes. In GNVQ lessons, where these qualities most definitely are required, few students prefer to learn in these ways. They prefer to operate by getting things done, taking risks and accepting the first solution that comes along (Figure 6.9).

Are there links between learning styles and subjects studied for A level and GNVQ?

Crowther's 'subject minded specialist' is firmly entrenched in the post-16 system. The dominance in A levels of the top ten subjects, in the related cognate groups of Arts and Sciences, is well known and firmly entrenched. It has recently become more common for students to combine subjects from different areas and for large numbers of students to take relatively new subjects that usually bear the cryptic label 'Studies'. The introduction of GNVQ has accelerated this trend. The result is that there has developed a kind of commonsense grouping of students by their course and subject(s) that implies particular 'types of mind'.

Ramsden reports research evidence that students

> have implicit theories about how subject specialities impose constraints on learning strategies. To oversimplify the findings somewhat, science and arts students have consistent views about the types of learning these two broadly defined subject areas demand; they also agree on what the differ-ences are. Learning tasks in science are typically described as hierarchical, logical, heterogeneous, and rule and procedure governed; humanities and social science tasks are seen to require interpretation, comparison, generalisation and self-direction.
>
> (Ramsden 1988: 173)

These descriptors fit well with those of Kolb's styles. Furthermore, if learning strategies are context dependent, do different approaches differ in different subject specialisms *and* across the academic/vocational domains? For example, some science tasks initially concentrate on technique and concrete procedural details (surface approach), whilst in the humanities the students seem more likely to be thrown in at the deep end where they are required to reinterpret material in a personal way. So, there may be conflict as the learning demands of

147

certain activities change as the students progress through a particular sequence, or as the students' preferences change over the two-year course, that would be valuable to explore.

Student preferences can be illustrated by examining two subjects that are often associated with each other across the A level and GNVQ line – Business Studies (at both A level and GNVQ) and Economics (A level only) (Figure 6.10). The A level students preferred a very traditional approach to learning – teacher presenting material and information, talking about it with them and illustrating it by getting them to do examples/exercises and make their own notes. They did not like dictated notes, presenting their own work or listening to others, using IT or reading. The GNVQ students preferred working in pairs/groups, following the teacher's presentation, doing exercises and practical work and using IT. They certainly did not like presenting their work to the class, or to a lesser extent reading or writing.

ALIS evidence has shown differences between A level subjects of the reported frequency of learning activities that seem to support the proposition that 'how

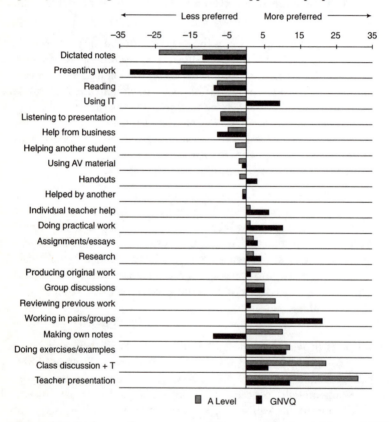

Figure 6.10 Student preferences compared between A level and Advanced GNVQ Business Studies

you teach depends on what you teach' (Fitz-Gibbon and Wright 1995a: 7). However, the predominance of those activities that are teacher-directed or teacher led appears to depart somewhat from the vaunted notions of independent and self-reliant activities traditionally associated with the post-16 stage. Taking together Science and Mathematics and contrasting them for the frequency of reported occurrence (routine or very frequent) with Humanities and Languages, a reanalysis of ALIS data (Figure 6.11) shows that in Science lessons there is a preponderance of working examples, and the teacher presenting material/information which the students take down as notes; whereas in the Humanities there is a lot of talk and discussion, using the teachers prepared handouts and making notes (see Frank Hardman's account of similarities and differences between English Language and Literature in Chapter 5). All these features, empirically derived, tie in with Ramsden's (1988) points made earlier about Arts/Science pedagogy.

Within the same curriculum area, Business Studies and Economics, can be seen clearly the students' reported different approaches to learning of GNVQ and A level courses (Figure 6.12).

Kolb (1984: 124) maintained that his research showed that the two main dimensions on which his theory of experiential learning was based were linked to the structure of different 'fields of enquiry'. On the gaining experience

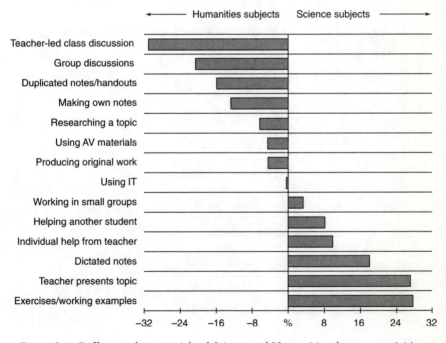

Figure 6.11 Differences between A level Science and Humanities classroom activities as reported by students

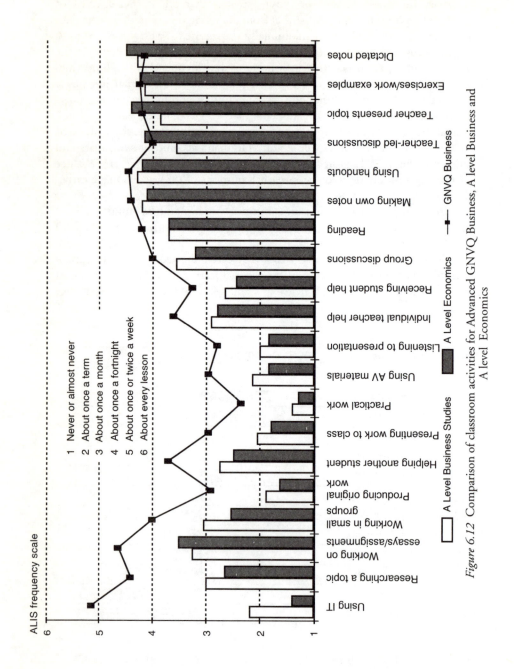

ALIS frequency scale

1 Never or almost never
2 About once a term
3 About once a month
4 About once a fortnight
5 About once or twice a week
6 About every lesson

■ GNVQ Business
■ A Level Economics
□ A Level Business Studies

Figure 6.12 Comparison of classroom activities for Advanced GNVQ Business, A level Business and A level Economics

dimension, Concrete Experience (CE) was associated with 'qualitative human-istic' enquiry, whilst the Abstract Conceptual (AC) dimension was associated with 'quantitative scientific' enquiry. On the transformation axis, Reflective Observation (RO) related to 'basic' enquiry and Active Experimentation (AE) to 'applied' methods. Furthermore, Kolb showed that the quadrants in the learning cycle closely corresponded to branches of study undertaken by undergraduates. So, for instance, the Divergers (Imaginative) were more likely to be Humanities and Social Science students; Assimilators (Logical) to be Natural Science and Mathematics students; Convergers (Practical) to be science-based professions, such as engineers; and Accommodators (Enthusiastic) to be associated with social professions and business. There is research evidence to support this categori-sation, so that it goes beyond commonsense stereotyping. In an earlier study, Wankowksi (1974) questioned university students about the prevailing patterns of subject teaching and learning that they had experienced in their sixth form, and their preference for active or passive methods. 'Humanities biased' (English, Languages and Geography) students significantly preferred and experienced more active styles of teaching and learning, whilst 'Science biased' (Mathematics, Physics and Chemistry) students preferred and experienced the 'one way' method of tuition. He also detected that 'the personality traits of extroversion and introversion seem to have a bearing on preference for methods of study and tuition' (1974: 58). These are the very factors associated with Kolb's dimensions of Active Experimentation and Reflective Observation. More recently, Burns *et al.* (1991) investigated sixth form students' understanding of learning Chemistry and found that 'in science subjects the acquisition of knowledge plays an important role because of the specialised terms and concepts involved' (1991: 285). Furthermore, the work of Tillema (1995) has shown that any reconstruct-ing of knowledge places a high premium upon the traits of 'accommodation' or adaptation rather than 'assimilation' or absorption of existing knowledge structures – or in other words, active rather than passive learning in the ways described earlier in this chapter.

Evidence from students' responses to the Kolb LSI showed overall a very loose connection between preference for learning activities and the subjects studied. This may be because students frequently crossed the Arts/Science divisions at A level. Many students at A level now study a kind of random *à la carte* curriculum, rather than the set Arts/Science *table d'hôte*, where they pick-and-mix subjects either out of a genuinely diverse interest in them or because they are counselled into taking three subjects – and subjects that will fit into the sixth form timetable – when they would prefer to take perhaps only two subjects. Nevertheless, there was some association for the Science cohort in the GNVQ study of FE colleges conducted by Meagher. Here, whilst the thirty-four students diverged equally on the transformation (extrovert–introvert) dimension, there was a definite trend towards the Abstract Conceptual end of the grasping experience continuum (twenty-two out of the thirty-four), which supports Kolb's claims noted earlier (Figure 6.13).

GNVQ Science students: n = 34   Science staff n: = 3

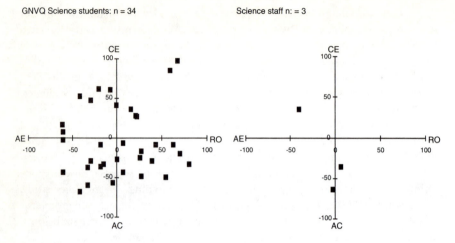

Figure 6.13 Advanced GNVQ Science FE cohort of staff and students' learning style practices

In certain individual classes there were close associations of students all favouring a particular learning style (for example, see Figure 6.7 for the A level Physics class and the GNVQ Business Studies class). Observation and interviews revealed a coherence and goal-directed focus of these classes that was appropriate for both learning activity and social atmosphere. Whether this led to over-dependence on one particular style of learning, to the exclusion of other valuable activities that Kolb stresses are part of the whole learning cycle, is difficult to ascertain with any degree of reliability, given our limited observation period, but is a question raised and examined later.

Whether learning styles assist with transfer of learning

In a sense, transfer is the holy grail of educators.

> Everybody believes in transfer. We believe that through experience in learning we get better at learning. . . . When one has acquired knowledge in one setting, it should save time and perhaps increase effectiveness for future learning in related stages. Transfer means applying old knowledge in a setting sufficiently novel that it also requires new knowledge.
>
> (Larkin 1989: 283–284)

The assumption is that problems occur in different settings, and that the mastery of a general set of principles in abstract terms 'automatically apply irrespective of context' (Saljo and Wyndham 1990: 245). Consequently, *metacognition*, a term introduced by Flavell (1976) to include how students know and monitor their conceptions of learning and their learning processes, is an important element of transfer, and increasingly explicit attention is being

152

given to transferable skills at A level (see Chapter 2). However, research into the problem of what competencies transfer between particular situations leaves the problem 'largely unsolved' (Saljo and Wyndham). The notion that transferable knowledge is a core of general problem solving skills has also been found to be 'historically unproductive' (Larkin). Similarly, Hennessy, McCormick and Murphy (1993), using Technology as an obvious area to which students are expected to transfer concepts from other subject areas, found little empirical justification for transfer taking place.

Part of the problem might be that 'flexible adaptation', as transfer is sometimes called, where students engage in 'near' transfer (knowledge from one context being applied to a similar context) and 'far' transfer (to dissimilar areas), requires the student to respond to anomalous data and contradictory information. These features form the very essence of the models of 'transformation' learning developed earlier in the chapter. Drawing on a wide range of studies about how scientists and science students respond to anomalous data, Chinn and Brewer (1993) argue that logically there are seven forms of response for a student who currently holds one theory and encounters data that cannot be explained by it. Only one response – accepting the data and changing the old theory, possibly in favour of a new one – they argue will lead to real learning or cognitive restructuring. Other, more common, responses suggest that the anomalous data could be ignored, rejected, excluded as irrelevant, held in abeyance, reinterpreted in terms of the existing theory, or have peripheral changes made to it. In other words, 'considerable effort is necessary to create the possibilities of restructuring knowledge in the face of experience' (Deforges 1995: 391), particularly if the new experience lacks the credibility of coming from an authoritative source such as the classteacher. If the potential rewards for transferring and transforming knowledge are not judged to be worth the effort, because the 'old' prior knowledge has proved rewarding in the past, then students will be tempted to settle for targets perhaps below their potential. In post-16 courses and their assessment procedures, however, a high priority is given in the GNVQ courses to developing transferable process skills in three critical areas that are supposed to lead to independent learning; but in separate A level subjects, little if any credit is given for making connections between subjects.

Our classroom observations showed that the Chinn and Brewer strategies were a common feature of life in post-16 classrooms, and that these are linked to Kolb's theories of experiential learning. Transfer means moving between the qualitatively different sectors of learning that feature in the Kolb cycle, particularly in the incorporation of diametrically opposed sectors, with their respective profiles of strengths and weaknesses. Thus a strong Converger (Practical) would benefit from paying more attention to some of the features associated with a strong Diverger (Imaginative).

Accretion, or encoding information in terms of existing schemata, is rather similar to the Piagetian concept of assimilation. Assimilators, according to Kolb, are likely to prefer engaging with theoretical models, inductive reasoning and logical explanations. As we have seen earlier, some Science and Mathematics lessons, both GNVQ and A level, followed this pattern if only because the theorists, teachers and students agreed that the acquisition of specialised terms and concepts was a necessary condition for successful performance. Transfer is not seen as an issue, as competence in Mathematics is usually a precondition of the course. ALIS (1995) data shows that Mathematics and Science are 'hard' subjects in the assessment stakes, and the message of working hard seems to be a commonly acceptable condition to staff and students. This is not to say that all the lessons observed were of this kind, and one could pick out the Physics teacher who taught both GNVQ Science and also A level Physics – but A level Physics following the principles of the Advanced Physics Project for Independent Learning (APPIL), which went further than passive transmission.

Transfer through restructuring and tuning is similar to the Piagetian concept of accommodation. This is a state of mind that allows for existing knowledge to be related to existing schemata and actively adapted. Kolb's Accommodators (Enthusiasts), that is those who score highly on the active and concrete dimensions, are supposed to prefer getting involved in new experiences and enthusiastically adapt to them, as they intuitively transfer what they know already. In theory, they are actively enthusiastic extroverts. In practice, the GNVQ students especially were, as noted earlier, often actively engaged in the sense that they were required to get on with a job of work (completing portfolios) that had been closely prescribed by their course outlines, and enthusiastic about doing something that they saw as occupationally related but that allowed for informal social interaction. Whether they transferred what they already knew, and how extensive this was, is difficult to ascertain because transfer is an on-going part of the learning process and not a specific event. Where it was an event, as in a GNVQ class of Health & Social Care students who mainly preferred to operate in Kolb's Accommodation (Enthusiastic) style, the research methods element was taught by a Sociology teacher in a separately time-tabled lesson. The integration of research skills into a Health & Social Care context became secondary to mastering (passing the end of unit test) a series of remotely presented basic skills necessary only for further progression.

In A level classes observed, the Accommodators (Enthusiasts) and Assimilators (Logical) engaged only implicitly with core skills. It was generally assumed and accepted by both the teacher and the students that the requisite generic skills were already in place as mental maps from which the students would draw upon as required. Specific lessons on developing and transferring generic core skills were often said to be covered in the General Studies course, in which all students were supposed to participate, but in practice A level students were mainly exposed only briefly to generic skills in sporadic outbursts in their separate subject lessons. It seemed that both staff and students accorded low priority to fostering transfer, and most regarded generic skills at best as distractions from the main business and at worst a waste of time.

Turning now to the other opposite sectors in Kolb's learning cycle – the Convergers (Practical) and the Divergers (Imaginative) – it might be expected that Convergers with their predilection for pragmatic activities would be readily involved in transfer within and between domains, whilst the Divergers with their tendency to favour imaginative activities might be particularly susceptible to transfer in the form of analogies and metaphors.

The A level Convergers' attitudes towards transfer may be illustrated from the comments of a student doing – in his order of preference – Physics, Mathematics and Chemistry. He was a very able student aiming to take up a place at a prestigious university to study Physics and said that he was good at Physics because he was good at Mathematics. He described transfer as exercising mental muscles built upon a hard mathematical base. Whilst expecting to achieve an 'A' grade in Chemistry, he regarded it as a 'boring subject because it is all about learning lists, formulae and things . . . Even the practicals don't stretch you like the Physics . . . Anyway Chemistry stinks!' A GNVQ Business student who was a clear Converger thought that transfer came into his studies only incidentally from other subjects and not from the core skills from the GNVQ course:

> I was thinking about doing an A level in Geography. I suppose it's linked to Business Studies through the economic side of Geography and also in the work outside school – like field work and project work. We had to do a survey in our GCSE Geography and in Business Studies we do the same sort of thing. . . . Yes, I think they have a lot in common besides this as well.

Divergers' attitudes to transfer can also be illustrated by student interviews. An able A level student of English, History and French commented on how she saw that English and History were linked in substance and method:

> In both we have to write a lot, but differently. Also both require us to read a lot, but it's a different kind of reading. In History it's facts and judgements, and in English it's life and feelings that have to be weighed up and interpreted. So in both your opinions count for a lot – but you have to back them up with lots of quotes and references. As Mr X (the History teacher) says we have 'got to climb over the wall of facts' and make up our own minds. . . . It's interpretation in both, but different interpretation although sometimes it's similar, that gets the good marks.

These comments from A level students are in direct contrast to those of a GNVQ student who, although she eventually passed her Health & Social Studies course, found it rather

> Heavy going with all that filling up of files we have to do. . . . There's a lot of copying, and it feels like cheating; but if that's what they want us to do then it's up to us to get on with it. I want to be a nursery nurse when I leave and I can't see the point of all this writing.

Here, for this student, transfer was naïvely taken literally. Copying and writing were not appealing, which is perhaps why she appeared more towards the active end of the transforming continuum on the Kolb scale, but she was prepared to stick with it, conforming to the pattern of Entwistle's (1994) surface learner with a strategic orientation.

The learning style cycle and the shift from teaching to learning

Kolb's work implies a shift from teaching to self-regulated learning. Gibbs, in a strong endorsement of that experiential approach, maintains that

> If it is intended that behaviour should be changed by learning it is not simply sufficient to learn new concepts and develop new generalisations. This learning must be tested out in new situations. The learner must make the link between theory and action by planning for action, carrying it out, and then reflecting upon it, relating what happens back to theory. It is not enough just to do, nor is it enough just to think. Learning from experience must involve links between doing and thinking.
>
> (Gibbs 1988: 38)

The implication is that there is a link between preference for knowing how and knowing that, because the one can sometimes be used to interrogate the other. This inter-relationship between *all* stages in a structured sequence is a central tenet in Kolb's theory of the experiential learning cycle. He also argues that 'Even a totally balanced profile is not necessarily best. The key to effective learning is being competent in each mode when it is appropriate' (Kolb *et al*. 1971: 29). To test this assertion we decided to examine the outliers, or those students whose scores on the LSI placed them towards the outer edges of the graph. It seemed reasonable to assume that extreme preference for one particular style might be to the detriment of three others. In one of the schools, eight students with extreme scores (four from each of the A level and GNVQ groups) were identified, observed in lessons and interviewed. They were also included in a 'triadic sort' whereby three names were picked at random and the teachers were asked to form two groups: one group to include two individuals who were alike, leaving one who was different from the other two. Each of the teachers was then asked what criteria they had used to arrange the students. In all respects the results were inconclusive. Perhaps the numbers of students involved were too small for patterns to emerge, or perhaps the LSI was insensitive to the changing and developing nature of the students at various contextually specific stages of their courses. So to test the stability over time of the LSI, a group of twelve GNVQ Health & Social Care students were measured on two separate occasions six months apart. All firmly remained on the Concrete (CE) dimension, with ten moving to a more extreme position and further away from the Abstract (AC) dimension. Also all of them moved further towards the extremes of the Active (AE) dimension, with three crossing over from the Diverger (Imaginative) to the

Accommodator (Enthusiastic) quadrant. These moves, even from such a small group, might indicate that students' preferred learning styles had changed during their course and that they had adapted to the style and ethos of the course they were following and also to the preferred style of their teacher. These particular students had moved from a rather tentative and unsure stance to a more confident position that, from observation, had unconsciously taken on the features of a continental vocational training programme called Leittext. This is designed to stimulate novices to learn in an active way by attempting to increase their independence and self-regulation in executing tasks and solving problems, and corresponds very closely to the 'Transaction' mode of learning discussed earlier (pp. 132–4).

A further question can be raised about Kolb's central tenet that effective learning requires the learner to follow an ordered cyclical sequence. So why students choose to take up a particular stance; how they cope with it when it matches the style of the teacher or is appropriate to the task, or not as the case may be; and why and when the students choose to move around the cycle during the course of their studies becomes relevant for the actual conduct of teaching and the learning as experienced by post-16 students.

To illustrate this in practice, the learning preferences of a class of GNVQ Business students can be examined and related to a series of lessons observed by Meagher. This is a group of mainly 'enthusiastic' learners, who preferred to obtain experience through Concrete Experience and deal with it by means of Active Experimentation, and as such are fairly typical of GNVQ students observed during the project. In a series of lessons observed, the Concrete Experience is the teacher's monologue, to which the students responded rather well. Although around half of them usually took no formal part in the question and answer session, there was a general hum of *sotto voce* comment and good humour. Clearly both the class and the teacher felt that this was the way in which the lessons should be conducted. Then the teacher would direct them to the next stage, which would normally be Active Experimentation, that is using the information gained and responding in a practical way. Typically, on an A level course, this might involve the completion of a worksheet or a set of exercises. In GNVQ, however, the next stage would involve individual research into the topic; this in turn would demand the exercise of a degree of Abstract Conceptualisation, handling symbols, words and numbers. This is clearly not within the preferred learning style of most GNVQ students, bearing in mind the sort of selection and enrolment procedures mentioned previously.

Ironically, a skilful teacher could, of course, lead students through a passage of reflection followed by a period of information gathering from abstract sources, to arrive at a point where Active Experimentation completed Kolb's learning cycle. In the GNVQ system, however, to do so would deny the students the opportunity of obtaining a distinction grade, which the teacher of these series of lessons outlined to a student during an individual review session

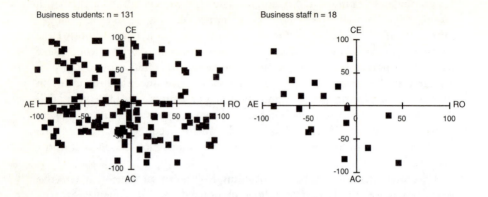

Figure 6.14 Learning preferences of Advanced GNVQ Business students

For a distinction you must be able to say, 'I understand; I have found the information; I have completed the work'; for a merit grade you have to say, 'I don't understand, and I have asked for help'; for a pass grade you say, 'I had the information provided.'

Furthermore, the gathering of information through a research programme and the presentation of the results is all that is subsequently demanded by the course. These GNVQ students know perfectly well that they will not be required to establish a small business in Italy, nor will successfully completing the course lead to their being asked to do so by a prospective employer. The learning cycle stops, as it must, with 'The preparation of a feasibility study for a British company wishing to sell a specific product in a specific European country' (BTEC: GNVQ3 Business Unit No. U1016531). Unfortunately, that is exactly what this group of learners is unable to do without a great deal of help, and this help is not forthcoming. Surely one of the most common procedures in real life if one does not know the way is to ask somebody who does! It would appear that not only is it possible to select optional units in GNVQ Business Studies, which depend for their satisfactory completion on students learning in ways that rely heavily on abstract conceptual thinking, but that the assessment requirements may inhibit the teachers from adopting their usual practices of providing much-needed assistance. If this is the case, then this particular group of active learners may not respond too well during those parts of the lessons set aside for them to work on their assignments.

Subsequent observation bore this out and showed that the students were uncomfortable with having to work like this. For example, an annotated summary of a typical lesson for this group revealed that after the first three minutes of the lesson, during which the teacher engaged in routine administrative tasks before going on to present the topic and review previous work, the students were told to work on their assignments for the rest of the lesson. The students then formed loosely coupled groups, membership of which was distinctly fluid, whilst the teacher circulated for a short time before leaving the room. Individual students used computer stations to copy from books, and less motivated students dropped off task and even out of the classroom. Of those that remained, the less socially accomplished students wandered between individuals and groups in an unhelpful way. 'It is difficult to detect learning' (field note).

To sum up, learning rarely followed that cycle of activity in which Concrete Experience (very common in our observations) was followed by Reflective Observation (extremely rare in our observations) before leading to Abstract Conceptualisation and further Active Experimentation. Instead, A level students tended to move 'backwards' (anti-clockwise) to Active Experimentation, where activity predominated and experimentation was less obviously present. On the other hand, GNVQ students tended to move 'forwards', missing out the Reflective Observation stage, and going straight to Abstract Conceptualisation, in so far as this concept describes their subsequent immersion in the portfolios of evidence where work is more apparent than learning (Doyle 1983). So, from the Kolb perspective, the most common sequence in both A level and GNVQ classes – where the teacher presents and demonstrates, followed by the students doing what they have been told or shown – seems largely to miss out the Reflective Observation stage unless, perhaps along with the teachers, one assumes that the students do this whilst being talked to or shown something.

The teachers' preferred learning styles and the students' learning processes

There is extensive evidence of teachers' devotion to the 'practicality ethic' of getting things to work in classrooms. 'Work' is a dominant word used both by teachers and students; 'learning' is rarely referred to. As Nisbet and Shucksmith pointed out in their empirical study

> Many children seemed blissfully unaware that there *was* any procedure at all in learning. They did what was required of them – or rather what they thought the teacher wanted: teachers teach and as a result students learn. Even where children did demonstrate some sophistication in their metacognitive knowledge they often showed little evidence of putting these procedures into action when faced with the demands of tasks set by their teachers. A classic case of production deficiency? Or were the children just being wiser than us in realising that classroom tasks are most efficiently performed and best rewarded by using the least sophisticated strategies geared to following instructions and getting finished in good time?
>
> (Nisbet and Shucksmith 1984: 6)

Although teachers can be dominant, recessive or even (sometimes) absent, they undoubtedly leave their imprint on the classroom milieu. Kolb (1976: 32) claims that 'there is a strong similarity between the student's learning style and that of the teacher who influenced him'. However, the extent to which the teachers' preferred styles of learning influence the students' learning experiences is not easy to assess. Certainly teachers do have preferred teaching strategies, either implicitly or explicitly acknowledged (Figure 6.15). It is clear that these strategies are driven by pedagogical considerations as well as by curriculum requirements.

To take an example, the Observer record was used in over thirty-two hours of A level classes in Biology, Business Studies, Economics and Psychology. Although twenty-nine categories of separate behaviours can be recorded, by amalgamating all the students' learning experiences in these four subjects, the record showed that almost half of the students' time (45 per cent) was spent in answering curriculum questions. If all the interactions of discourse and questioning (teacher-led discussion, answers a curriculum question, answers a management question, asks a management question, asks a curriculum question, adds to another's response, initiates a contribution, students discuss their work), the figure rises to nearly three-quarters of the time. Obviously the teachers involved were firmly locked into the A level style of discourse, and the students duly complied. There is, however, evidence of variation between the subject areas. In this case the Biology students were significantly involved more in answering curriculum-based questions, whilst the Psychology students were significantly less involved in discourse and questioning than the other students. This might suggest that, in these classes at least, the teachers go beyond the dictum that 'what you teach determines the way you teach' to incorporate the pedagogic preferences of individual teachers.

Kolb LSI questionnaires were completed by a total of eighty-five teachers and lecturers from a wide range of curriculum areas. Overall, the teachers preferred

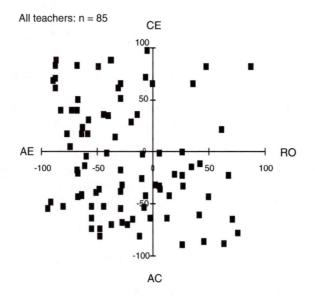

Figure 6.15 Teachers' answers to Kolb LSI questionnaires

160

to acquire information that was abstract rather than concrete (61 to 38 per cent); and to transform it actively rather than reflectively (72 to 28 per cent). Of the eighty-five teachers only four fitted into Kolb's Divergers sector, twenty into the Assimilator sector, twenty-nine into the Accommodator sector, and thirty-two into the Converger sector. Such a distribution indicates the importance attached by the teachers to theoretical knowledge and to doing something useful with it – which just about sums up the image of traditional professional pedagogy.

An interesting comparison can be made between the preferred learning styles of staff and students for different subjects and for A level and GNVQ subjects (Figures 6.16 and 6.17). The GNVQ Hospitality & Catering preferences accord well with the vocational area – the preparation of food in a busy kitchen, the operation of a fast-food outlet or hotel reception, for example. The A level students of both Physics and Chemistry rely heavily on logical thinking, manipulating symbolic language and Abstract Conceptualisation for the acquisition of information, as do most of their teachers. Once they have obtained information, the teachers prefer to transform it through active, practical applications rather than mull it over in reflective introversion.

There were very few teachers who taught subjects both at A level and GNVQ in the project cohort. Those that did were mainly enthusiasts campaigning for a more active style of learning, and all appeared on the Active Experimentation side of Kolb's transformation dimension. What proportion of transfer there was from GNVQ or A level to the other was impossible to ascertain. The teachers did see a clear difference between A levels and GNVQ, especially in terms of the assessment regime and in the amount of time allocated to them. However, there was close agreement between these teachers and the students in all their post-16 classes about the characteristics of the lessons.

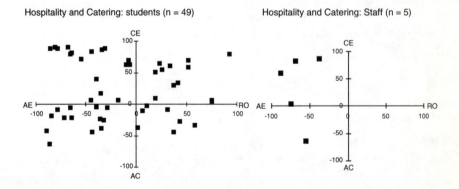

Figure 6.16 Preferred learning styles of GNVQ Hospitality & Catering staff and students

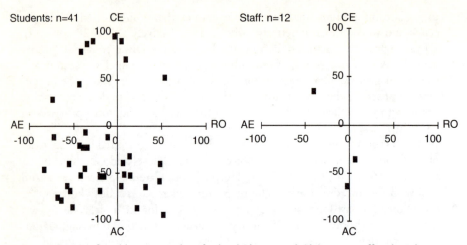

Figure 6.17 Preferred learning styles of A level Physics and Chemistry staff and students

CONCLUSIONS

Advanced GNVQs have been promoted as appealing to students who are inclined towards more active and applied forms of learning. Their responses to both the questionnaires about preferred activities and to the Kolb Learning Styles Inventory showed scores on both sides of the traditional divide to be widely dispersed. Nevertheless, there is considerable evidence that GNVQ students have a marked preference for avoiding Abstract Conceptualisation – which their overwhelming engagement with coursework research activities seems to require. In contrast, the A level students appear to be under-employed on these same abstract conceptual activities, which their predominant expressed preferences indicate would be most welcome, perhaps because of the teachers' over-riding concern to transmit to the students an inert and over-loaded subject content during their tightly scheduled class-time, leaving the students to 'transform' it for themselves in their own time – either in study periods or for homework.

7

CONCENTRATED AND DISTRIBUTED RESEARCH
Reflective observations on methodology
Carol Taylor Fitz-Gibbon

In this book, Edwards, Haywood, Meagher and I each consider the question of how students learn. It is almost implicit that teaching should be that process or activity that promotes learning in the student-learning broadly conceived. In searching for clues as to the nature of that illusive construct 'good practice', we must also entertain the possibility that some learning could be not only ineffective but also damaging to future competence. This is an issue that is not irrelevant to the issue of methodology, as I hope will become apparent.

How do students learn? And how do teachers learn? How, for that matter, do researchers learn? How does society become a learning society? How has humankind learned through the ages? And how has humankind learned, so very recently, such an amazing amount about the physical world? I shall suggest that most learning, perhaps all, is accomplished by behaving in a way that we have come to know as scientific. The more scientific, the better the learning, other things being equal.

Kolb's interesting cycle of learning, introduced to this book by Roy Haywood in Chapter 6, postulates a cyclical (or spiralling?) process in one of the convenient two axis representations that fits so well on the flat page (Figure 7.1). Kolb postulated that effective learning cycled through Concrete Experience to Reflective Observation to Abstract Conceptualisation to Active Experimentation. This is also the process of science, cycling through from data/observation to creative activity, data analysis, and thence to theory building (Abstract Conceptualisation), through to theory testing (Active Experimentation) and back to more observation. Whilst a cycle can start anywhere, the general principle that 'if you want to understand anything, try to change it', which would suggest that once you know what it is that you wish to understand you should start with Active Experimentation. Frequently, however, science begins with the kind of careful, systematic descriptions that have been aimed for in this project. Indeed, a noted ethologist, Lorenz, argued strongly for description in a piece entitled 'On the fashionable fallacy of dispensing with description'. Description tentatively identifies the variables and leads to the formulation of hypotheses.

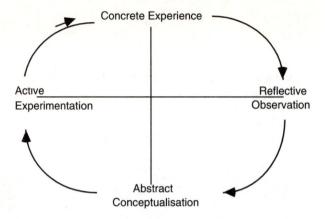

Figure 7.1 Kolb's learning cycle

Experimentation tests hypotheses, and our capacity to measure the variables we can think about.

How have we learned to apprehend, if not understand, so much about the world in which we live? Humankind has been a collection of rare animals for about 98 per cent of its existence as *homo sapiens*. Prior to recorded history, we apparently made very little progress in providing comforts or documenting carefully acquired knowledge. The 2 per cent of our species' existence that comprises history could be characterised by a very slow start on science, yielding to the current crescendo. Concrete Experience could not be avoided even in pre-history, even in the years before concrete existed. Almost certainly, even Neanderthal man reflected and made stabs at representing life and death: Abstract Conceptualisation. These abstractions were much aided by the development of language. But where the stage of Abstract Conceptualisation has not been passed, learning is neither efficient nor effective. Arguments about angels on pin heads spring to mind – observation, reflection and Abstract Conceptualisation are all there. Superstitions represent Abstract Conceptualisation and, when embodied in ethnocentrism, do great harm. Active experimentation, the remaining all-important step, occurs because of a dissatisfaction with Abstract Conceptualisation, a need to test it, to doubt it, to deny that grand theory, deep beliefs or off-the-top-of-the-head solutions are adequate guides to action. (Politicians have recently suggested homework, caning, contracts and various other nostrums off the top of their heads.) Science requires first the admission of ignorance (even after book-loads of Concrete Experience, reflective observation and Abstract Conceptualisation) and then a research design to obtain adequate evidence. Evidence disconfirms most over-generalised prejudices, in-group cohesions and outgroup hatreds. Evidence of a sound kind, based on Active Experimentation, is approached by the methods we call 'research methods'.

I fear that it may misrepresent the classical civilisations, but my weakly grounded impression of the culture of ancient world is that there was an approach to attempting to understand the universe that urged thought as the method. This led to plausible but off-the-top-of-the-head Abstract Conceptualisations of the world being at the centre of a universe with the stars rotating on perfect spheres – a nice model if not upset by Active Experimentation. Another approach urged authority such as, for example, the authority of those, later, who would not look through Galileo's telescope.

This may all seem remote from Advanced GNVQs but it is not. A major concern is that students should be taught in Advanced GNVQs and in A levels, not to rely on their own experience or their intuition, nor to accept authority, but to go on from these stages to interrogate the world scientifically. This teaching of thinking as science underlies the promising work of Michael Shayer and Phil Adey in CASE (Cognitive Acceleration through Science Education).

Researchers often adopt strategies that are almost like the old theological disputations. In his presidential address to the British Educational Research Association, Michael Bassey attacked the scholarly practice of citing the opinions of other researchers, calling this 'sand-bagging'. It is essentially like much medieval disputation an appeal to authority or putative expertise. Only *evidence* should be cited, not opinion. (I am uncomfortably aware as I write that I am trying to persuade you by sand-bagging.)

If teaching A levels or Advanced GNVQs discounts evidence and information, and almost despises 'facts', then this could damage long-term prospects for learning, producing students who believe too confidently that solutions can be found by thinking with words, as long as those words are elegant and impress people. Politicians epitomise that damaged style of learning, and we have to conclude that most have been poorly educated, imbued with Abstract Conceptualisation untested by Active Experimentation. 'This, from my personal experience, is a solution to the problem of low achievement/poor teaching/indiscipline/ vocational qualifications/the weather, etc.' Is this irrelevant to Advanced GNVQs? A notable authority in vocational education wrote an entire book of personal ideas without reference to research, to pilot studies, to evaluations – just Abstract Conceptualisation uncluttered by Active Experimentation by himself or others. It may have set vocational education back by years and resulted in the damaging report from FEFC detailing the inefficiencies and unwieldliness of the assessment procedures. A review of the criterion reference testing literature and the behavioural objectives literature from the US could have at least alerted him to many of the pitfalls, especially if combined with some respect for such slowly evolved and now valuable methods of Active Experimentation as have been carefully developed in this century.

Reliability and validity may not be the catch phrases of the moment, but they underpin all efforts at collecting evidence, whether of observations or judgements (e.g. inspections). Neglect of them leads to oppressive and wasteful systems. Any system that neglects them will run into trouble because reality catches up with poor methodology. But the most important step in methodology is the necessary caution of interpretation. In the absence of carefully designed experimentation, all kinds of charming associations can be seriously misleading. The correlation reported in Rutter *et al.* 1979 between whether or not schools used lines for punishment and the delinquency rates, was statistically significant and not insubstantial. Can we therefore reduce delinquency by setting lines? It is as reasonable an interpretation as 'good schools have strong leadership', equally based on the fallacious interpretation of correlation as causation. The same method – interpreting association as indicating cause – can lead us to see larger classes, from all the survey evidence, as getting better results, both in absolute terms and Value Added. Why is that data so consistent? Perhaps because schools allow classes of biddable pupils to become large, and keep small the difficult classes – and the association with achievement follows. Low achievement is causing small classes, not vice versa.

The research methods represented in this book go to the point of Reflective Observation but none of us has gone further. The use of questionnaires and tests are merely ways to improve the observation technique by acquiring more information that can be readily checked for kinds of reliability and validity. (From the point of view of the researcher, this is another form of passive observation, but from the point of view of the student the testing and the questionnaires are interventions into their lives, as is having someone observing their class. These interventions are made from the researchers' point of view merely to observe what is happening with the least possible disturbance – except in the case of testing, which is often used as a way to motivate students to learn, and a rather effective method it appears to be.)

One of the issues from which researchers shrink is the cost-effectiveness of the research methods chosen, and this issue will eventually lead us back to the question of how people learn. We can be fairly sure that in most human activities there is rich complexity but that also there are some broad simplicities (Fitz-Gibbon 1996).

The ALIS data enables the broad context, the landscape on which schools and colleges function, to be mapped. This is done by ensuring the administration of questionnaires under confidential conditions to students, questionnaires that are then returned to the CEM Centre (now at Durham University) where they are combined with examination data. The patterns in the data are then located *and reported back* to the heads and teachers in hundreds of schools and colleges. The data casts light on many questions, as is clear throughout this book. The ALIS data showed, for example, without any of the expense of classroom observation, that Advanced GNVQs are indeed taught differently from A levels, a conclusion that had begun to emerge from the study of the BTEC National Diploma in Business and Finance (Lacy 1993). As Frank Hardman's chapter makes clear, how you teach is not well represented by Abstract Conceptualisations and rhetoric. Despite efforts to create more student-centred syllabuses (e.g. English Language as opposed to Literature, Salter's Chemistry as opposed to other

Chemistry syllabuses), differences at A level between these syllabuses have rarely if at all been evident (Tymms and Vincent 1994).

As argued elsewhere, what appears to be different with the Advanced GNVQs is not just the rhetoric but, influentially, the consequences. The assessment demands project work and almost forces teachers not to help students who are capable of helping themselves. Such students may, if this self-reliance is demonstrated, achieve a 'distinction'. We are all keen on students becoming independent learners and, often, on teachers becoming independent researchers. How can we help? Our project's research methods report card reads as follows:

Research methods used in the book

Concrete Experience	observing/experiencing	done
Abstract Conceptualisation	thinking	done
Reflective Observation	reading	done
	observing systematically	done
	questioning	done
	testing	done
	evaluating	done
	writing	done
Active Experimentation	intervening, conducting experiments,	
	finding out what works,	yet to
	evidence-based education	be done

The summer 1989 issue of the (US) *Journal of Educational Statistics* (14, 2) was devoted to methodology, and the consensus was:

> there is *no substitute* for properly designed experiments. No fancy statistical analysis can work magic on a badly confounded set of data. The best message to convey is that many interesting and important questions must remain doubtful until experimenters obtain the funding, control and authority to carry out the proper research. (emphasis added)

I would like to predict that research councils in the social sciences will eventually wake up to this scientific necessity and will go through a period of funding primarily Active Experimentation. The gains will be disappointing but real. Rhetoric is so much more dramatic than the small gains that experimentation can show. But if that is reality, we need to confront it.

Will this book, going no further than passive observation of the world and ending with Reflective Observations, contribute substantially to the learning of researchers or teachers or society? I fear the contribution could be largely academic: a book read by teachers doing advanced degrees and finding the topics of interest. If we took the view that Active Experimentation was necessary for understanding, there would be little to read on MEd courses.

Must we wait for Active Experimentation to find out what is effective in education? Probably yes. However, in the meantime more accurate observation on which to reflect can be helpful *but only, perhaps, to those who are so close to the complexities that they can interpret the data.* To the extent that work has provided information directly back to those doing the work of teaching, it may already have been directly useful. Feedback has long been a step in qualitative methodology, a methodology that has frequently included the teacher, as has action research. The highly quantitative ALIS project has now been feeding back findings (the Value Added, student by student, subject by subject, plus attitudes and much more) to schools and colleges since 1983. It is with this idea that we return to the title of this chapter. Just as large mainframes have given way to *distributed computing,* is it perhaps time that concentrated, centralised research, hoping to advance by the thinking of a small number of researchers, gave way to *distributed research* in which high quality information, carefully analysed to sort out the simplicities, is fed back to those who know full well the complexities, but who welcome a clear picture of the simplicities? Then they will be able to adopt Active Experimentation and move our understanding of what works forward faster, by the application of the whole of Kolb's cycle, the whole method of science.

8

CONCLUSION
Different and unequal?

Carol Taylor Fitz-Gibbon preceded this concluding chapter by using the Kolb model to express provocative doubts about styles of research that avoid Active Experimentation. Our own non-experimental findings have been reported directly to the schools and colleges in which we worked, with no expectation that those receiving them would be greatly surprised by what they read, but in the hope that some familiar practices and dilemmas might become clearer from having been systematically explored. We now go beyond that evidence to draw some tentative conclusions about differences between A levels and their GNVQ alternatives, and about the prospects for parity between them.

The conclusion of Chapter 3 is that A levels and Advanced GNVQs are 'slightly different and equally useful'. Other chapters concentrate on some of the differences. These are not consistent, so that generalisations about the distinctiveness of learning experiences on either side of the divide are necessarily cautious and hedged around with qualifications. They are sufficiently clear, however, to indicate that in so far as both qualifications pass the test of fitness for purpose (a claim made explicitly for A levels in the Dearing Review) and in so far as they are indeed 'equivalent' in level, then rather different purposes are being served for different categories of student through rather different modes of learning. If they are indeed to be 'equally useful', then the special claims made for GNVQs' direct relevance to the needs of employment must confront traditional objections to giving anything like parity of esteem to practical knowledge in comparison with the higher-order skills and understanding associated with advanced 'academic' study.

It was in this context that we became more acutely aware during our research of the extraordinary mixture of change and continuity in English post-compulsory education. Certainly the changes have been dramatic. Participation rates which long prompted bleak comparisons with other industrial countries seemed to be catching up, although a levelling out since the peak of 1993 has caused concern about reaching national targets for qualifications at levels 2 and 3 which are notably ambitious by national (though not international) standards. A levels 'may already be approaching the ceiling of academically-minded young people for whom [they] were designed' (Dearing 1995: 5), but if they are, then they have already displayed a remarkable flexibility of design because they now accommodate one in three of the age-group in pursuit of a qualification initially thought suitable for only about one in twenty. Alongside the rising numbers of candidates for that venerable qualification towards a possible ceiling, Advanced GNVQs have secured a niche in the market more rapidly than their promoters initially expected, even though a less substantial one by 1996 than they had hoped. NVQs have certainly not replaced traditional qualifications to anything like the extent that some advocates predicted, but they have proliferated sufficiently for disputes about how many students have actually achieved them or are working towards them to involve confrontational exchanges of very large numbers indeed (Robinson 1996). Beyond this mass tertiary stage, Britain has become (as claimed in the 1995 *Competitiveness* White Paper) 'a European leader in graduate output'. This is itself a remarkable transformation in a country traditionally inclined to believe in a natural rationing of high educational achievement.

Taken together, these changes have been welcomed on democractic grounds as promising a better educated citizenry and moving the country towards becoming a 'learning society'. But, as argued in the two opening chapters, the main political momentum behind expansion has come from analysing the needs of employment and then prescribing the kind of workforce that a modern competitive economy is believed to need. Like another recent publication (Tomlinson 1997), this book began with descriptions of the sharp separation of leaders from followers that selective secondary education and an exclusive view of sixth forms reflected and did much to reproduce. Fifty years later, a competitive economy is seen to need 'thoughtful workers' at most levels of employment. Thus 'developed abilities' once reserved for an educated elite are to be much more widely diffused. 'Learning to compete', to take the title of the latest *Competitiveness* White Paper, therefore insists that all 14–19 education and training should develop self-reliance, breadth and adaptability.

Yet beneath and within these changes, an old divisiveness remains to provide conspicuous continuity. The Conservative Government continued to insist on retaining three types of post-compulsory qualification, despite the connotations of a hierarchy of gold, silver and iron, because (as Secretary of State Gillian Shephard put it in 1996) while each deserved respect, it was also 'right that they remain distinct'. Wanting them to be different but also equal, Sir Ron Dearing recognised that the obstacles to achieving that objective were maintained by 'the very different value placed on achievement in the academic and vocational pathways' and the continuing assumption that they were taken respectively by 'the able and the less able'. Supporting the case against merging them, which has been seen from some quarters as the only remedy for their persistent inequality, he claimed that strong 'academic' bias of the English system would skew a single qualification too heavily in that direction to the detriment of those 'who have not yet responded well to academic learning' (Dearing 1995: 12). He sought instead a more 'consistent' distinctiveness of purpose and form.

170

Advocates of a real alternative to A level understandably object to the familiar polarising of the academic and the vocational, with its implication that vocationally oriented studies are inherently non-academic. Dearing's tactical solution was to recommend replacing both the formal label of Advanced GNVQs and their ministerial designation as Vocational A levels with the new brand-name of Applied A levels. This would simultaneously avoid confusion with NVQs, emphasise the value that society placed on vocational education, and celebrate 'a distinctive approach to learning based on the application of knowledge'. As noted in several preceding chapters, the 1996 Conservative Party Conference then provided a convenient illustration of old attitudes not even dying hard but positively flourishing. The Dearing proposal was flatly rejected by ministers, with an accompanying claim that Sir Ron had also changed his mind. Ostensibly this was because it would be confusing to change a name that was only just beginning to be understood in the marketplace. In different circumstances, it might also have been taken as indicating a new credential now able to stand on its own feet. Instead, the decision was generally interpreted as resistance to 'diluting' A level, and was soon followed by government proposals to 'redeem an ailing qualification' by making its assessment more rigorous – predictably, by making it conform to more traditional academic practices (*The Times Educational Supplement* 8 November 1996). It is also reasonable to suspect, however, that 'maintaining the rigour of A levels' (as Dearing's remit required him to do) prohibited undermining the position of the established market leader. Dearing's proposal would have entailed some reallocation of existing A levels to the alternative route. And in so far as calling that route 'applied' would hold fewer connotations of inferiority than calling it 'vocational', then the change of label would dissatisfy those wishing to maintain the separation of A level from any alternative intended to provide a less demanding 'ladder for the less able to climb' (Raffe and Surridge 1995: 5).

Yet that is exactly the stereotype that Advanced GNVQs are intended to challenge. Distinctiveness in English post-compulsory education has come from providing separate categories of selected and self-selected students, with qualifications at different levels offering unequal prospects (Macrae *et al.* 1997). Beginning with BTEC National, however, the declared intentions have been not only to raise participation rates by diversifying provision so as to recruit a much wider constituency of students, but also to provide for many able, ambitious and practically minded students drawn to the traditional academic route largely because nothing else of comparable status was available. Advanced GNVQs have therefore been promoted as appealing to those who want their studies to have a direct and visible relevance to a broad area of employment, and whose abilities would not previously or otherwise be 'developed or recognised' (NCVQ 1994: 18). They are also claimed to produce outcomes that are rated highly by 'modern' employers, but to do so through a different kind of learning experience that is nevertheless of the same standard as A level.

That is the challenge of parity of esteem. As previous chapters have shown, the A level route continues to attract almost all the high attainers at GCSE. It also attracts many who 'have not yet responded well to academic learning' and for whom the risks of 'disappointment' are high. The large database on which Carol Taylor Fitz-Gibbon drew in Chapter 3 indicates that while GNVQ students often rated the 'interest' of their courses highly, few had GCSE results comparable even to those taking the 'easier' (or more leniently graded) A levels and many had results below the level conventionally taken as evidence of suitability for advanced academic education. To summarise the evidence, students taking the Advanced GNVQ route are generally less well qualified by prior attainment, feel less secure academically, and are also less optimistic about their chances of a job afterwards, despite being more confident than their A level contemporaries about the occupational relevance of their studies. As we noted earlier, however, they were more confident than their A level contemporaries about being prepared for employment should they get it – in particular through the use of IT and through collaborating with others in projects and problem solving. It was with the prospect of finding such differences in learning experience that our research began.

On the reasonable working assumption that A levels were already familiar enough, the alternatives have been promoted with unusual explicitness about the kinds of learning experience that those choosing them can expect. As defined by Dearing (1995: 14), they should appeal to students 'whose approach to learning is by doing and by finding out', and to employers who give priority to core skills and to 'more interactive learning styles'. Designed for a different kind of student, they are also claimed to be better adapted, or at least much more overtly adapted, to the kinds of workplace literacy demanded of an ever higher proportion of the workforce. Roy Haywood reports evidence in Chapter 6 of students' implicit theories about how different subject specialisms 'impose constraints on learning strategies', and of how they may be drawn towards some subjects rather than others for that reason. ALIS data certainly indicates differences between A level subjects in the frequency of various perceived learning activities. For example, class discussion appeared as infrequently in Mathematics as did teacher presentation in English Literature, while dictated notes were commonplace in the first and rare in the second (Fitz-Gibbon and Wright 1995a; Tymms and Vincent 1995). A liking for discussion or for more orderly linear learning might then draw students not committedly subject minded in one direction or the other. But we found no evidence of such differences being 'advertised' even informally within schools or colleges, whilst a predominance of 'finding out' is advertised quite explicitly in the promotion of GNVQs. The detailed consideration given to research into learning styles in Chapter 6 raised obvious questions about whether different preferred ways of perceiving and processing information, and of approaching learning tasks, might lead students to one side of the academic vocational divide because of what they 'know' A levels to be like and because they have been persuaded that GNVQs

172

will be different and educationally more suited to them. The promotion of GNVQs has certainly involved the promise of both intrinsic and extrinsic benefits. Some of its outcomes, especially in relation to transferable core learning, might be expected to bestow a relative advantage in some circumstances on holders of that award when compared with the products of traditionally academic courses.

Yet, as the two opening chapters described, there is a long tradition of regarding 'practical' (less 'academic') knowledge as being more easily acquired, and as motivating 'less able' students. A monitoring of GNVQ 'standards' which has seemed obsessive to many of those involved, though still inadequate to its critics (Smithers 1997), reflects a concern not only to establish the general credibility of a new qualification but also to gain acceptance as 'equivalent' to A level despite the latter's advantages, epitomised by Dearing as 'long life and innate quality'. GNVQ must therefore be seen as accrediting the same 'level' of performance, even though the actual performance will be different, involving 'distinctively' different modes of learning, and being fit for somewhat different purposes (Coles and Matthews 1996). At the same time, some kinds of learner should find a more 'active' approach congenial.

Roy Haywood describes learning styles as being both fairly stable and yet permeable – that is, open to being changed through experience of different ways of working or in response to (for example) more problem solving classroom tasks. His own evidence illustrates the difficulty facing teachers who may wish to adapt their own approach to what they perceive as the preferences of their students when those preferences are likely to be widely scattered. He suggests that A level might be expected 'in theory' to emphasise reflective observation and Abstract Conceptualisation, and GNVQs to emphasise Concrete Experience and Active Experimentation. He then describes lessons on each side of the 'divide' that confound that neat distinction. In general, our research has both softened and complicated the 'commonsense' contrasts from which it began. Certainly we found evidence of differences, not consistent but enough to confirm the relevance of Carol Taylor Fitz-Gibbon's question – what had given teachers the signal to teach in different ways? The extensive ALIS+ data shows considerable differences between A level subjects in the balance of perceived learning activities and the frequency of some of them. It also indicates that GNVQ students generally make much more use of IT (although what they do with it beyond word-processing assignments is not clear), make public presentations of their work more often, and are more likely to give and receive help in preparing their work. Given the value that employers claim to place on potential recruits' experience of IT, communication and presentational skills, teamwork and collaborative learning, these would appear to be differences well worth celebrating. That they appeared in comparisons of pairs of subjects selected to represent each side of the 'divide', but which might also be expected to have some common content, such as Business and Business Studies, makes them the more persuasive. And the striking similarities that Frank Hardman found between two purportedly different forms of A level English lends support to the existence of what Dearing referred to as 'the A level approach', an approach to which he believed many of those exposed are unsuited (1996: 3.5). As described in Chapter 5, the new A level of English Language was intended to encourage investigational, independent and collaborative forms of learning of the kind associated with advanced vocational education, and to display a greater concern for application and practicality. Yet its predominant mode of instruction remained transmissional, with the teacher no less directive and students no less receptive than in the supposedly more purely academic study of English Literature.

Something like a pervasive GNVQ 'approach' might certainly be expected, attributable to an 'assessment regime' that has been dominated by the portfolios of evidence on which students' performance is assessed even if not to the persuasiveness of NCVQ advocacy of 'active' learning. The strong tendency of classroom practice to regress to the familiar is well documented, as is the pressure on both teachers and students not to take risks where the stakes are high. In Advanced GNVQs, the costs risked by taking time away from Smithers' (1993) 'conventional teaching' or from vigorous tutorial interventions have to be balanced against the requirement on students seeking high grades to demonstrate a sufficient measure of 'independence' and effective self-direction in compiling and presenting evidence of their performance. The qualification has been criticised for relying too heavily on 'testing in' desirable forms of learning, rather than 'building them in' through carefully constructed programmes of study (Sparkes 1994). But the weight given to students' portfolios means that they are socialised early and thoroughly into the 'workplace' activities demanded by projects. Indeed, Nick Meagher's interviews with GNVQ admissions tutors during the research supported by the NCVQ indicated that while GCSE performance was formally the prime criterion, students' past record for attendance and completing assignments on time was also given considerable weight in assessing suitability for that route.

The observational evidence reported by Nick Meagher in Chapter 4 describes very different lessons on the same side of the 'divide', but it also supports some generalisations about differences between them. Classroom activities in GNVQ classes were heavily skewed towards the preparation and production of assignments, and in A level classes towards more discursive forms of learning centred on teacher exposition and sequences of teacher-directed question and answer arising from it. The tempo of A level lessons was faster, with more frequent changes of activities of shorter duration. Over a series of lessons, GNVQ students were engaged in a greater variety of activities – a difference that also appears in the ALIS+ data – but those activities were generally of longer duration. An apparently more relaxed pace gave more scope for time off task, students' greater control over the pacing of their individual work and the likelihood of that work being done in groups, providing regular opportunities for conversation. The brisker, more intensive character of A level lessons produced apparently more consistent busyness but also seemed sometimes to crowd out consolidation and reflection. The students might or might not do a great deal of 'research' as homework, but in class the teacher expected and was expected to 'instruct, interpret and direct'. While students were sometimes encouraged to question and challenge, in line with idealised notions of A level teaching, our evidence generally offers little support to that version of independent learning. And while GNVQ students enjoyed more control over the processes of learning, they seemed to have fewer opportunities to take any responsibility for its content.

Carol Taylor Fitz-Gibbon argues that qualifications should signal clearly to potential users what has been learned – the 'developed abilities' reasonably attributable to that programme of study and the level to which that development has been taken. But as her 50 per cent framework suggests, qualifications are also quite reasonably taken as evidence of the kinds of student likely to have pursued them. Certainly GCSE results were used in the schools and colleges we visited as strong indicators of suitability for different post-16 routes, without much sign of that careful assessment of suitability for a particular 'approach' to learning that GNVQ publicity seems to require. To borrow from a now familiar vocabulary, the market value of credentials is affected by the kinds of customer it is believed or even assumed to attract. We suggested earlier that A level has been widely used as a proxy measure of the ability, ambition, working capacity and social background of those who succeed in obtaining it. It may develop occupationally relevant skills in 'analysis and the critical evaluation of information', as Dearing was certain it did. But it is also taken as evidence of much more general characteristics, most obviously a capacity to learn, which go well beyond the particular kinds of learning that A level may develop and (at least indirectly) test. In fact, it has been taken for granted that A level develops higher-order skills appropriate to the positions of leadership and responsibility for which most of those taking it were destined. Although the traditional notion that these skills were properly reserved for an academic minority has proved hard to shift, the emergence of alternatives has marked an apparent acceptance that the steep pyramid of a few leaders and many followers is now obsolete.

Vocationally oriented general education at a suitably advanced level has therefore become in its declared purposes more theoretical, more knowledge based and more focused on conceptual understanding. Our research interest in 'contrasts in learning' took into account a great deal of uncertainty about what differences to expect. A levels and GNVQs come from very different curriculum traditions, and are portrayed as suitable for students with different perspectives on knowledge and different preferences for ways of learning. Yet there should also be a considerable convergence in intended outcomes, especially in relation to the less tangible but supposedly transferable core learning that has traditionally been associated with and largely reserved for 'the thinking classes' (Tomlinson 1997). If the more ambitious and humane purposes of post-compulsory education are to be achieved, then careful monitoring of processes and outcomes is essential. It will also require much more thought than has been evident behind the high pace of reform about the scale, scope and especially the coherence of expanded provision. Certainly the problem of establishing parity for 'vocational' study is not solved, and is barely alleviated, by the technical solution of more 'rigorous' assessment (predictably interpreted as making it more conventionally academic). Nor is it overcome by throwing a common bridge of core skills across a divide still constructed from 'separate and unequal forms' of knowledge and understanding.

REFERENCES

Abbott, A.J. (1994) *Learning Makes Sense: Recreating Education for a Changing Future*, Letchworth: Education 2000.

Ainley, P. and Corbett, J. (1994) 'From vocationalism to enterprise: social and life skills become personal and transferable', *British Journal of Sociology of Education* 15, 3: 365–374.

Anderson, R. and Haywood, R. (1996) 'Advancing GNVQs', *Forum* 38, 81–83.

Ashford, S., Gray, J. and Tranmer, M. (1993) *The Introduction of GCSE Examinations and Changes in Post-16 Participation*, Sheffield: Employment Department.

Ashton, D., Maguire, N. and Spilsbury, M. (1990) *Restructuring the Labour Market: Implications for Youth*, London: Macmillan.

Atkins, M. (1984) 'Pre-vocational studies: tensions and strategies', *Journal of Curriculum Studies* 16, 4: 403–415.

Audit Commission and Her Majesty's Inspectorate (1993) *Unfinished Business: Full-time Educational Courses for 16–19 Year Olds*, London: HMSO.

Ausubel, D.P. (1960) 'The use of advanced organisers in the learning and retention of meaningful material', *Journal of Educational Psychology* 51: 267–272.

Ball, C. (1990) *More Means Different*, London: Royal Society of Arts.

Ball, C. (1995) 'Developing the learning society', Presidential address, North of England Education Conference (4 January).

Barnes, D. and Todd, F. (1995) *Communication and Learning Revisited: Making Meaning Through Talk*, Portsmouth, NH: Heinemann.

Bates, I. (1995) 'The competence movement and the national qualification framework: the widening parameters of research', *British Journal of Education and Work* 8, 2: 5–13.

Bennett, N., Desforges, C., Cockburn, A. and Wilkinson, B. (1984) *The Quality of Pupil Learning Experiences*, London: Earlbaum.

Berliner, D.C. (1988) 'Implications of studies on expertise in pedagogy for teacher education and evaluation', *New Directions for Teachers Assessment*. Proceedings of the 1988 EIS Institutional Congress, Princeton, NJ : Educational Testing Service.

Bernstein, B. (1990) *The Structure of Pedagogic Discourse: Volume IV, class, codes and control*, London and New York: Routledge & Kegan Paul.

Bernstein, B. (1995) *Pedagogy, Symbolic Control and Identity*, London and Bristol, PA: Taylor & Francis.

Biggs, J.B. (1993) 'What do inventories of students' learning processes really measure? A theoretical review and clarification', *British Journal of Educational Psychology* 63, 3–19.

Bloomer, M. and Morgan, D. (1993) 'It is planned, therefore it happens. Or does it?', *Journal of Further and Higher Education* 17, 1: 22–37.

Blue, G. (1995) 'Language after Sixteen', in C. Brumfit (ed.) *Language Education in the National Curriculum*, Oxford: Blackwell.

Board of Education (1943) *Curriculum and Examinations in Secondary Schools (Norwood Report)*, London : HMSO.

Boud, D. and Feletti, G. (eds) (1991) *The Challenge of Problem Based Learning*, London: Kogan Page.

Brody, C.M. (1995) 'Co-operative learning and teacher beliefs: a constructivist view'. Paper presented to the American Educational Research Association, Chicago. Quoted in J. Berry and P. Sahlberg (1996) 'Investigating Pupils' Ideas of Learning', *Learning and Instruction* 6, 19–36.

Brown, P. and Lauder, H. (1995) 'Post-Fordist possibilities: education, training and national development', in L. Bash and A. Green (eds) *Youth Education and Work: World Yearbook of Education*, London: Kogan Page.

Brown, P. and Lauder, H. (1996) 'Education, globalisation and economic development', *Journal of Education Policy* 11, 1: 1–25.

Burchell, H. (1992) 'Reforming the A-level curriculum', *Educational Studies* 18, 1: 57–69.

Burns, J., Clift, J. and Duncan, J. (1991) 'Understanding of understanding: implications for learning and teaching', *British Journal of Educational Psychology* 61: 276–289.

Canwell, S. and Ogborn, J. (1994) 'Balancing the books: Modes of assessment in A-level English literature', in S. Brindley (ed.) *Teaching English*, Buckingham: Open University Press.

Chinn, C.A. and Brewer, W.F. (1993) 'The role of anomalous data in knowledge acquisition: a theoretical framework and implications for science instruction', *Review of Educational Research* 61, 1–49.

Chitty, C. (1991) 'Towards new definitions of vocationalism', in C. Chitty (ed.) *Post-Sixteen Education: Studies in Access and Achievement*, London: Kogan Page.

Chorlton, W. (1994) *GNVQ: Is It for You?*, London: Careers Research and Advisory Centre.

City Technology College Trust (1991) *The City and Guilds Technological Baccalaureate*, London: CTC Trust.

Cockett, M. and Callaghan, J. (1996) 'Caught in the middle: transition at 16+', in R. Halsall and M. Cockett (eds) *Education and Training 14–19: Chaos or Coherence?*, London: David Fulton.

Cohen, G., Stanhope, N. and Conway, M. (1992) 'How long does education last? Very long term retention of cognitive psychology', *The Psychologist: Bulletin of the British Psychological Society* 5: 57–60.

Coles, M. (1996) 'Do advanced science qualifications meet the requirements of employers and tutors in higher education?', British Educational Research Association Annual Conference, Lancaster University.

Coles, M. and Matthews, A. (1996) *Fitness for Purpose – A Means of Comparing Qualifications*, London: School Curriculum and Assessment Authority and the NCVQ.

Coles, M., Duffy, B. and Matthews, A. (1995) *Report on Regional Conferences for Higher Education Science Admissions Tutors on GNVQ Science*, London: NCVQ.

Collins, A., Brown, J.S. and Newman, S. (1989) 'Cognitive apprenticeship: teaching the craft of reading, writing and mathematics', in L. Resnick (ed.) *Knowing, Learning and Instruction: Essays in Honour of Robert Glasser*, Hillsdale, NJ: Erlbaum, 453–494.

Committee of Vice-Chancellors and Principals (1995) 'A Strategy for Vocational Higher Education', *Competence and Assessment* 29 (June): 16–32.

Confederation of British Industry (1989) *Towards a Skills Revolution*, London: CBI.

Confederation of British Industry (1995) *A Vision for our Future. A Skills Passport*, London: CBI.

Corno, L. and Snow, R.E. (1986) 'Adapting teaching to individual differences among learners', in M. Wittrock (ed.) *Handbook of Research on Teaching* (3rd edition) London: Collier Macmillan.

Cornwell, J.M. and Manfredo, P.A. (1994) 'Kolb's learning style theory revisited', *Educational and Psychological Measurement* 54, 317–327.

Croll, P. (1986) *Systematic Classroom Observation*, Lewes: Falmer Press.

Crombie-White, R., Pring, R. and Brockington, D. (1995) *14–19 Education and Training: Implementing a Unified System of Learning*, London: Royal Society of Arts.

Dean, J., Bradley, K., Choppin, B. and Vincent, D. (1979) *The Sixth Form and its Alternatives*, Windsor: National Foundation for Educational Research.

Dearing, R. (1995) *Review of the 16–19 Qualifications Framework: Interim Report and Issues for Consideration*, London: School Curriculum and Assessment Authority.

Dearing, R. (1996) *Review of Qualifications for 16–19 Year Olds: Full Report*, London: School Curriculum and Assessment Authority.

De Corte, E. (1995) 'Learning theory and instructional science', in P. Reimann and H. Spada (eds) *Learning in Humans and Machines: Towards an Interdisciplinary Science*, Oxford: Elsevier Science.

Delamont, S. and Hamilton, D. (1984) 'Revisiting classroom research: a continuing cautionary tale', in S. Delamont (ed.) *Readings on Interaction in the Classroom*, London: Methuen.

Department for Education and Employment (1995) *Value Added in Education*, London: DfEE.

Department of Education and Science (DES) (1986) *A Survey of the Teaching of 'A' Level English Literature in 20 Mixed Sixth Forms in Comprehensive Schools*, London: HMSO.

Department of Education and Science (1987a) *Experiencing A-Level: Aspects of Quality* (A Report by Her Majesty's Inspectorate), London: DES.

Department of Education and Science (1987b) *Experiencing A-Level: Aspects of Quality* (A report by Her Majesty's Inspectorate), London: DES.

Department of Education and Science (1987c) *Non-Advanced Further Education in Practice: an HMI Survey*, London: HMSO.

Department of Education and Science (1988a) *Advancing A levels (The Higginson Report)*, London: HMSO.

Department of Education and Science (1988b) *Secondary Schools: An Appraisal by HMI*, London: HMSO.

Department of Education and Science (1991) *Programmes of Students on GCE Advanced-level Courses (AS and A level) 1989–90* (A report by Her Majesty's Inspectorate), London: HMSO.

Department of Education/Department of Employment (1991) *Education and Training for the 21st Century*, London: HMSO.

Desforges, C. (1995) 'How does experience affect theoretical knowledge for teaching?', *Learning and Instruction* 5: 385–400.

Dillon, J.T. (1994) *Using Discussion in Classrooms*, Milton Keynes: Open University Press.

Doyle, W. (1983) 'Academic work', *Review of Educational Research* 53, 159–199.

Drake, K. and Edwards, A. (1979, 'Eighteen-plus examinations: innovation without change', *Educational Studies* 5, 1: 217–224.

Dunkerton, J. (1981) 'Should classroom research be quantitative?', *Educational Research* 23, 2: 144–151.

Edwards, A. (1983a) 'An elite transformed?: continuity and change in 16–19 education policy', in J. Ahier and M. Flude (eds) *Contemporary Education Policy*, London and Canberra: Croom Helm.

Edwards, A. (1983b) 'The reconstruction of post-compulsory education and training in England and Wales', *European Journal of Education*, 18, 1: 7–20.

Edwards, A. (1995) 'Changing pedagogic discourse', in P. Atkinson, B. Davies and S. Delamont (eds) *Discourse and Reproduction*, Cresskill, NJ: Hampton Press.

Edwards, A.D. and Westgate, D.P.G. (1994) *Investigating Classroom Talk* (2nd edition), London: Falmer Press.

Edwards, A. and Whitty, G. (1997) 'Marketing quality: traditional and modern versions of educational excellence', in R. Glatter, P. Woods and C. Bagley (eds) *Choice and Diversity in Schooling*, London and New York: Routledge.

Entwistle, N. (1987) *Understanding Classroom Learning*, London: Hodder & Stoughton.

Entwistle, N. (1994) *Teaching and the Quality of Learning*, London: Committee of Vice-Chancellors and Principals and Society for Research in Higher Education.

Entwistle, N.J. and Ramsden, P. (1983) *Understanding Student Learning*, London: Croom Helm.

Eraut, M. (1994) *Developing Professional Knowledge and Competence*, London: Falmer Press.

Fielding, M. (1994) 'Valuing difference in teachers and learners: building on Kolb's learning styles to develop a language of teaching and learning', *The Curriculum Journal* 5, 3: 393–417.

Finegold, D. (1992) *Breaking Out of the Low-Skill Equilibrium*, London: National Commission on Education, Briefing Paper 5.

Finegold, D., Keep, E., Miliband, D., Raffe, D., Spours, K. and Young, M. (1990) *A British Baccalaureat: Ending the Division between Education and Training*, London: Institute for Public Policy Research.

Fitz-Gibbon, C.T. (1991) *Evaluation of School Performance in Public Examinations: A Report for the Scottish Office Education Department*, CEM Centre, School of Education, University of Durham.

Fitz-Gibbon, C.T. (1996) *Monitoring Education: Indicators, Quality and Effectiveness*, London and New York: Cassell.

Fitz-Gibbon, C.T. and Lacy, M. (1993) *The BTEC Added Value Project: Comparisons with A-level* (Report for Business and Technology Education Council No. 7), Newcastle upon Tyne: Newcastle University School of Education, Curriculum, Evaluation and Management Centre.

Fitz-Gibbon, C.T. and Vincent, L.S. (1994) *Candidates' Performance in Science and Mathematics at A-level*, London: School Curriculum and Assessment Authority.

Fitz-Gibbon, C.T. and Wright, M. (1995a) *Advanced GNVQs and A-levels: Evidence from the A-level Information System* (A Report for NCVQ), Newcastle upon Tyne: Newcastle University School of Education, Curriculum, Evaluation and Management Centre.

Fitz-Gibbon, C.T. and Wright, M. (1995b) *Characteristics of Students Taking Advanced GNVQs*, Newcastle upon Tyne: Newcastle University School of Education, Curriculum, Evaluation and Management Centre.

Flanders, N. (1963) 'Teacher influence in the classroom', in A. Bellack (ed.) *Theory and Research in Teaching*, Columbia: Teachers College Press.

Flavell, J.H. (1976) 'Metacognitive aspects of problem solving', in L.B. Resnick (ed.) *The Nature of Intelligence*, Hillsdale, NJ: Erlbaum, 231–236.

Fuller, A., Helsby, G., Machell, J. and Saunders, M. (1991) 'Standard class', *Education* 177, 24: 484.

Further Education Funding Council (1994) *General National Vocational Qualifications in the Further Education Sector in England*, London: FEFC.

Further Education Funding Council (1995) *General National Vocational Qualifications in the Further Education Sector in England*, London: FEFC.

Further Education Unit (1992) *A Basis for Credit*, London: FEU.

Further Education Unit, Institute of Education and Nuffield Foundation (1994) *GNVQs 1993–4: A National Survey Report*, London: FEU.

Galton, M. (1979) 'Systematic classroom observation: British research', *Educational Research* 21, 2: 109–115.

Geekie, P. and Raban, B. (1993) *Learning to Read and Write Through Classroom Talk*, Stoke-on-Trent: Trentham Books.

Gibbs, G. (1988) *Learning by Doing: A Guide to Teaching and Learning Methods*, London: FEU.

Gibbs, G. (1992) *Improving the Quality of Student Learning*, Bristol: Teaching and Educational Services.

Glass, G.V. (1978) 'Standards and criteria', *Journal of Educational Measurement* 15, 4: 239–261.

Goddard, A. (1993) *Researching Language: English Project Work at 'A' Level and Beyond*, Lancaster: Framework Press.

Graham, D. with Tytler, D. (1993) *A Lesson for Us All: The Making of the National Curriculum*, London: Routledge.

Green, A. (1995) 'Core skills, participation and progression in post-compulsory education in England and France', *Comparative Education* 31, 1: 49–67.

Green, A. and Ainley, P. (1995) *Progression and the Targets in Post-16 Education and Training*, London: London University Institute of Education Post-16 Education Centre.

Greenwell, B. (1988) *Alternatives at English 'A' level*, Sheffield: National Association for the Teaching of England.

Gregorc, A.F. (1985) *Inside Styles: Beyond the Basics*, Maynard, MA: Gabriel Systems Inc.

Handy, C. (1984) *The Future of Work: A Guide to a Changing Society*, Oxford: Basil Blackwell.

Harkin, J. and Davis, P. (1996) 'The impact of GNVQs on the communication styles of teachers', *Research in Post-Compulsory Education* 1, 1: 97–107.

Harrison, B.T. and Mountford, D. (1992) 'Consultative Patterns of Guided Learning in English Post-16 Studies', *Educational Review* 42, 2: 195–204.

Hennessy, S., McCormick, R. and Murphy, P. (1993) 'The myth of problem-solving capability: Design Technology as an example', *Curriculum Journal* 4: 74–89.

Her Majesty's Inspectorate (HMI) (1991) *The TVEI in England and Wales*, London: DES.

Higham, J., Sharp, P. and Yeomans, D. (1996) *The Emerging 16–19 Curriculum*, London: David Fulton.

Hirst, P. (1993) 'The foundations of the National Curriculum: why subjects?', in P. O'Hear and J. White (eds) *Assessing the National Curriculum*, London: Paul Chapman.

Hodgson, W. (1994) 'Gender differences in Mathematics and Science: a study of GCE Advanced-level examinations in the United Kingdom', unpublished Ph.D thesis, University of Newcastle upon Tyne.

Hodkinson, P. (1991) 'Liberal education and the new vocationalism: a progressive partnership?', *Oxford Review of Education* 17: 73–88.

Hodkinson, P., Sparkes, P., Andrew, C. and Hodkinson, H. (1996) *Triumphs and Tears: Young People, Markets and the Transition from School to Work*, London: David Fulton.

Holland, G. (1979) 'More than half our future: 16–19 year olds in employment', *Oxford Review of Education* 5, 2: 147–156.

Holland, G. (1994) 'Young people and work: towards post-16 coherence', keynote speech to the CRAC Conference, *Young People and Work*, CBI Conference Centre, London (3 December).

Holt, M. and Reid, W. (1988) 'Instrumentalism and education: 14–18 rhetoric and the 11–16 curriculum', in A. Pollard (eds) *Training and the New Vocationalism*, Milton Keynes and Philadelphia: Open University Press.

Hunter, J.E. and Hunter, R.F. (1984) 'Validity and utility of alternative predictors of job performance', *Psychological Bulletin* 96, 1: 72–98.

Hustler, D. and Hodkinson, P. (1996) 'Rationales for student-centred learning', in R. Halsall and M. Cockett (eds) *Education and Training 14–19: Chaos or Coherence?*, London: David Fulton.

Hyland, T. (1993) 'Vocational reconstruction and Dewey's instrumentalism', *Oxford Review of Education* 19: 89–100.

Hyland, T. (1994) *Competence, Education and NVQs: Dissenting Perspectives*, London: Cassell.

Jessup, G. (1991) *Outcomes: NVQs and the Emerging Model of Education and Training*, London: Falmer Press.

Jessup, G. (1995) 'Outcome based qualifications and the implications for learning', in J. Burke (ed.) *Outcomes' Learning and the Curriculum: Implications for NVQs, GNVQs and Other Qualifications*, London: Cassell.

Johnson, M. (1974) 'Bases for comparing approaches to curriculum development', in P.H. Taylor and M. Johnson (eds) *Curriculum Development: A Comparative Study*, Slough: NFER.

Jones, R. (1992) *Post-16 Provision in City Technology Colleges: Bridging the Divide*, London: CTC Trust.

Joyce, B.R. and Showers, B. (1984) 'Transfer of training – the contribution of coaching', in D. Hopkins, and M. Wideen (eds) *Alternative Perspectives on School Improvement*, Lewes: Falmer Press.

Joyce, B.R. and Showers, B. (1988) *Student Achievement Through Staff Development*, New York: Longman.

Kaplan, A. (1964) *The Conduct of Enquiry*, Aylesbury: Chandler Pub.

Kelly, A. (1976) 'A study of the comparability of external examinations in different subjects', *Research in Education* 16: 50–63.

Kingdon, M. (1991) *The Reform of Advanced Level*, London: Hodder & Stoughton.

Kolb, D.A. (1976) *The Learning Style Inventory: Technical Manual*, Boston, MA: McBer.

Kolb, D.A. (1984) *Experiential Learning: Experience as the Source of Learning and Development*, Englewood Cliffs, NJ: Prentice Hall.

Kolb, D.A. and Fry, R. (1975) 'Towards an applied theory of experiential learning', in C.L. Cooper (ed.) *Theories of Group Processes*, London: John Wiley, 33–58.

Kolb, D.A., Rubin, I. and McIntyre, J. (1971) *Organisational Psychology: An Experiential Approach*, Englewood Cliffs, NJ: Prentice Hall.

Kyriacou, C., Bennansour, N. and Low, G. (1996) 'Pupil learning styles and foreign language learning', *Language Learning Journal* 13: 22–24.

Lacy, M. (1993) *Teaching and Learning Activities and Resources* (BTEC Added Value Project No. 5), Newcastle upon Tyne: Newcastle University School of Education, Curriculum, Evaluation and Management Centre.

Lacy, M. and Fitz-Gibbon, C.T. (1993) *Achievement Levels and Added Value* (BTEC Added Value Project No. 4), Newcastle upon Tyne: Newcastle University School of Education, Curriculum, Evaluation and Management Centre.

Larkin, J.H. (1989) 'What kind of knowledge transfers?', in L.B. Resnick (ed.) *Knowing, Learning and Instruction: Essays in Honour of Robert Glasser*, Hillsdale, NJ: Erlbaum, 283–306.

Leach, S. (1992) *Shakespeare in the Classroom*, Buckingham: Open University Press.

Lewis, T. (1994) 'Bridging the liberal/vocational divide: an examination of recent British and American versions of an old debate', *Oxford Review of Education* 20, 2: 199–218.

Macrae, S., Maguire, M. and Ball, S. (1997) 'Competition, choice and hierarchy in a post-16 education and training market', in S. Tomlinson (ed.) *Perspectives on Education 14–19*, London: Athlone Press.

McCulloch, G. (1989) *The Secondary Technical School: A Usable Past?*, Lewes: Falmer Press.

McCulloch, G. (1991) *Philosophers and Kings: Education for Leadership in Modern England*, Cambridge: Cambridge University Press.

McCulloch, R., Mathieson, M. and Powis, V. (1993) *English 16–19: Entitlement at A-level*, London: David Fulton.

Macfarlane, E. (1993) *Education 16–19 in Transition*, London: Routledge.

McGuiness, C. and Nisbet, J. (1991) 'Teaching thinking in Europe', *British Journal of Educational Psychology* 61: 174–186.

McNeill, P. (1994) 'GNVQ: some implications for higher education', *Journal of Education Policy* 9, 4: 381–388.

Maguire, M. and Ashton, D. (1981) 'Employers' perceptions and use of educational qualifications', *Educational Analysis* 3, 2: 25–36.

Marton, F., Dallialba, G. and Beaty, E. (1993) 'Conceptions of learning', *International Journal of Educational Research* 19: 277–300.

Mathieson, M. and Bernbaum, G. (1988) 'The British disease: a British tradition?', *British Journal of Educational Studies* 26, 2: 126–174.

Melton, R. (1995) 'Developing meaningful links between higher education and training', *British Journal of Educational Studies*, 43 1: 43–56.

Mercer, N. (1992) 'Culture, context and the construction of knowledge', in P. Light and G. Butterworth (eds) *Context and Cognition*, London: Harvester.

Merson, M. (1995) 'Political explanations for economic decline in Britain and their relationship to policies for education and training', *Journal of Education Policy* 30, 3: 303–315.

Messick, S. (1984) 'The nature of cognitive styles: problems and promise in educational practice', *Educational Psychologist* 19: 59–74.

Ministry of Education (1959) *15–18 : A report of the Central Advisory Council for Education (Crowther Report)*, London: HMSO.

Murray-Harvey, R. (1994) 'Learning styles and approaches to learning: distinguishing between concepts and instruments', *British Journal of Educational Psychology* 64: 373–388.

National Commission on Education (1995) *Learning to Succeed: The Way Ahead*, London: National Commission.

National Council for Vocational Qualifications (1994) *A Statement by NCVQ on 'All Our Futures'*, London: NCVQ.

National Union of Teachers (1996) *The Road to Equality: 14–19 Strategy for the Future*, London: National Union of Teachers.

Newstead, S.E. (1992) 'A study of two "quick and easy" methods of assessing individual differences in student learning', *British Journal of Educational Psychology* 62: 299–312.

Nisbet, J. and Shucksmith, J. (1984) *The Seventh Sense: Reflections and Learning How to Learn*, Edinburgh: SCRE.

Norcross, L. (1990) 'The egalitarian fallacy', in *GCSE London Institute of Economic Affairs Education Unit*, London: IEA.

North, J. (ed.) (1987) *The GCSE: An Examination*, London: Claridge Press.

Nystrand, M. and Gamoran, A. (1991) 'Student engagement: when recitation becomes conversation', in H.C. Waxman and H.J. Walberg (eds) *Effective Teaching: Current Research*, Berkeley, CA: McCutchan.

O'Hear, A. (1987) 'The importance of traditional learning', *British Journal of Educational Studies* 35, 2: 102–114.

REFERENCES

O'Hear, A. (1991) *Education and Democracy: Against the Educational Establishment*, London: Claridge Press.

O'Hear, A. (1993) *An Entitlement to Knowledge*, London: Centre for Policy Studies.

OECD (1989) *Pathways for Learning: Education and Training from 16 to 19*, Paris: OECD.

Office for Standards in Education (1996a) *Business Education and Economics: An Inspection Review 1993–1995*, London: Ofsted.

Office for Standards in Education (1996b) *Effective Sixth Forms*, London: HMSO.

Ohlsson, S. (1995) 'Learning to do and learning to understand: a lesson and a challenge for cognitive modelling', in P. Reimann and H. Spada (eds) *Learning in Humans and Machines: Towards a Interdisciplinary Learning Science*, Oxford: Pergamon.

Pearlman, K., Schmidt, F.L. and Hunter, J.E. (1980) 'Validity generalization results for tests used to predict job proficiency and training success in clerical occupations', *Journal of Applied Psychology* 65, 4: 373–406.

Peterson, A. (1973) *The Future of the Sixth Form*, London: Routledge & Kegan Paul.

Pilkington, P. (1991) *End Egalitarian Delusion: Different Education for Different Talents*, London: Centre for Policy Studies.

Pring, R. (1993) 'Liberal education and vocational preparation', in R. Barrow and P. White (eds) *Beyond Liberal Education: Essays in Honour of Paul Hirst*, London: Routledge.

Pring, R. (1995) *Closing the Gap: Liberal Education and Vocational Preparation*, London: Hodder & Stoughton.

Raffe, D. and Surridge, P. (1995) *More of the Same? Participation of 16–18 Year Olds in Education*, London: National Commission on Education Briefing Papers (new series) 6.

Ramsden, P. (1988) 'Context and strategy: situational influences on learning', in R.R. Schmeck (ed.) *Learning Strategies and Learning Styles*, New York: Plenum Press, 159–184.

Reid, W. and Holt, M. (1986) 'Structure and ideology in upper secondary education', in A. Hartnett and M. North (eds) *Education and Society Today*, Lewes: Falmer Press.

Riding, R. and Buckle, C. (1990) *Learning Styles and Training Performance*, Assessment Research Unit, Faculty of Education and Continuing Studies, University of Birmingham.

Riding, R. and Douglas, G. (1993) 'The effect of cognitive styles and mode of presentation on learning performance', *British Journal of Educational Psychology* 63: 297–307.

Robinson, P. (1996) *Rhetoric and Reality: Britain's New Vocational Qualifications*, London: Centre for Economic Performance, London School of Economics.

Rumelhardt, D.E. and Norman, D.A. (1978) 'Accretion, tuning and restructuring: three modes of learning', in J.W. Cotton and R.L. Klatz (eds) *Semantic Factors in Cognition*, Hillsdale, NJ: Erlbaum.

Rutter, M., Maughan, B., Mortimore, P. and Ouston, J. (1979) *Fifteen Thousand Hours: Secondary Schools and Their Effects on Children*, London: Open Books.

Saljo, R. and Wyndham, J. (1990) 'Problem-solving, academic performance and situated reasoning, a study of joint cognitive activity in the formal setting', *British Journal of Educational Psychology* 60: 245–254.

Sanderson, M. (1994) *The Missing Structure: Technical School Education in England 1900–1990s*, London: Athlone Press.

Scarth, J. and Hammersley, M. (1988) 'Examinations and teaching: an exploratory study', *British Educational Research Journal* 14, 3: 231–249.

Schmeck, R.R. (ed.) (1988) *Learning Strategies and Learning Styles*, New York: Plenum Press.

REFERENCES

School Examinations and Assessment Council (1992) *Qualifications post-16: Choice and Coherence (Conference Report)*, London: SEAC.

Schools Council (1970) *Sixth Form Survey: Volume 1, Pupils and Students*, London: Schools Council Publications.

Schools Council (1972) *16–19 Growth and Response: Curricular Bases* (Working Paper 45), London: Evans/Methuen.

Schools Council (1980) *Examinations at 18+: Report on the N and F Debate*, London: Methuen.

Scott, P. (1989) *Reconstructing 'A' Level English*, Milton Keynes: Open University Press.

Semin, G. and Fiedler, K. (1992) *Language, Interaction and Social Cognition*, London: Sage.

Shayer, M. (1991) 'Improving standards and the National Curriculum', *School Science Review* 72 17–23.

Sheeran, Y. and Barnes, D. (1991) *Discovering the Ground Rules*, Milton Keynes: Open University Press.

Simon, A. and Boyer, G. (ed.) (1970) *Mirrors for Behaviour: An Anthology of Classroom Observation Instruments*, Philadelphia: Research For Better Schools Inc.

Sinclair, J. and Coulthard, M. (1992) 'Towards an analysis of discourse', in M. Coulthard (ed.) *Advances in Spoken Discourse Analysis*, London: Routledge.

Skilbeck, M., Connell, H., Lowe, N. and Tait, K. (1994) *The Vocational Quest: New Directions in Education and Training*, London: Routledge.

Smithers, A. (1993) *All Our Futures: Britain's Education Revolution*, London: Channel 4 (*Dispatches* Report).

Smithers, A. (1997) 'A critique of NVQs and GNVQs', in S. Tomlinson (ed.) *Perspectives on Education 14–19*, London: Athlone Press.

Smithers, A. and Robinson, P. (1991) *Beyond Compulsory Schooling: A Numerical Picture*, London: Council for Industry and Higher Education.

Sparkes, J. (1994) *The Education of Young People aged 14–18 Years*, London: The Royal Academy of Engineering.

Spours, K. (1993) 'The recent background to qualifications reform in England and Wales', in W. Richardson, J. Woolhouse and D. Finegold (eds) *The Reform of Post-16 Education and Training in England and Wales*, Harlow: Longman.

Stenhouse, L. (1975) *An Introduction to Curriculum Research and Development*, London: Heinemann.

Stubbs, M. (1983) *Language, Schools and Classrooms* (2nd edition), London: Methuen.

Taylor, P.B., Reid, W. and Holley, B. (1974) *The English Sixth Form: A Case Study in Curriculum Research*, Windsor: National Foundation for Educational Research.

Tillema, H.H. (1995) 'Changing the professional knowledge and beliefs of teachers: a training study', *Learning and Instruction* 5: 291–318.

Tomlinson, S. (ed.) (1997) *Perspectives on Education 14–19*, London: Athlone Press.

Tymms, P. (1992) 'The relative effectiveness of post-16 institutions in England', *British Educational Research Journal* 18, 2: 175–192.

Tymms, P.B. and Vincent, L.S. (1994) *The Comparability of Examination Boards at A-level: A Report for the GCE Boards*, Newcastle upon Tyne: Newcastle University Department of Education, Curriculum, Evaluation and Management Centre.

Tymms, P.B. and Vincent, L.S. (1995) *Comparing Examination Boards and Syllabuses at A-Level: Students' Grades, Attitudes and Perceptions of Classroom Processes*, Belfast: Northern Ireland Council for the Curriculum, Examinations and Assessment.

Waldrop, M.M. (1992) *Complexity: The Emerging Science at the Edge of Order and Chaos*, London: Penguin.

Wankowksi, J.A. (1974) 'Teaching method and academic success in sixth form and university', *Journal of Curriculum Studies* 6: 50–60.

REFERENCES

Weinstein, C.E. and Mayer, R.E. (1986) 'The teaching of learning strategies', in M.C. Wittrock (ed.) *Handbook for Research on Teaching* (3rd edition), London: Collier Macmillan.

Wells, G. (1993) 'Re-evaluating the IRF Sequence: a proposal for the articulation of theories of activity and discourse for the analysis of teaching and learning in the classroom', *Linguistics and Education* 5: 1–37.

West, A. and West, R. (1996) *A Comparison of GCE A/AS-level Examination Results of Assisted Place and State School Pupils*, London: Centre for Educational Research, London School of Economics and Political Science.

Westgate, D. and Hughes, M. (forthcoming) 'Identifying "quality" in classroom talk: An enduring research task', *Language and Education*.

Whiteley, M. (1990) 'Wither A-level literature?' in NATE Post-16 Committee *A-Level English – Pressures for Change*, Sheffield: National Association for the Teaching of English.

Whitty, G., Edwards, T. and Gewirtz, S. (1993) *Specialisation and Choice in Urban Education*, London: Routledge.

Wiemann, J. and Giles, H. (1992) 'Interpersonal communication', in M. Hewstone, W. Stroebe, J.P. Codol and G. Stephenson (eds) *Introduction to Social Psychology* (2nd edition), Oxford: Blackwell.

Willcoxson, L. and Prosser, M. (1996) '*Kolb's Learning Style Inventory* (1985): review and further study of validity and reliability', *British Journal of Educational Psychology* 66: 247–257.

Wolf, A. (1991) 'Assessing core skills: wisdom or wild goose chase?', *Cambridge Journal of Education* 21, 2: 189–201.

Wolf, A. (1993) *Parity of Esteem: Can Vocational Awards Ever Achieve High Status?*, London: Institute of Education: International Centre on Assessment.

Wolf, A. (1995) *Competence-based Assessment*, Milton Keynes: Open University Press.

Wolf, A. and Rapiau, M-T. (1993) 'The academic achievement of craft apprentices in France and England: contrasting systems and common dilemmas', *Comparative Education* 29, 1: 29–43.

Wood, D. (1992) 'Teaching talk', in K. Norman (ed.) *Thinking Voices: The Work of the National Oracy Project*, London: Hodder & Stoughton.

Young, D. (1990) *The Enterprise Years: A Businessman in the Cabinet*, London: Headline Press.

INDEX

ability 1, 56, 61
abstract conceptualisation 163
academic excellence 9
academic standards 12
academic-vocational continuum 70;
  'divide' 1, 11
active experimentation 163–4
active learning 39
admissions officers 43, 51–2, 60
age distribution 37–8
A level 'approach' 174
A level Biology 77; Business Studies 77,
  85, 87; Chemistry 34, 167; Economics
  24, 74, 77, 85; English Language 46,
  166, 174; English Literature 46, 174;
  Mathematics 98; Psychology 77
A level/GNVQ comparisons: classes
  88–91, 174–5; courses 80, 84–6
A level pass rates 3, 9, 11
ALIS (A level Information System) 96,
  98, 102, 109–10, 122, 173;
  questionnaire 66, 71
applied A levels 6, 14, 63, 171
aptitude 61
Art and Design 29, 43
assessment 20, 22–3, 58–9, 174
attrition 31
Audit Commission 12

Board of Education 128–9
Boswell, T. 14
BTEC 4–5, 30, 58, 75, 97, 140, 166,
  171
Business Studies 16, 29, 34, 38–44,
  47–9, 52–5

Capey Report 20
careers 39

chance 40, 43, 52
Chances graphs 52–3
city technology colleges 19, 23
classroom observation 68–70, 80–3,
  166
college/school comparisons 86
Committee of Vice-Chancellors 132
Communication Studies 97
competences 20
Competitiveness White Paper 3, 170
computer-assisted observation 68
concrete experience 163
Confederation of British Industry 11
core skills 22, 26, 39, 51, 59, 61
correlations 54, 166
coursework assessment 102
credentialism 4–5, 9, 11–12, 144
Crowther Report 2, 25, 110

Dearing 1, 3–4, 9, 14, 19, 26, 169, 170–1
deferred vocationalism 17
Department for Education 2
developed abilities 51–2, 56
dictated notes 46
didactic teaching 97, 100, 116, 123
difficulty (level of) 14, 56, 60, 172
discourse analysis 24, 96, 102–8, 110
distinction 47, 57
distributed 30, 163, 168

economic imperatives 23
Education 2000 23
effectiveness 47, 50, 60, 166
employers 51
employment 30, 48, 54, 169
enrolment 32
epistemological frame of reference
  112–13, 118, 121–2

equivalence 13, 169, 173
evidence 164, 167
exercises 46
experimentation 163–4
external marking 61

FEFC (Further Education Funding Council) 30–1, 40, 44, 59, 165
FEU (Further Education Unit) 18, 30
fifty per cent framework 29, 52, 57, 61
Flanders Interaction Analysis 68–9
Fordism 129
Forth, E. 11
Further Education 30, 48

GCSE (General Certificate of Secondary Education) 2, 31–7, 50–8, 175
Girls Schools Association 9
GNVQs (Advanced) Business 29, 34, 40–1, 43, 48, 80, 85, 87; Health and Social Care 29, 80; Hospitality and Catering 80; Human Biology 52–5; Science 63
gold standard 4, 9, 14, 22
good practice 59, 163
grading 58
Graham, D. 8–9
grammar schools 8

Handy, C. 10
Headmasters Conference 9
Higginson Report 26
higher order skills 10, 175
Higher School Certificate 4
HMI (Her Majesty's Inspectors of Schools) 17, 19, 25–6, 98, 123

independent study 7
indicators 49
induction 38
information technology 41, 43, 46–7, 52, 173
initiation-response-feedback/evaluation 104, 114, 116, 118–19, 122–4
insecurity 49
International Test of Developed Abilities 54, 56
interview structures 71

Jessup, G. 130

knowledge: applied 16, 18–20;
disciplined 18; practical and propositional 126, 138, 147, 149–51, 153–7, 159, 161; pure and applied 16–17; regionalised 15–16; relevant 15, 18, 22, 26; specialised 15; useful 18–19
Kolb, D. 126, 138, 147-51, 153-5, 156–7, 159, 161, 163, 168–9, 169

leaders 7, 9–10
learning: active 15; autonomy 21, 24–5; deep and surface 27; models 20–1, 23; strategic 27
learning cycle 156–9
learning society 170
learning styles 136–47, 172–3; subject bias 147–52; teachers' influence 156–62
Learning Styles Inventory 138–9
leittext 157
lesson tempo 82, 87, 174
level of performance 51, 60
liberal education 12, 24
linguistics 97, 115, 122
literary canon 97, 122

Manpower Services Commission 19
media studies 97
metacognition 152
methodology 163, 166–8
modernisation 23
motivation 18–19

National Curriculum Council 8, 26
National Education and Training Targets 1, 9
National Union of Teachers 2
NCVQ (National Council for Vocational Qualifications) 21, 30
Noldus Information software 68
Norwood Report 18–19, 128
NUS/UWT 20
NVQs (National Vocational Qualifications) 14, 20–1, 170, 171

observer effects 67
observing 166–7
Open University 48
original work 46

parity of esteem 2, 6, 9, 13–15, 16, 20, 51, 169–71

participation rates (in post-compulsory education) 2–3, 9, 12–13, 169
pedagogic conservatives 25
Peterson, A. 8–9
PLAs (perceived learning activities) 98, 100–2, 109
portfolios 31
private sector 8
problem solving 41, 59, 60
progressive education 18, 22, 24
project work 48, 167

recitation 102, 110–14, 119, 124
reflective observation 163
regression 54–5
relevance 14
reliability 165
reporting 58
residuals 50
resources 41

Schools Council 137
scientific research 163–5, 167–8
Shephard, G. 13
sixth forms 9, 12; 'new' 3
skill 40, 47, 52; skills revolution 11
Smithers A. 2, 7, 21, 63
social constructivist theory of learning 110, 124
specialisation 1–2, 8–9
standards 51
Stenhouse, L. 129

student-centred learning 116
student satisfaction 30, 38–9, 43–4, 49
study in depth 8
subject cultures 123; discipline 100; mindedness 17, 25; paradigms 103, 115

targets 54
teacher assessments 50
teaching exchanges 103–9, 114, 116
teaching styles 97–8, 103–4, 111, 123
team work 40, 47
technical education 19
topic presentations (by teacher) 46
transfer of learning 152–6
TVEI (Technical and Vocational Education Initiative) 6, 19, 23, 97

unemployment 49, 52
universities 48
university demands 23

validity 44, 61, 163, 167
value added 30, 48, 50
vocational A levels 4, 14, 63, 171
vocational education 1, 9

work experience 40
workforce (modern) 10–11, 170

Young, D. 19
youth unemployment 10